Additional Comments of Support and Praise for This Work

"I have had the good fortune to work with Dick Knowles and to use the Process Enneagram for near on 6 years in my work with clients around the world. Put simply-it works, it really works. I have used it in companies and communities in Australia, South Africa, Namibia, New Zealand, Canada, USA, Mexico, Japan, Malaysia, Thailand, Singapore, China, Germany and Indonesia with groups as diverse as coal miners and steel makers through to lawyers, accountants and those charged with shaping the future of South Africa for the next 20 years. In every single case, I have been able to achieve results with clients that would have been unheard of using other processes. This work represents a significant advance in thinking about both underlying models and the attendant processes for helping groups in corporations and communities realize their desires, to take a holistic and systemic view of their problems and to marshal commitment to act to achieve results."

Tim Dalmau, CEO Dalmau Network Group, Australia

"The central problem has always been, 'How do we get people to live and work constructively together? How do we get people to live in healthy relation one with another?' In the *Leadership Dance,* Dick Knowles shines a very bright light down a path we will all want to follow. For those of us who cherish the dream that business and organizations can be a source of vibrant growth and learning, of life in full bloom – indeed, that they must be – Dick's wisdom on how we might live that dream is a rare and welcome gift."

Thomas J. Hench, Ph.D. Former Business Manager and now Associate Professor of Management

"*The Leadership Dance,* by Richard N. Knowles, Ph.D. is a refreshing approach to guide eclectic leaders in their important governing function. The leadership team of the City of Niagara Falls, USA in particular, is developing under this philosophical, creative model. It is through the use of this dynamic and open support model that we are rebuilding our City located at a Wonder of the World, Niagara Falls."

Irene J. Elia, Ph.D., Mayor of Niagara Falls, NY, USA

"The importance of this searching book, *The Leadership Dance*, is that, contrary to most books on organization and leadership, it isn't primarily about what should be done to improve an organization, but about how organizations of any type and size actually do function, whether that's what is intended or not and whether anyone knows it or not. The point about describing organizations as 'living systems' rather than 'machines' is that living systems is what they are and treating them as machines eventually and inevitably doesn't work well. Once this basic fact is recognized, changes follow, as organizations learn to work according to their real nature, thus brought within the scope of consciousness awareness. It is a simple idea – yet complex, because living systems are complex. Richard Knowles has made this complexity available and understandable."

Rosemary Haughton, Co-Founder and Co-Director Emeritus, Wellspring House, Gloucester, MA and author *The Passionate God*

"If we adopt the perspective of organizations as living systems, the Process Enneagram provides a useful lens into the heart and soul of an organization. Each week our management group meets and uses the Enneagram to co-create a context to help us deal with issues such as funding, difficult clients, inter-agency relationships, staff morale, etc. Using it, we constantly re-affirm who we are and what we're trying to achieve."

Barrie Evans, Ph. D. Director, Madame Vanier Childrens Services, London, Ontario

"*The Leadership Dance* is a personal story about the conversion of one man to a more open and inspired form of leadership. Dick Knowles came to be at home in the world of chaos and complexity and brought to bear a form of systems thinking called *systematics* derived from an English philosopher and innovator named John Bennett. This provides a way for people to talk about and to understand their situation together; it brings the principles of self-organization into practice."

Anthony Blake, Teacher and International Consultant and author of *The Intelligent Enneagram*

The Leadership Dance

Richard N. Knowles

The Leadership Dance

Pathways to Extraordinary
Organizational Effectiveness

Third Edition

The Center for Self-Organizing Leadership
Niagara Falls, New York
2002

Published by
The Center for Self-Organizing Leadership
6989 Rebecca Drive
Niagara Falls, NY 14304
Internet www.centerforselforganizingleadership.com
The Center for Self-Organizing Leadership and its logotype are trademarks.

© 2002 by Richard N. Knowles
Third Edition
Edited by Andrew A. Moyer

Library of Congress Control Number 2002094083
ISBN 0-9721204-0-8

Previously published as
What's Going on Here?
A Deeper Pattern and Processes in Living Systems
First Edition: © 1998 by Richard N. Knowles
Leadership in These Turbulent Times:
Thriving in the Midst of Chaos
Second Edition: © 2001 by Richard N. Knowles

Printed in the United States of America

This book is dedicated to all those who have helped me on this journey of discovery and growth.

The support and understanding of my daughters, Elizabeth, Dorothy and Cynthia, and stepdaughter, Christine is deeply appreciated. It is dedicated especially to my wife and partner Claire, whose insight, wisdom, patience and faith supports and sustains me in this journey.

Richard N. Knowles
August 24, 2002

Contents

Contents

Contents

List of Figures

List of Tables

Foreword

The Story of the Journey

It's hard to pick a specific point when my journey into this way of thinking and being began. My first memories of my father and mother, Frank and Dorothy Knowles, are around treating people fairly and with respect. My father was a DuPont Plant Manager for a number of years. We often heard stories about the Plant people over dinner and in long drives in the car. He had great respect for the people at his Plant. He had modest beginnings and a hard farming life as a teenager; he really connected with the people close to the work.

My two brothers and I had a reasonably good time growing up. My older brother Frank graduated from Duke University in chemical engineering and received a Master's Degree in chemical engineering from the University of Delaware. Our careers came together now and then over the years; a story about one of these times is told in a later part of this book. Frank worked for DuPont for about 35 years in a variety of manufacturing and research assignments. Late in his career, he was the Manager of the process control R & D group that was responsible for developing and supporting the installation of new chemical process control computers in our plants. My younger brother John studied Spanish and received a Bachelors Degree form Rutgers University, a Masters Degree from Middlebury College and a Ph. D. from Rutgers University. John taught Spanish culture, language and literature for about 38 years at the McDonogh School in Maryland, Rutgers University, the University of Delaware and Salisbury University in Maryland. He's a wonderful teacher.

My interests in High School and Oberlin College led me into scientific work. I received a Ph. D. in organic chemistry from the University of

Rochester in 1961. I joined DuPont to do exploration for new products. The move into DuPont seemed quite natural; I must have had a DuPont oval stamped on my rear when I was born. For my first 14 years in DuPont, I did research looking for new agricultural chemicals, flame-retardants, animal repellants and polymerization initiators. I also did a lot of process development work. By 1973, I'd received 40 US patents for my work. In 1974, I was promoted to become a Research Supervisor, and my journey into the people side of things began.

I never received any formal supervisory training up to this point. and I didn't receive any until around 1978. So as a new supervisor, I did what many people do and that is to wing it. Sometimes, I knew intuitively how to work with people to get things done. Other times, I was a hard-line manager. Things went okay, except I found that I was getting harsh with people to push them to get better results. This was the way I'd experienced and seen other DuPont managers function, so I learned that this was the way to do things. I never worked for my father, but he may also have functioned this way at work in those days.

As time moved on and I seemed to be doing okay in my career, I moved to other supervisory assignments in marketing, and manufacturing. I did receive some formal supervisory training in 1978. In January 1983, I was appointed Assistant Plant Manager at the DuPont Chambers Works in Deepwater, NJ.

We had two Assistant Managers then, one for operations and I was there for strategic planning. A year later, the Operations Assistant Manager moved on to become the manager at another Plant and I became the remaining Assistant Manager responsible for the operations of the 3,000-person facility. We made about 700 organic chemical products there.

During this period of career growth, things at home were not right. My wife Alice Keith and I were becoming disconnected. We had been college sweethearts and were married the summer after we graduated. She's a fine violinist and teacher. Our first daughter, Beth, was born in 1958 while I was in graduate school, so finances were tight. I had a nice teaching grant, and my wife did some music teaching in the Rochester schools. When I joined DuPont in October 1960, I thought we were in clover. I was focused on the research work earning more than I ever thought possible—all of $790/ month. I guess I didn't appreciate how hard it was for her to put her musical career aside while the kids were young. Our next two daughters, Dorothy and Cynthia, were born in 1961 and 1963. I felt such pressure from my wife to be with the family and do my duties that I dropped out of the Company golf leagues and turned down some transfer opportunities, difficult choices in those days in the Company. I really tried to focus a lot on the family, but often felt alone and guilty that I was not carrying my part of the load. I felt I could never quite measure up no matter how hard I tried. To the outside world, things were just fine; we were good at covering up our circumstances.

During this period, several of my close work friends committed suicide. Both my mother-in-law and my mother died in 1968 within 10 weeks of each other. That was also the year Martin Luther King was assassinated, which impacted me deeply.

The interplay of this personal struggle combined with my efforts to be the best manager I could be was a heavy burden. I felt that I really didn't know how to be a good father, husband or manager, but I put on a good front. I was becoming more and more demanding of the people who worked for me, insisting on superior work performance and having little patience if they didn't get things done to my standards in the times I required.

There was so much that I didn't understand; I was deep into my own downward spiral of depression. I guess that it was tough to see what was going on around me after falling into such a deep hole.

Moving on to Niagara Falls

In August 1983, I was offered a transfer and promotion to become the Plant Manager of the DuPont Plant in Niagara Falls, NY. Although I'd refused other transfers requiring relocation outside of the Wilmington, DE area, I felt that I had to grow and that this move was necessary for me. It was hard on my wife because it meant that she had to give up her position as Principal Second Violinist in the Delaware Symphony Orchestra, as well as leaving the Suzuki violin program she'd helped to start at the Wilmington Music School. At this point, all the girls were in college, so I think that the move didn't impact them as much.

The move put more pressure on our marriage. My wife became involved in a strong Suzuki violin-teaching program in Buffalo, played in a good chamber orchestra and substituted some in the Buffalo Symphony Orchestra, but things didn't improve.

The Niagara Plant was a tough assignment. It had the worst labor relations history in the Company. There were two strikes in its history, one of which lasted for 6 months in 1970-1971. The Plant's safety performance was not good. When I arrived in the Buffalo Airport on my first day, I was informed that we'd had a lost workday injury because a man had cut off his finger in the Sodium Shop. So at 10 P.M. on my first day, we were doing a safety inspection in the Plant. I became really uptight. The Sodium Shop, the area where we made metallic sodium by electrolysis, was a shock to me. This was the first time I'd seen it. The process is a tough one and the work difficult. We handle lots of salt (like table salt) and it was scattered all over the floor. Sodium reacts with moisture in the air forming sodium oxide, which is corrosive to the skin and eyes; there were rinds of sodium oxide on lots of the equipment. The operating area had been in use for 85+ years and showed the wear and tear. The attitude of Plant Management towards the injury seemed pretty casual. It was clear we were in a pretty deep safety hole.

The day that our furniture was moved into our home in November 1983, I had to leave my wife and the movers, pick up my top VP and the top lawyer of the Legal Department to take them to Niagara University to meet with the University's President. About a year before I'd moved to the Plant, there had been an environmental release in which a small chlorine cloud had come down to the ground right in the middle of a Niagara University/Siena College football game. It had caused the game to stop and resulted in a lot of bad publicity for the Plant, the Company and the community. The enrollment of new students at Niagara University had fallen off, and they felt that DuPont had contributed to the problem. The meeting was pretty tense. During the meeting, my VP remained quiet and listened. I did as well. After the meeting, my boss let me know that if my management of the Plant ever put him through anything like that, he'd have my backside. I got the message!

Shortly after this meeting, I went to a public meeting at the fire hall near the Love Canal area on its current status. There were about 200 people there including lots of media and all three TV stations from Buffalo. The EPA engineers were droning through boring technical stuff and were not addressing the issues of the people who were wondering what was going to happen to them. I sat at the back; no one knew me at this point, so I could be inconspicuous. After the engineers talked, questions poured out. They ranged all over the place. One lady wanted to know what they were going to do about her house; all her assets were in it and she was having a hard time because she couldn't sell it. At the other extreme was a guy sitting in front of me who talked to his buddy about the Monday Night football game for most of the session. At one point, he jumped up, ran to the front of the fire hall and screamed about all the injustices. The TV people raced up to get him on camera. After about 2-3 minutes, he went back to his seat and picked up on the next play of the football game. He got onto TV, which was his objective. It looked to me that no one was trying to really solve the problems and help the people who had been impacted by the tragedy. This was another good lesson; we need to be connected to the people involved when we're into something that's as difficult as this issue.

Shortly after this episode, I learned that our Plant had serious environmental problems stemming from production operations that had been discontinued 15 years earlier. I had my first press conference. I had to tell the community and our Canadian neighbors that chlorocarbons like chloroform and methylene chloride were leaching from the soil under the plant, and about 50 pounds a day were going into the Niagara River. Our news of the material leaching from under the Plant was not well received.

I tried to be as open and honest as I could be about the problem. The Buffalo News environmental reporter, Paul MacClennan, was at the conference and recognized that I was trying to put the cards on the table and to address the issue. I learned that sharing the information openly, talking honestly about it, and sharing the plans to do something about it were really important. I continued to work this way, and Paul always treated me fairly.

Taking on an issue like this by openly sharing the information and plans was not normally done in the chemical industry in 1983, so I felt that I was way out on a limb. The other Plant Managers were not very happy with me for being as open as this.

One of the positives coming out of this work was a call from Sister Margeen Hofmann OSF, who headed the Ecumenical Task Force in Niagara Falls. This was an organization formed by 17 or 18 churches to address the human side of the Love Canal disaster. Sister Margeen was brought in from the Boston area to lead their effort. As she tried to work with the companies involved and the regulators, she met constant resistance. The more she pushed to get the information that was needed by the Love Canal people, the more she met resistance and criticism. By the time of my arrival in Niagara Falls, Sister Margeen and the Ecumenical Task Force had become a vocal, powerful, local environmental force.

When she called, I was afraid that I had somehow fallen into the soup with them. I didn't need any more trouble right then. However, she called to tell me that she had noticed that I was behaving differently from the other managers and she wanted to meet me. I began to talk with her and learned that she was really a very nice person who wanted to help the people in these environmental matters. We talked a lot about DuPont and I tried to help her to understand the situation. As we talked, I began to realize how important it was to try to build personal relationships with folks. I discovered that we had a lot in common. We all wanted clean air, clean water, good schools, a good government, etc. I also learned how fragile that trust really is. Now and then, I'd make a mistake and she'd take a piece out of my rear; we'd then keep talking and work things through. She wanted to keep talking just as I did.

Things inside the Plant were beginning to get under better control. Chet Kodeski, who had been the Union President for a number of years, and I began to develop a respectful and more open relationship. The Plant had a history of grieving just about everything. We had a backlog of over 200 grievances at the third step, which is when the Plant Manager got into the process. We began to have third step meetings every Tuesday and Thursday mornings for 2 hours. The Grievance Committee had about 12 union officers on it. I had some one from the employee relations group with me to help me understand the details of all the procedures that were being challenged.

In Western New York there are lots of people of Eastern European descent. These good solid folks often take pretty strong positions when expressing their views. Many of these folks were on the Grievance Committee, and we'd have some pretty heated discussions. We'd shake hands at the beginning of the meetings, argue like the dickens and then part on reasonable speaking terms. These guys were tough, and the meetings were not ones to which I looked forward. However, they began to see that I was trying to find the truth as best I could and was trying to listen. I denied a lot of grievances, but I also decided in favor of the Union on a lot of them. The historical relations between the Union and Management had often been contentious, so many times the Union grieved about mistreatment by the supervisors. The Union was often right. We'd argue intensely, but we stayed in the heat to find the best answers we could.

At social affairs, like retirement parties and the Plant Picnic, we all got along quite well. I began to learn that, person-to-person, we did pretty well. But, functioning in our roles, we had a pretty low trust level. I didn't understand this either, but trust and our relationships were better person-to-person.

Yet, when there was a crisis, people put all the problems down and worked together in quite astonishing ways. Then after we'd overcome the crisis, we'd go back and behave badly again. We'd often talk together about how great things were during the crisis. I wondered why we could behave this way at those times, but not all the time. This puzzle stayed with me for years. It was great when I discovered how we could work this way all the time, but more on this later.

I spent a lot of time walking around the Plant talking with people and trying to break down the barriers between the people and management. Some days I did better than others. One time I got a good lesson in how some supervisors blindly followed the Manager in trying to make a good impression. Our Plant was started in 1896 to make sodium using the newly-developed hydropower from Niagara Falls. One day as I was walking down the stairs in the sodium shop, I asked why we didn't have a door in the right wall at the foot of the stairs so that we could go easily into the next room. No one commented, but the next time I walked down these stairs, there was a new doorway. It probably cost us several thousand dollars. There was a lot of fixed equipment opposite from where the door had been cut, so there was no way we could use the door. Everyone knew the idea was dumb, but no one had the courage to tell me it wasn't good idea. I really learned that I had to be out in the Plant and get to know it and the people very well, if I were to make good decisions. It was clear that information flowing up and down the hierarchical chain wasn't as reliable as I'd thought.

Our safety began to get better and our folks felt pretty good about the improvements. My Management felt better as well, which was good.

At about this time in the middle of 1984, the Company began a new management program called organizational effectiveness. The idea was to develop teams, get everyone involved and improve the safety and the business. The material was developed from the work of a consultant named Charlie Krone. His work was derived, in part, from the work of John Bennett, an Englishman who worked from around the 1920's to 1974 when he died. Bennett developed a way of thinking he called Systematics. This was difficult material to understand and Bennett was hard to read. Some very good courses were developed, however.

At Niagara, we called it the Management Training Process. It was a three-week program for everyone to learn how to solve problems and to work in teams. As we developed this course, there was a lot of training at the Corporate as well as the Plant level. Many of us found this was really a good advance in what we were trying to do. At Niagara, I was deeply involved in planning our work and in leading some of the sessions. I believed in modeling the new behavior, and one way for me to do that was to teach many of the sessions. Over the next 18 months, I spent about 100 days teaching. An unintended consequence of this was that it looked like a one-man show and an ego trip for me to some people. This didn't help me improve my relationships with the Plant Staff.

In October 1984, just two days before Senator Mondale, the Democratic Presidential Nominee, brought his campaign to Western New York (WNY), a scientist in the EPA in Washington, DC issued an unauthorized report stating that the DuPont dump at Necco Park was leaking hazardous wastes and was destroying the secure landfill liners of the nearby CECOS hazardous waste dump cells, and that this would cause another Love Canal. The adjacent community went nuts. Was another environmental tragedy hanging over them? What was going to happen?

It was true that the Necco Park dump was leaking. DuPont had used it for many years as a dump for barium salts and the waste from C 1 and C 2 chlorocarbons production. They had stopped using it as a dump in about 1980, had capped it and were doing some remediation work. The Company had put in several study wells and had begun to collect waste to reduce its movement off-site in the ground water 20-30 feet down in the rock formations. A phased study process was in place. We were continuing to address and correct the problem. We had no indication that the CECOS landfills were being impacted.

Region II EPA, whose main office was located in New York City, came to the Falls to have a public meeting two days later. It was held in a large meeting room in the Post Office near Congressman LaFalce's office. The room was packed, but as I entered, the crowd parted like the opening of the Red Sea. No one wanted to talk to me except Sister Margeen, who came over and told me she was glad I was there. She introduced me to a lady who'd lived in the Love Canal area and had lost a baby at 6 months from a brain tumor. I thought to myself, I don't need this right now. Then Sister Margeen told her I was different and would talk with her. The lady now lived near, but not on the Necco Park site; there were no homes built on it. Reporters from the WNY region and as from as far away as Philadelphia were there. All the local politicians were there as well.

Then the hearing began and it was ugly. The EPA Region II Administrator was trying to tell the people that he didn't think there was a serious problem and that they'd study it. This was the story at the beginning of the Love Canal experience and the people didn't want to hear the same old thing again. I kept a low profile and tried to look inconspicuous.

After the session was over, I went to Sister Margeen and told her that I didn't think this was another Love Canal and that we needed to share our information with the neighbors to help them understand what we knew and what we were doing. We went over to talk to the Administrator and urged him to let us tell more to the neighbors than just that the EPA was going to study things. It got really tense, since he didn't want to deal with the issue this way. I realized that I was in a pretty strange place for a manager. A young woman Rabbi was on my right, Sister Margeen was on my left and the woman environmental reporter for the Niagara Gazette was on her left. All four of us were arguing intensely with the Administrator that we needed to talk further on this. He finally agreed to have a meeting the next morning at 7 A.M. in the same meeting room in the Main Post Office in Niagara Falls.

I lay awake most of the night trying to figure out what to do next. The DuPont Public Affairs manager from headquarters was going to meet me at the Post Office at 6:30 A.M. to review the situation with me before the meeting. On the way, I got a chart pad, pens, and doughnuts since I'd been learning about how to prepare for meetings in our Management Training Course. We met in the pre-dawn hours on the Post Office steps. As we were finishing, he asked me "What if any neighborhood homes are contaminated?" I knew how the Company felt about its intense responsibility to be a good corporate citizen, so I said "Then the we buy the damn homes." He turned white as a sheet. We went in.

About 16 or 17 people had gathered. There was the Public Affairs Officer for the EPA in Region II, the Love Canal Coordinator for the NY Department of Environmental Conservation (DEC), Sister Margeen and others from local community environmental groups. The tension was palpable!

As I was setting up the chart pad, the EPA fellow came up and said that he was going to run the meeting. I responded that it wasn't his community and to please sit down. After we all introduced ourselves to each other, I suggested three questions that had come to me in the night.

1. Is this another Love Canal?
2. If it is, as a homeowner, what does it mean to me?
3. If it is, what should I do next?

No one could answer the first question just as it stood, so I suggested we look at it from two perspectives: what makes it like Love Canal and what makes it different from Love Canal?

As we explored these two questions, the things that made it look like Love Canal were:

· fear of the unknown;

· surprised again; and

· not knowing any information about the specifics of the situation.

The things that made it look different from Love Canal were:

· there were no homes built on Necco Park;

· the Plant Manager was talking with them;

· there was some remediation work under way; and

· there was some information we could and would share.

After about 2 hours, there was general agreement that there was not a crisis here. The EPA fellow complimented me on how open and well the meeting went. I asked him what he was going to tell the neighbors now. He said he was going to tell them not to worry, which was the same message that he was going to tell them the day before. I told him I wanted to make the calls with him. He said I couldn't do that, to which I replied, "I'm going to call as well. I'll either walk beside you or behind you." He called the New York office of the EPA. After about 30 minutes, he came to me and said that we could make joint calls. It had never been done before.

One of the people there was so excited about the prospect of joint calls that she wondered if the people from CECOS would also be willing to go with us. So, we called them and they agreed to have lunch with us to talk about it. We met at the Howard Johnson's near the landfill area to talk. There were four of us, the EPA public affairs person, the Love Canal Coordinator for the DEC, the CECOS public Affairs person and me. Things went well and we agreed to make the calls together.

Just as we were leaving the restaurant, Don Postles, a prominent TV anchorman in Buffalo came in the door. My heart dropped. He wanted to know what we were up to. So, after we told him, he wanted to come along with his cameraman. Things were escalating! Calls like this had never been made before, and now we were going to be doing them live and in color.

We began our calls by going up onto the porch of one of the homes. Upon knocking, the door opened. There was a guy about 6 feet 3 inches tall, with a bright red sweatshirt, no front teeth, and about 4 days of stubble. I thought this was going to be the end; I feared that I was going to get killed, right there in living color. But, after a couple of minutes, when he realized why we were there, he said he didn't have any problems and brought his kids out to meet the Don Postles.

There were no negative interactions at the next house or the next or the next. The reporter stopped me on the sidewalk and said "There's no Love Canal here and we're going to stop the panic tonight." We did the interview, called on a few more homes, and I went home to see what the TV folks were saying. He reported the news very factually and said that there was no Love Canal here; the panic stopped just as if someone had turned off a switch. Openly sharing the information and being involved in the process were two an important lessons that I'd learned from this. This is like a participative sport!

Wilmington Management couldn't believe how well we'd done. We made our calls on a Friday; the weekend was quiet.

On Monday, the New York Times called to set up an interview. The reporter could come only on one day, Wednesday, at the same time that I'd already scheduled a meeting with the Rabbi who wanted to look at the data we had about the remediation work. When I called her to reschedule our meeting, she said she wanted to come with the reporter. I felt I had to go ahead with them both, so we met on Wednesday. I hadn't slept much worrying about this; the New York Times is the big league!

We introduced ourselves, and the reporter and the Rabbi started to visit. He had grown up in the same neighborhood where the Rabbi had attended divinity school. It was like old time's week. As he interviewed me, she kept telling him that I was really trying to do the right thing. Our article was a good one!

I was learning that it is when you participate in the process and are fully into it that things came forth that you never expected. This is called emergence and synchronicity and it only happens when you're in the process.

Things got quiet for me around this issue, but the EPA and the New York DEC were going at it. It was a complicated situation because Necco Park and the CECOS landfills were adjacent to each other, and the DEC had jurisdiction over Necco Park and the EPA had jurisdiction over the CECOS landfills. In December, I was called into the Region 9 DEC Director's office in Buffalo. The Director said that DuPont had to sign, right then, a Consent Decree to cover the work we were doing to remediate Necco Park. As I read it, I could see that there was a problem with the Decree so I gave it back to him and said I couldn't sign it in that form on behalf of the Company.

Several weeks later, I was called again to report to the Buffalo office of the DEC. This time, Rich Gentilucci, one of our environmental managers, and I were meeting with the DEC lawyer who was pretty unfriendly and was very pushy. They gave me a new Decree that was much worse than the first one; it required us to put in about 50 monitoring wells, look at old drainage ways and sewer line trenches.

Our remediation consultants had recommended that we put in 22 more wells, for a cost of around $200,000, so that we could do the next phase of the studies. This Decree was going to cost us around $500,000. I tried to resist and avoid the more expensive approach to solving the problem. We were doing a lot of remediation already, believing the phased study was the best approach for both the community and the Company. After about 5 weeks of tense meetings, I agreed, with Management support, to do the work they were requesting. They then gave me the Decree to sign, and the last part said that I also was agreeing on behalf of the Company to give up our rights to appeal any future decision of the DEC. I didn't feel that the Company should agree with this Decree.

The very next day we received a Consent Order from the EPA, who'd taken jurisdiction for Necco Park away from the DEC, saying that this was an environmental emergency (covered under CIRCLA) and that we'd have to put in 100 wells to cover a much larger area than we were impacting. This would have cost us over $1,000,000. It looked like they wanted us to do a regional ground water study to cover all the questions raised in the original EPA report issued in October.

This seemed very unfair, and we didn't agree that there was an emergency, so with Management support, we began to plan to appeal their decision. We had 30 days to sign the Decree. In the second week, the newspapers started to put the pressure on us, wanting to know what we planned to do. In the third week, I was teaching an organizational effectiveness workshop in Wilmington, DE. The DEC announced a community meeting to update the community on what was happening in the school near Necco Park for Thursday of that week. On Monday of that same week the EPA called to order me to come to a meeting in their New York office on the following Friday.

I planned to fly to Erie, PA on Wednesday evening to do some organizational effectiveness teaching on Thursday before going to Niagara Falls for the meeting of the DEC in the school. After 5 P.M. on Wednesday, the EPA called the plant to say that they'd found chemicals in a well under the school. When I landed in Erie, Claire Stoelting, who was also teaching, met me to break the news. I sat in a phone booth trying to get in touch with the school and City officials without any luck. I had frightening visions of women with baby strollers and big signs picketing the meeting, telling the world that DuPont was a bad neighbor.

Claire drove me the 100 miles back to Niagara Falls so I could be there first thing in the morning. But the first thing in the morning, the EPA called to say they'd made an analytical error and there were no chemicals under the school. Nevertheless, the newspaper ran a story that there was contamination under the school. All this pressure was piling up just before the New York meeting with the EPA. The school meeting turned out to be one where, to my surprise, the community scolded the officials for the way they were treating DuPont. The relationships that I'd developed with the community really helped us.

Friday morning several of us from the plant caught the first plane to New York to meet my Wilmington Manufacturing Director and the lawyer who'd come up with him from our headquarters in Wilmington, DE. The EPA meeting was ugly. There were around 20 of them and 4 of us. They put huge pressure on us to sign the Consent Decree. We said we were still studying it. The meeting lasted most of the day. I flew home that evening all worn out with the whole thing.

Our plan was to file an appeal the next Friday, which was the last day of the 30-day period. I think that this was the first time the DuPont Company had gone to court against the EPA. We had a press conference at Necco Park on Friday morning to announce our plan to appeal. At the same time, we also announced that we were going to begin the remediation work we'd agreed to do for the DEC. So we had three drilling rigs begin the drilling as we spoke to the press. Our lawyers filed their appeal in the Federal District Court declaring that this was not an emergency, and that we were entitled to a pre-enforcement review of the Order.

The EPA didn't seem to know what to do with us at the Plant. The community loved that we were going ahead with the remediation. The EPA environmental engineers came to Necco Park to watch what we were doing. I told our engineers to let them know what we were doing so they could see that we were doing high quality work. Each day that we hadn't signed the Decree, we got a $5,000 fine.

The days dragged on; the fine got bigger and bigger. The papers were all over this like a big football game. My VP of Manufacturing called to find out what we were doing and to learn how the legal case was coming. He was pretty anxious about the growing size of the fine. At day 37, the Judge issued his decision that this was not an emergency and DuPont was entitled to a pre-enforcement review. The fine had reached $ 185,000. The case came under the Court's supervision to work out the remediation plan. I signed the agreement on behalf of the Company. We had to pay a fee of $25,000, but the EPA agreed not to call it a fine.

About a year later, we reached an agreement with the EPA on the remediation program. The ability to work together to try to do a sensible, technically sound job saved the Company over $1,000,000 in ongoing costs, and fully addressed the environmental needs for the community.

I'd learned that being open and standing on your principles was the best strategy for us. The community knew what we were doing because we'd had so many meetings with them. I ate a lot of coffeecake in the homes in the evenings. More and more the trust between us grew, and we began to understand each other better. At one point, we offered the community a grant of up to $50,000 to cover their costs for hiring an environmental engineer to help them independently review and under-stand the data we were sharing with them. We set this up through their lawyer. The offer was that they would pick the person to do the work, and if we agreed that the person was a competent environmental engineer with a well-known reputation, we'd pay the fees. They wanted to find a person who was free of both industry and Government influence, but they couldn't find anyone who hadn't done work for one or the other. I don't know if they ever actually exercised the offer, but making the offer was an important step in helping us all move to a better level in our relationship.

As Sister Margeen and I continued to talk, we came up with the idea that it would be good if the Plant Managers could sit down with the Love Canal residents and begin a dialogue. The Love Canal issues were so intense that we decided that no media or public relations people should be with us. So on March 9, 1985, we had a meeting at 3:00 in the after-noon. We rented a conference room in a local hotel that had windows overlooking the Niagara River. As people began to gather, I sensed the extreme tension in myself and in everyone else. As I looked out the win-dow, 9 Whistling Swans flew past; I took that as a good omen. Although we had a good open meeting, it was a difficult one. There had been so many hurt feelings, so much fear of what the chemicals would do to people—especially the children—so much anger at having been stonewalled on information requests that people had to get a lot off their chests. Sharing information, listening to each other and building our relation-ships seemed to be making a difference.

Sister Margeen and I then decided to continue these dialogues. We set up a process through the Niagara Falls Area Chamber of Commerce, called the Environmental Liaison Committee. We met many times and learned to talk about these difficult issues. We had Plant visits, and the environmental people got to know the plant people and vice versa. In our first plant meeting with the Environmentalists, one of our more competent engineers talked about his environmental work. He was so frightened by the whole thing that he lost his voice just as he started to talk. Sister Margeen revived him with a glass of water and we heard his presentation.

This interactive work with the public was pretty hairy as we struggled to learn how to engage in dialogue with them. As this work continued, the Ecumenical Task Force decided to have a conference called a Blue Print for Action. The idea was to have former Love Canal, NY and Times Beach, MO residents come into dialogue with people from the plants and the regulatory community. At the time, the regulators were also in the doghouse with the community folks because they wouldn't talk openly with them.

The process for planning this conference took over a year. No one seemed able to trust anyone else to do things, so we all went around and around. We finally set the date for the conference in Niagara Falls and sent out the invitations. A psychologist from Atlanta came in to help us; another local chemical company had hired him to help the process. He was trying to help us develop a process for the dialogues. He was pretty firm about a particular process and pushed the group hard. The whole thing blew up on him, so he went home to Atlanta. With only three weeks to go before the conference, we went into crisis mode.

The process he was trying to get us to use was a good one and was similar to one we'd learned in DuPont in our Management Training Process. So, I made a proposal to the group that I could bring in around 10 people from DuPont to facilitate the process so we could go on with the conference. I promised that they'd play a neutral role facilitating the dialogue and not try to take over the conference. The environmental folks really struggled with this, but after several days agreed to my proposal. So I sent out the calls for help and was pleased to have the rest of the DuPont organization support me in this effort. About 300 people came to the conference. Practically everyone felt that it had been a real success in bringing so many diverse people together to talk about these difficult issues. Even so, some of the anti-corporate folks criticized DuPont for looking like they had taken over the Conference. I had roamed about during the three days, and I am quite sure our folks did a credible, neutral job in facilitating the meeting.

In the interviews after the conference, the reporters interviewed many people, but ignored the DuPont facilitators and me. Everyone else took credit for the success and DuPont didn't get a public word of thanks. We'd done the right thing, and as Sister and I kept trying to help, the relations between the plants and the community got better.

All through this stressful time, I was feeling more and more alone and depressed. No one seemed to understand the pressure I felt. No one seemed to give a damn. We were doing things in the community that no one else was doing in the chemical industry; we were bringing people together. We were in dialogue. We were doing things that upheld the good reputation of the Company. I felt like I was really hanging out all alone, but we were making progress. Under these pressures, I became increasingly demanding of the folks reporting to me. I'd get frustrated and angry at their slow progress.

At home, things continued to get much more difficult. Being a strong, white male, I felt that I just had to tough it through; this was how I was brought up. I prayed a lot, but felt that I was moving away from God as well. I was low, confused, lonely and in trouble. One Saturday morning in February 1985, I was painting the louvered shutters in the powder room, when I asked my wife about going to the Auction in Niagara Falls for the Boys and Girls Clubs. I was on the Girls Club Board of Directors. She said, in no uncertain terms, that she wasn't interested in going to this event in Niagara Falls with my friends. I think that was the straw that broke my back. I cried all day as I tried to paint. I realized that I'd have to leave this situation because I didn't know what else to do, and it was going to kill me. Leaving my wife was one of the things I thought I'd never do—that was done by weak bums who had no moral fiber. Now I was one of them. What would the girls say? What would the Company say? I felt like I was in the Valley of the Shadow of Death. I was at a low point in my life. It was now finally clear to me that my wife had chosen her path; I needed to choose my own.

On the morning after the March 9th meeting with Love Canal residents and Plant Managers that I mentioned earlier, I was talking to Claire Stoelting, who was in the HR Group and had helped to scribe the meeting for me. As we talked, she looked at me in a rather peculiar way and said, "You better sit down. You're in trouble. I can see what it is that you're trying to do and how important that is. I can see that you have a mission to fulfill, and bringing people together is the start of it. But you need help—you need to start talking about what is going on in you." I almost fell through the floor. I think it was the first time in my life that anyone had seen what I was trying to do and cared enough to talk to me like that. I almost cried. We began to talk. We talked almost every morning for a few minutes before the workday began. A great weight began to lift from my shoulders.

Another stress during this period was related to the chlorine-caustic plant that DuPont wanted to build to use the low-cost hydropower which was available to the Company. After the Niagara Falls Schoelkopf Power Station slipped into the Niagara River in 1957, a huge project to build new hydroelectric stations to use the great power of the Niagara River was begun. As part of the project, several different power rates were established. The lowest rate was called replacement power and was intended to encourage industrial growth in Western New York. The cheap rate would last until 2006. There was a block of power available, so DuPont felt it would be a good business decision to use it to make chlorine and caustic. The other raw material we needed was salt. Western New York has giant salt deposits lying about 1000 feet below grade level in zones up to 50 feet thick. Salt mining, both dry mining in underground mines, and solution mining (drilling into the formation, pumping water into the salt and pumping brine out) were already done in the area.

When I arrived at the Niagara Plant, this project was already in the planning stage. During my orientation with the previous manager, he mentioned that as things stood with the project, one of my big challenges would be to get a permit to discharge 50,000 pounds of salt an hour, as spent brine, into the Niagara River. I thought to myself that I wouldn't even try to do this; the idea was appalling to me. I talked this over with Barbara Northan, Rich Gentilucci and Dick Diamond who were our environmental managers. We all agreed that we should try to find out how to do it with no salt discharges to the River. With this shift in thinking, our folks found a way to use solution brine mining, by pumping the saturated brine to the plant through a 60 mile, 12 inch diameter pipeline. We could then return the spent, depleted brine back to the mine through another similar pipeline and return the waste salts to where we'd gotten them. The engineers did an outstanding job; it looked as if we'd have almost no impact on the environment. This was a great step forward. The project progressed to the point when we needed to go after the appropriation of money from DuPont and the permits from the DEC to build and operate the plant. The plan called for a solution brine mine near a beautiful town named Wyoming about 60 miles to the east of Niagara Falls. We'd pump the salt solution across the 60 miles using a dual pipeline so we could return the depleted brine to the mine. In Niagara Falls, we'd build the facility to produce the chlorine and caustic by an electrolytic process. We'd use about as much electricity as a city of 30,000 people.

Based on what I'd learned from my previous community work, we began to have meetings with the communities of Niagara Falls and Wyoming. We talked about all aspects of the project, particularly the environmental impact. We built models of the pipeline showing how we'd lay the pipe and clean up the areas as we went. We talked to the people in Wyoming. John Halberstadt, the project design manager and I went to a fundraiser there for their historic town hall and made a modest donation to it's remodeling. We had more coffee and cakes in the homes.

Along the pipeline route, we met with a number of people to talk with them about the project. Texas Brine Company was the contractor who would develop and operate the mine and lay the pipe. The guys laying the pipe put down 5-6 miles a day of pipeline. The trench diggers operate several miles ahead of the men laying the pipe. They are followed by the people who cover it and restore the land with grass. We had to buy the rights of way and work around wetlands and the pieces of property where we couldn't get them.

One summer night as we were drilling the monitoring wells in Wyoming, the drillers ran their big diesel drilling engines all night and woke up a lot of people. A lot of the good will we'd worked to develop went out the window. Several of the neighbors decided to try to block the work in court. They hired a Buffalo lawyer named Lewis Steel, a dedicated environmental attorney. Lewis was active in all the environmental activities in Niagara Falls, so I knew him pretty well. Even though I was sharing a lot of information with the neighbors and was getting to know them, Lewis and I bumped heads fairly often; it was respectful but intense.

We had a lot of public meetings in Niagara Falls. While some meetings were small, one had over 200 people in attendance. At that meeting, we made a complete review of the project for the community. It lasted for over two hours. Lewis spent an hour questioning me, finally sitting down only when the other citizens at the meeting got after him for taking up so much time and not asking new questions. I kept my cool very well and felt I'd done a good job in providing the information in an understandable and open way. By now I'd gotten to like Lewis; he deeply believed in what he was doing and tried to live his beliefs. I think he came to respect me in the same way. At his brother's funeral several months later, I met his mother. Lewis and I connected pretty well there.

We had about 22 public meetings with the communities and shared all we could with them. When it came to the public hearing step in the permitting process, the DEC, who'd been at most of the public meetings as observers, said we'd answered all the questions and a special public hearing was not needed. Lewis didn't like this and challenged this in court, but the court upheld the DEC decision. The permits were finally issued and the opening of the wells and the construction of the plant and pipeline began.

To open the mine, we intended to pump water down the well pipe drilled into the salt formation under enough pressure to lift the overburden and crack the salt formation. Once the formation was cracked, water could be pumped into the salt. After a few days, we could establish contact with another pipe that could then pump the brine out of the well. This area of New York has 10-12 very small earthquakes each year. They are measured by the Columbia University Seismology Lab, which is located in WNY. We felt the chances of a small quake were very low, but some of the neighbors challenged us in the Federal court in Warsaw, New York. Lewis was working hard to stop the work. We had a great environmental attorney named Dan Darraugh helping us all through the project. He knew the law, he knew the people involved in Western New York, and he knew where the goal line was. If it was right to move forward, Dan moved; he didn't equivocate. Dan had been our lawyer on the Necco Park activities as well, so we knew each other pretty well.

During the afternoon in the Warsaw, NY courtroom where Lewis was trying to get a Stay to stop the drilling, Dan called to tell us he thought we would be okay. We planned to fracture the mine that evening. We had a number of seismographs located around the site to monitor what we were doing. The judge ruled that we could go ahead, so that evening the pumping began. The work progressed well and the formation was cracked. There were no disturbances shown by the seismographs. About two weeks later, we established contact with one of the other wells so we could pump brine.

Construction at the plant was progressing, but previous ground contamination caused the work to be slower than we'd anticipated. Each time we dug a hole we had to be careful to discharge any ground water through a waste treatment plant because of the chlorocarbons I mentioned earlier.

Each week the engineers would meet with the DEC engineers to review what we were doing. On each Thursday, Barbara Northan, Dick Diamond, Rich Gentulicci and the other DuPont engineers would meet to prepare what they'd talk to the DEC engineers about on Friday. We were all learning to be more open, so one day Dick Diamond mentioned that they'd quit having the Friday meetings and had invited the DEC engineers into the Thursday meeting. I'm glad they hadn't asked me about this because I might not have approved it; they were becoming more open than I was. This process worked very well.

More learnings came. Sharing information, building relationships where we could work together, and building our shared future seemed to help things go much better.

By now, Olin Corporation had become a 50/50 partner in the project. They had a chlorine-caustic plant right next to our plant. They planned to ship the caustic in their rail car fleet, and we planned to ship the chlorine in our tank car fleet. Their Plant Manager, Mickey Norsworthy, was a great partner. When the project received the final permits and approval of the New York Power Authority on the allocation of power, we had a community party. Employment had declined so much in Niagara Falls over the years that we wanted to celebrate a new plant. Niachlor, as it was now known, had a big banner in the Convention Center. We had all the business leaders, politicians, community folks and environmental folks together for the community party.

In mid-1985, we in DuPont began to work with Niagara Falls' Mayor O'Laughlin to form a Hazardous Materials Advisory Council to help the community prepare for a potential hazardous materials incident. It was the third Advisory Council in the US. DuPont had played a strong role in setting them up, first in Memphis, TN, then in Newark, NJ and now in Niagara Falls. This was another big step in helping the community come together.

One interesting thing we did was to have a joint meeting with the City Councils of Niagara Falls, Ontario and Niagara Falls, NY. It was the first time that the two City Councils had ever met together. We talked about potential plant and transportation incidents and how the two communities would react.

After I'd left for my next assignment, the Niachlor Plant started up successfully, and met all the environmental requirements.

My marriage continued to deteriorate. I'd decided that I had to leave my wife, so in January of 1986, I moved out! I was terrified and wondered what would happen. When I left my wife, I made it a point to go to talk to my management in Wilmington. When I told my boss, we were sitting in his office. He was messing with some papers on his desk. When I told him I was moving out, he looked up and said he was sorry and if he could be of any help to call him. Then he went back to his papers. We just didn't know how to connect and help each other. In the Company at that time in the mid-80s, we were so uptight that personal problems didn't even get on the radar screen until things hit the fan.

I had several good Assistant Managers at Niagara. The first was really very good and was a big help in all the work we were doing. He helped to keep things going inside the plant while I was spending so much time trying to open up our freedom to operate. When he moved on, another Assistant Manager was assigned. I knew this fellow from our work in New Jersey at the Repauno Plant. He'd been the plant manager of one of our smaller plants, and Management wanted to give him experience in a larger plant. He was really quite good with the people and helped to improve the relations with the Union. He and Chet Kodeski agreed to have a "blue sky" type of meeting to talk about what the Plant could look like in ten years.

As a result of this meeting, we had about 20 all-day meetings with everyone at the Plant to talk about the future. I led these, and we all came together pretty well. I was not so easy to be with, however, back with my staff. I became increasingly concerned with my own temper for it just broke out now and then.

Claire and our Relationship

Claire and I kept talking, and we developed a special kinship. Her own marriage came undone during this same time for a variety of reasons. Ultimately, our respective roads to divorce, though disconnected one from the other, are what caused our relationship to be misconstrued by many people around us. Our relationship became a problem for the Company. Several people from the Plant sent letters to the CEO telling him their views about me; I suddenly was in deep trouble. They scolded me and in February 1987, I was put on special assignment in Headquarters for 2 months until the Plant Manager position opened up in Belle, West Virginia. Claire was well regarded by the plant people and the top management; she was doing the HR Senior Supervisors job. But eventually, her career was adversely impacted by our relationship as well.

After my transfer to Belle in April, we kept up our relationship. I was divorced by now and she was in court trying to extricate herself and her daughter from their situation. It was a bitter custody battle over their 3-year-old daughter, Christine. After over two years, the divorce was settled with each parent having joint custody of Christine. She would spend alternate weeks with each parent. Claire and I tried to see each other on weekends, our relationship grew, and we wanted to get married. Over a year after I'd been sent to Belle, she was demoted a full salary level with no credible explanation, and put into a training assignment for the Niachlor group. She was moved into an office trailer next to the contractors in the back of the Plant. This was devastating for her, and I could do nothing to help. She held her head high though with courage and dignity. She didn't give in and quit. She made lemonade out of the lemon. She became an inspiration to the other women in the organization for her courage and the way she worked and held herself. After several years, new management came into the picture. Her HR, labour relations and people skills were recognized. Her supervisor went to bat for her, and she was promoted back up a half level. She was a key, staff leader in the Niachlor Plant.

Claire had started her work career with DuPont right out of high school, beginning as a switchboard operator. She now decided to get her college degree. The State University of New York has an external degree program called Empire State College of the State University of New York. This fit her needs so she enrolled. She was interviewed and granted credit for her 2-year professional secretaries' degree, as well as given credits for some of her life and work experiences. For example, they recognized her being an OSHA certified safety training professional. She majored in Business Management and Economics. In just 2 years, she received her BS degree. She passed 15 challenge exams and took 8 courses getting 7 A's and a B+. I am really proud of her for overcoming the adversity she encountered for having the courage to love me.

Several years later, she had the chance to apply for an HR job at the DuPont plant in Buffalo where the product, Corian®—a material for making solid surface counter tops of superior quality—is made. There are around 750 people working there. Within 4 years she'd been promoted 2 levels and was the site Administrative Services Superintendent responsible for human resources, labor relations, safety, health, environmental performance, employee assistance, purchasing, snow plowing; any thing that didn't make money, as she'd say. She had risen to a higher level than she'd achieved at

Niagara, and she'd done it on her own!

We were married on New Year's Eve in 1988. We built a home in Niagara Falls near her former husband's house so that Christine could go back and forth easily, go to the same schools and have the same friends. We decided to try a commuter marriage, not knowing whether we could do it. We traveled almost every weekend between Niagara Falls and Belle. The Pittsburgh Airport, where we had to make the airline connections between Charleston and Buffalo, became our home away from home. Some people buy boats for recreation; we bought airplane seats. Claire was a certified Occupational Safety and Health trainer so we often made safety audits at the Belle Plant on the weekends. The Belle people liked her much better than me, so these were good for all of us. We became close friends with many of the people there. Christine also often joined us in West Virginia for the weekends.

Wilmington

My Special Assignment in the Wilmington headquarters prior to being transferred to Belle consisted of working with the Production Division Staff in developing some leadership principles. We did several half-day sessions on these principles and I spent a lot of time trying to write and get input from the 6 or 7 Production Managers. I also sat in on the Production Staff meetings, which were an eye-opener. These fellows weren't functioning any better than we were at the plant levels. I somehow still had the belief that these higher ups would do this stuff better, but I discovered that they were just another bunch of fellows trying their best to make sense of the world. Another learning from this work was seeing how deep the patterns and behaviors we all engage in really are; they show up at many levels.

After doing some good work and developing some good principles, I suggested that we post these around the offices. I was startled to find that they didn't want to share them with anyone. Beginning to open up is hard work. Sharing information and building relationships isn't that easy.

Moving on to Belle

The assignment to Belle came in April 1987. Belle was not in the same Department I'd been part of, but it made many products for my old Department's business groups. Their performance was not good, and the plant received a lot of criticism. Belle was viewed as being very unresponsive, and it didn't seem to understand the need to get better. One reason for my being sent there was to address this problem. Belle was a big, old plant that was started in 1927 to make ammonia. Believe it or not, this was the newest plant in which I had ever worked.

The older plants in DuPont had developed through many organizational changes, so most of them made products for several different businesses. In some plants, the organizations were divided up to report to the various businesses so they'd have better control. Belle was fully under the control of the Agricultural Chemicals Department but made products for 3 or 4 other businesses as well.

Belle's strength was that the plant could handle and make highly hazardous chemicals safely. Belle had been in decline for years, and its employment had dropped from over 5000 people in World War II to about 1300 when I was sent there. They had not hired hourly people for about 10 years. Although I wasn't told this, I think that management expected the plant to fail and shut down. All its products were made in other places around the world, so we had little competitive advantage. When I got there, I found a broken organization and a sick plant.

The safety performance, for example, was about 8 times poorer than the Company as a whole. I found this very interesting. How could they have survived so long this way? They didn't even realize that they were so far out of line.

My first days on the job happened to coincide with the annual management visitation. This involved hosting about ten people from the head offices and other plants who listened to talks and took tours for 2 days. These were attempts to learn about what was happening and to help the plants get better. The visitors were there to help. As I watched and listened, I realized that I had my work cut out for me. The plant management put on quite a show that included spreading thousands of dollars of new crushed stone all over to make the plant look better. The newly painted areas still smelled strongly of fresh paint. I could see the symptoms; they were trying to paper over a lot of deep problems and issues.

Like many DuPont plants, Belle had jumped into the organizational effectiveness (OE) effort in a big way. They had taken all 1300 people off their regular jobs for three weeks of training over the previous year. Expectations were raised high as a kite; a new day was dawning and everyone would have a say in how the plant was run. For many reasons, the effort fell apart, and the people became quite cynical about the whole effort.

My first goal was to get to know people, so I embarked on an effort to meet everyone and talk with them in the first 6 weeks or so. Everywhere I went I was asked if I believed in OE. I said that I did, but that right now we had to get back to the basics in all aspects of our performance, beginning with safety. This was a struggle for almost all of the people because they thought their performance was okay. Having no family with me, I spent long hours at the plant talking and doing audits. Each morning, we had a morning wrap-up meeting to review the previous day's performance and talk about the plan for the new day. I noticed quite quickly that one guy took over the meetings and tried to control everything. He was very angry with me because he thought he deserved the manager's job. The fact that I was an outsider was also a problem for him. I began to notice his misinformation and game playing, his bullying and pushing people around. One morning I'd had enough and angrily called him down in front of the rest of the people, which was not good performance on my part. Once he tried to bully me by coming into my office, sitting on my desk over me and giving me a lecture. That never happened again; in fact, he was on the desk for only about 10 seconds.

In another morning meeting, one of the General Superintendents reported an injury that had happened the previous day. When I asked about the person, he didn't even know the man's name. His indifference and arrogance towards the people angered me, and I let him know it right then—not good!

I did many things to drive home that I was in charge. I took the head seat at the table for our weekly management meetings and for the morning report meetings. I drove safety by fear. I did things to let them know that safety was important to me. In our huge parking lot, for example, the tradition was to park diagonally heading in. This meant, that in the evenings as people were going home at shift change, they had to back their cars out into the flow of traffic and people. I felt this was not safe and turned the parking around so people would back in the mornings and be headed out frontward where they could see better in the evenings. We come to work in the mornings one or two at a time, but there was a mass exodus in the evenings and a lot of crowding. Being able to see where you were going during the most crowded time seemed to make safety sense to me. Wow, that really upset people. I even had one General Superintendent come in and tell me he didn't know how to back his car into the parking spots. I could hardly believe the lame behavior.

Soon after coming to the plant, I began to expand the number of business meetings well beyond what my predecessors had done. We began to hold two each week in various areas of the Plant. We'd meet in control rooms, shops, labs and offices, meeting wherever the people were. Everyone in the particular group was invited, including all the supervision. The meetings were held each Wednesday; one at 7:30 A.M. and the other was at 9:00 A.M. They lasted about an hour. We'd begin with a rundown of our safety and environmental performance followed by a brief summary of the business conditions. We'd then open up the meeting to questions. All questions were okay and we tried to answer each one. My secretary would come along to take the notes in shorthand. We didn't want to tape record the meetings because we feared that this would cut down on the participation. We'd publish the minutes of the meeting within 36 hours. This was a big effort, but well worth it; the minutes became a great communication process, uniting the plant and lifting up critical issues.

These meetings were very difficult at first because people were so frustrated and angry about the way things had been going. After a year or so, the flavor began to improve and people gradually became more purposeful. Sometimes people in the meetings made a point of testing each other to see if we were for real.

Several years into these meetings, I was scheduled to talk with a maintenance group who prided themselves on being ornery. Unbeknownst to me, their supervisor had told them that particular morning "Don't make waves for Knowles." The meeting started normally, but when I got to the question part, it came apart. I asked for any questions, and all 40 of them got up, turned their chairs around and sat down with their backs to me. My stomach turned into a knot. If I blew up, I was finished. If I walked out, I was done. My intuition told me that something was going on between them and their supervision so I said "Okay, everyone in supervision please get out." They moved into the hall and I shut the door. Still, there was nothing but backs and silence. I got a cup of coffee and sat down—just backs and silence. It seemed like ten years, but was probably more like a minute when I said, "Fellows, this is a pretty lonely job. Is anybody going to talk to me?" Within a minute, everyone had turned around and we had a great meeting. I learned what had happened with their supervisor.

After the meeting, I had a back-to-basics hour with the supervisor and managers. Treating people this way just wasn't acceptable. So there was another lesson. People behave in the way we treat them: tit-for-tat.

At about this time, a funny situation developed. My management team and I made a poor decision about something—I don't even remember what it was at this point. The plant people were raising quite a fuss over it. I do remember sitting in the staff meeting as they discussed the situation, trying to come up with an explanation that would convince everyone that we really hadn't made a mistake. I began to see how funny this was, so I stopped the meeting and told the folks that we were going to go out to the people. We'd tell them we'd made a mistake and would try not to do it again. Some members of the staff were shocked with this approach. We did it and the issue immediately disappeared. Another thing we learned was that Covey is right. It's not the first mistake that gets you into trouble. It's the second one where you try to tell your people that you hadn't made a mistake when everyone knows you did.

My secretary, Debbie Fisher, was great in helping me to keep my balance. We'd connected quite well in my first weeks in the plant. We became a good team. One day she brought a visitor into the outer office when I was in one of my uptight moods and was giving someone the devil on the phone. They overheard my frustration and bad language. When I hung up the visitor came in; I was still upset so I guess I wasn't very courteous to the visitor. After he'd left, Debbie came in and gave me a lecture about my behavior; this really shook me up and helped me to try to do a better job on this front. She told me a few years later that I looked like a little boy who gotten into trouble. We laugh about that now.

After about a year, I decided to relocate the Manager and General Superintendent's offices from the old main office building into the manu-facturing plant to be closer to our people and the operations. The old main office building was a three story brick building located outside the plant fence along the main road. Each time I went into the plant I had to show my pass to get in the main gate. As I look back, I realize that this move was a significant signal to the plant that things were changing. We all became more accessible, and we interacted with many more people. We removed ourselves from the seat of the old culture, the place where 70 years of memories and protocols resided.

Debbie also found that this move freed her up to shape the office in a more workable and smooth way. She was only the third Plant Manager's Secretary in the last 50 years, so there was a lot she wanted to change. Before the move, she felt that she was living under a heavy, stale, moldy blanket. The stuffy atmosphere of the old main office was behind us. Several people who'd worked for years to get close to the manager's office were quite upset with the move. This move helped to remove the old we vs. them culture.

In just 2 years, the injury rate came down from around a total OSHA recordable injury rate of about 5.8 to about 0.7. I applied the safety standards to everyone as equally as I could. Supervision had shoved this off to others for years, so this new approach was pretty upsetting to them. I learned that several people had written to the DuPont CEO telling him I was causing a lot of trouble and was crazy. My immediate management was with me and they supported the improvements we were making.

Then we suddenly faced a major problem. Over about a three-week period in early 1988, we had a series of serious safety incidents that really shook us. We had one operator who was in a drug rehabilitation program and tested positive for a controlled substance. His job was to unload hydrogen cyanide tank cars. Shortly after this, our locomotive removed a tank car from a rail loading spot without disconnecting the loading hoses. Fortunately, we were not transferring any material since it was a toxic product. We drug tested both the operator on the ground who cleared the car for the railroad and the railroad man, who also cleared the car for removal. Both of them were on a controlled substance. A few days later, two electricians were working on a 12,000-volt switch. One dropped a wrench into it. The voltage going to ground caused a big explosion and destroyed the switch, which shut down about half the Plant. One of them was also on a controlled substance.

We were really frightened and sobered by these events. We handled the sorts of hazardous materials that could kill people, and drugs like marijuana and cocaine just didn't belong in this environment. Our neighbors lived right next to the Plant.

We went to the plant people and said that we had to do something about this. We needed a mandatory, random drug-testing program to drive drugs out of the Plant. We talked about it in the weekly business meetings. Maybe it would be more accurate to say that we did a lot of fighting about it in the weekly meetings. Everyone seemed pretty upset with the idea of having his or her personal rights violated. We pointed out that those working at the plant and the neighbors working nearby had the right to a safe working environment and a safe community.

We drafted the first proposal for the program and shared it with everyone. We asked who should be in the program. We asked for ways to be sure we didn't get any false positives. We got back to everyone that made inputs on the procedures. We ran the procedures through 3or 4 different iterations. I was tested at one point. Although the test was negative, I remember that during the test, I too worried about a false positive, so I was very sensitive to that issue. I was bragging to a mechanic about having peed and passed. He asked, "Who told you to do that?" When I said I'd done it to show leadership around the issue, he asked if others could do that as well.

The next day we announced a voluntary testing program. About 150 people volunteered. Each one had their social security number put on a card that was placed in a bingo basket, which we then took to the business meetings. Each week about 5 numbers were drawn in the meetings, so people could see that the system was open and fair. We decided to use two labs to test for us. The urine specimens were collected under a chain-of-custody procedure using nurses to administer the sampling. People were not observed delivering the specimen, but the temperature of the urine was measured to try to prevent cheating. Each specimen was split into two and each one was sent to a different lab. The first lab ran a qualitative test. If it was negative, the process stopped. If it was positive, they ran a quantitative test to identify the particular drug. If that was negative, the process stopped. If it was positive, we'd ask the second lab to verify the test. If that was negative, the process stopped. If it was positive, then the person was sent to a team of psychologists in Charleston, WV for consultation. After they tested free of drugs, they returned to work in their own work group doing work that was not safety-critical. The person also went into a two-year drug rehabilitation program.

Everyone in safety-critical assignments was included in the testing. This amounted to about 92% of the people. Secretaries, for example, were not included because they were not in safety-critical assignments.

The drug testing laboratory selection process involved the plant quality control laboratory union visiting them to see if they were qualified. We did everything we could to include people around the whole effort in developing the processes. It was a wide-open process so everyone knew what was going on. In the fall, the Lab Union took us to court over what they felt was the violation of personal rights. The Federal Judge ruled that we'd properly balanced the rights of all individuals and had met the guidelines of the Constitution. We began the site-wide program the next week.

Over the next 5 years that I was at Belle, we tested about 20 people a week. Throughout the testing process, only about 15 people ever tested positive. We were relieved that the number of people testing positive was so low. Unfortunately, most of those who did test positive couldn't get through the 2-year probation period. It was hard to see them leave because many of them were quite nice people, but mind-altering drugs and hazardous chemicals don't mix. We did have several others leave as well. Two guys tried to cheat and two operators in safety-critical assignments refused to be tested, so we parted company with them. The rules applied to everyone.

By 1988, with all the changes taking place, the level of dissatisfaction among some of the employees was high enough for them to try another union organizing campaign. The campaign was intense; we did almost nothing but work on relationship building and sharing information about why we felt a union would hurt our ability to compete. This drew our focus inward away from the customers. The Plant had been through 18 other campaigns since 1948. Some of the staff acted as if this was just another game while others did their best work during the campaign. After a 6-week campaign, we came to the vote.

Part way into the campaign, my 89-year-old father who lived in Florida, came down with a gall bladder attack. With his heart condition, the doctors didn't feel they could operate. Both Claire and Debbie insisted that I go to see him. An opportunity came during the campaign when I thought I could be away for a few days, so I went to see him. He was in hospital and not very coherent. He was strapped in the bed with his arms tethered so he couldn't pull out the IV needles. It was sad to see him this way. I stayed with my stepmother and visited him several times. I told him I loved him and finally at one point he said he loved me; we had never talked that way while I was growing up. I had to head back to my post at the Plant to resume the effort to convince the folks that, for many reason, voting for the union was not in their or the Plant's best long-term interests.

I've worked at many unionized facilities and deeply believed we didn't need one, providing that there was the open communication, trust and mutual respect that we were building at Belle. We felt that a union would cause us to focus internally so strongly that we wouldn't compete effectively in the markets we were in. I saw this as a struggle for the long-term survival of the plant. I felt responsible for trying to make the site as healthy and competitive as possible, so that we'd have a viable business and a good place to work. I spent hours and hours with the people talking about these issues. Gary Lewis, Elbert Price and others on the Leadership team played a major role in this effort.

At one point, someone accused me of being on an ego trip with all the changes we were trying to make. I just looked at him in amazement and said, "No one in his right mind would be doing all these things on an ego trip. The stakes are way too high for that. If we fail on these things, we could lose the whole Plant."

The voting took place on a Thursday and Friday so that all the shift workers could vote. Officers of the National Labor Relations Board supervised the election and voting. The polls closed at 7 P.M. on Friday, so at about 7:30 P.M. we gathered to observe the vote count. As I was leaving my office at about 7:15, there was a loud clap of thunder. In a chemical plant, electrical storms are a worry because you can loose power and that causes environmental incidents and spoils our products. I looked up—there was only a single dark cloud in the sky and there was no rain.

The vote count was very deliberate. Each one was read and the vote announced. The HR Superintendent, Elbert Price, was next to me keeping track of the votes. Some of the naysayers on my staff were predicting we'd lose (maybe hoping to embarrass me) so I was on the edge of my seat. The vote came out with about 66% voting against a union. What a relief!

I went back to the office to call my father with the news. My stepmother answered the phone. When she found out it was me, she said "Didn't your brother call you? Your father died at 7:15." I just sat there, devastated. We'd won an important battle and I couldn't even tell him about it. The HR management people from Wilmington headquarters called to congratulate the team, and me, but I could hardly talk I was so choked up and crying.

The next week my brothers and I gathered in Florida to be with our stepmother for the memorial services. Several days later, the funeral was held in Wilmington where we'd all grown up and where my father wanted to be buried next to my mother. My Manufacturing VP and one other person from the Agricultural Chemicals Department came to the funeral. I appreciated that they came. Claire and her two sisters also came. My daughters were also there, which was so good. I needed their support as well. Even though they still hadn't sorted everything out about Claire and me, I was deeply grateful that they came to support me and to honor their grandfather.

At Belle, we'd made good improvements in restoring the safety and other standards, but it had taken a toll on us. We'd hired a consultant I'd known in Buffalo, named Alan Gilberg, who began to help us learn how to talk to each other and be more open. We'd also realized that we needed to move into a team environment if we were going to make the further progress we needed to survive. One of the staff members suggested that if we were going to go to teams, we should try it ourselves. We quickly discovered that being a team was a lot more difficult than talking about being a team. We talked about our team play each week and rated our performance as a team on a scale of 0-10, with 10 being best. While it was a subjective rating, it was a good measure of how we were doing. For weeks, our score averaged around a 7.5. I was getting more and more frustrated with the guys for not getting better. One day as I was talking to Alan, I wondered if I was the problem and was blocking the team's progress. I then asked them if they would be willing to tell me what I was doing that was getting in the way of our improvement. All but one of the 9 on the staff spent an hour with me telling me what a jerk I was. It was great when I wasn't there. They really didn't like the way I was managing even though they recognized we were making strong progress in the safety and the businesses. This really hurt for I was doing the best I could and working 65-70 hours a week to do it. What a lousy report! It really hurt. Claire was a vital support for me.

I spent a lot of time lying awake trying to figure out what to do. After a week or so, I sat down with the staff and gave them a summary of their report. I said I wanted to change and needed their help. As I mentioned before, a few weeks after I came into the Plant as the new manager, I took the chair at the head of our meeting table to make it quite clear that I was in charge. One thing I said I wanted to do now was to move away from the head of the table and to sit at the side of the room. Each week the leadership of the team rotated among them. The leader could call meetings and was the key communicator with Wilmington and the community if I wasn't around. They would also sit at the head of the table. If anyone had a special meeting subject to lead, he or she would sit at the head of the table. That could also be me now and then. They all agreed to try this. Alan kept helping us to be civil and helpful.

The first week after having made the change, our team's report on how we were doing was much better and the score jumped to over 8.5. It was clear that I had been causing many of the team's problems in my drive to improve and save the plant. I was glad we'd begun to find a way out of the morass, but embarrassed that I'd been a barrier to our progress. We moved on and they helped, which was critical because I couldn't have done it by myself.

Not long after having arrived at the plant, the Company asked me to be their representative on the Chemical Manufacturers Association (CMA) Community Awareness and Emergency Response (CAER) Task Group. The CMA is now known as The American Chemical Council and has as its members the larger chemical companies that account for about 85% of the chemical production in the US. My involvement with the CAER Task Group was intended to help the industry benefit from and build on my experiences while I was the manager at Niagara. This Task Group was intended to help guide the industry in developing community outreach and emergency response procedures. This group was the first step in what later became Responsible Care®. This is a solid initiative of the industry towards self-regulation in process safety and emergency response. My major contribution was to keep a plant focus to the efforts. We met roughly every two months. I was on this group for about 9 years. There will be more on this later.

After I was at Belle for about a year, I was invited to be on the Board of the National Institute of Chemical Studies (NICS) in Charleston, West Virginia. On December 3, 1984 the Bhopal, India tragedy occurred, which was a result of an accidental release of methylisocyanate. It had killed several thousand people and injured many more. Union Carbide (UCC) made methylisocyanate in South Charleston, WV, so there was a lot of concern in that community about the safety of the local plant. UCC had talked with the community about their safety procedures, which had given the community the confidence that this sort of thing couldn't happen in South Charleston.

Then in 1985, UCC had the Aldecarbe® release in South Charleston. It happened during the day, and the toxic cloud drifted across the Kanawha River into the parking lot of a large shopping mall. Somewhere between 50 and 100 people went to hospital because of their exposure. The community went right through the roof. They felt that they weren't as safe as they had thought. Several large, tense community meetings were held, including one with the UCC CEO. This release led to the creation of the National Institute of Chemical Studies (NICS), and later to the passage by the US Congress of the Clean Air Act of 1990. NICS was formed out of the wreckage by a number of community leaders who didn't want the community to fall apart. Board members came from the broad community and from business, as well as from churches and the political community. The conversations among these people really helped to bring the community back together. When I joined the Board in 1988, people were talking about the issues of the 13 chemical plants located in the Kanawha

Valley near Charleston. The Board felt that the local issues were merely a microcosm of those in the rest of the country. What we were learning locally had national implications. This was a correct observation. I met with the Board at their monthly meetings, and got to know some of the business leaders and the environmentalists. My connections with the community became closer and healthier.

One of NICS's efforts was to encourage the formation of local community advisory councils (CAC's), so that the plants and their neighbors could establish ongoing dialogues. This was also aligned with the CMA CAER Task Group recommendations. We formed one in the Belle community in about 1988. There was a lot of interest in what we were doing. Our CAC was a joint one with Occidental Chemicals who were in an adjoining but much smaller plant. We had plant tours and open houses so people could see for themselves what we were doing, see what the facilities looked like and get to know the people better.

Early in 1988, we decided that we needed a much closer connection with all the DuPont businesses functioning at Belle. We had about 4 different businesses involved, as well as 2 or 3 research and manufacturing groups. Traditionally, they functioned quite independently and made decisions that were appropriate for them, but they were often disconnected from the other businesses. This sometimes caused big disruptions at the plant, which then affected the other businesses.

We formed the Belle Coordinating Team to try to bring everyone together to hear about the work we were trying to do, as well as to talk together about plans. This way we could begin to develop a coordinated effort. Ken Cook, Bob Brown, Gary Lewis, Elbert Price and others from the Plant put together our thoughts and the supporting information about what we felt needed to be done. We worked hard in between these quarterly meetings to keep everyone together. By this process, we were able to have a profound impact on the future of the plant. We discovered that we at the Plant were the only ones with a comprehensive picture of what needed to be done, so we were able to step out and really lead the whole effort. We talked about technical issues, the production issues and the long-term business issues in these meetings. Over the 3 to 4 years when these were most active, we were able to make huge progress in developing a coordinated plan of action. We proposed bold initiatives and delivered on them, so we built our confidence that we could take the lead. This was a great example of providing the leadership from below in the organization. We were able to open up the space for us to have a major impact on the shape of our future. In these meetings, we were able to generate the support for and the freedom to do the innovative work we were doing. The Coordinating Team was very supportive during the Union Campaign I discussed earlier.

Sometimes the meetings were very difficult, but as long as we all stayed in the process of trying to find the best solutions for the business and plant issues, we accomplished a lot. One of the first big challenges involved a business that was one of our largest in terms of production quantities. It was an old business where we were no longer the major supplier. The Business Team felt that significant changes to all parts of the business were necessary to justify remaining in the business.

We decided, with the Business Team in one of the first Belle Coordinating Team meetings, to make the required changes in the production part of the business. We were the second largest producer of the three related products. We had higher costs than our competitor did, and our quality was not quite as good. Our part of the improvement effort at the Plant involved changing the process control instrumentation from pneumatic to electronic controls. The pneumatic controls were state of the art 30 years ago, but were now obsolete. This system measured process control parameters such as temperature and pressure by using changes of nitrogen gas pressure in a closed system of sensors, valves, probes, tubes and the like. These changes were measured in the control room and converted into readings of temperature and pressure in the process. We could only measure the temperatures, for example, to within a range of several degrees. This didn't give us the control we required to produce the top quality products we needed.

The electronic controls would give us much better accuracy and precision. We'd be able to read the temperatures, for example, to within a few tenths of a degree. This would provide much better distillation column control so we'd be able to make better separations of the products. Projects like this are usually expensive, and retrofitting them to old, existing production lines is difficult.

We asked our Engineering Department people to come in to do a study and make a project proposal. They said that it would take two years and cost around $6,000,000. They would build a second control room and we'd run the units using the instruments from the old process until we'd learned how to use the new ones. From my previous experience, I knew that the operators would take a further two years before they accepted the new process and really learned to use it.

XLVII

This was both too expensive and took too long so we thanked them and said "No thanks." Then, working with a process control group in our research division, led by my older brother, Frank, (synchronicity again) and a group from Honeywell Corporation who'd supply the instruments, we began the project ourselves. The Engineering folks were not happy with us for taking this route and began to spread the word that we'd fail.

We had Project Status Reviews in the operating control room each week, so everyone was knowledgeable and could contribute. Our engineers didn't like this because they felt the room was too crowded and too noisy—which it was. It was exactly the right place for the meetings, however, because everyone was involved. Most of us stood up during the 1-2 hour meetings each week. I mostly listened because I didn't have the technical expertise to contribute that way. My role was to hold open the space for these conversations to take place and to ensure that we paid attention to each other. I also prayed a lot, a whole lot.

We decided that we would not run parallel processes. This meant that when the changeover came, we'd tear out the pneumatic system and replace it with the electronic system. If that strategy failed, we were out of business and my career path would have changed, again.

Part way through the work, we sent about 15 operators and a few mechanics to the Honeywell Instrument School in Arizona for three weeks of training. We had to learn how to install, run and maintain the new instruments. I then had to explain to my higher management why I'd sent these people to sunny Arizona in the middle of the winter.

The excitement and interest built as we moved. At one point, the operators said that they wanted to design their remodeled control room. I said that was fine, providing it was operable, neat and clean and that they didn't put their coffee cups on the instrument keyboards. It was their place, so I was okay with them doing this. The operators were involved with the engineers in designing the graphics for the monitor screens. The mechanics worked with the engineers to help decide on the placement of the instruments.

In late June, we signed off on two projects for the work totaling just under $3,000,000. We did this in about 10 minutes on each other's backs during one of the meetings instead of the 8 weeks this usually took us to go over projects. We were all very close to this work and knew all that was happening. The business team member from Wilmington took the projects back to have the Business Division VP sign them. She did an excellent job and they were signed the next day. We were moving!

The energy and activity built as we approached the late October shutdown. In addition to changing over the instrumentation, we'd also did our other annual maintenance tasks like inspecting the insides of the distillation columns and checking the safety relief devices. It was elbows and knees all over the place. Everyone was committed to this being a successful effort.

The mechanics were now pulling the wires and helping do the loop checks for integrity. The last minute programming was being done and the training was complete. I was still praying a lot. We went into the shutdown and there was stuff everywhere. I just looked on in amazement hoping they could get it all back together again. As a chemist, I didn't know much about this kind of work.

After the two weeks of the shutdown, we had changed the 100 or so loops that required the entire plant to be down, the distillation columns were checked and back together—everything was ready. We started up without any environmental incidents or injuries and were in full production in just 4 days. It was awesome to me to see what these folks had done. The teamwork and learning were extraordinary. Here was a powerful lesson in the importance of sharing all the information, building trust and having everyone involved in the whole process.

Ken Cook, the General Superintendent for this area of the Plant and his team played an extraordinary role in the success of the changeover. Ken's quiet, strong leadership helped us all to keep our feet on the ground. Pretop Gobel, the lead engineer, also played a key role.

I was almost as fascinated by the reaction of the Engineering Department people that we had sent away. They were telling people we were having trouble and that the project was failing. When my boss called to find out what was happening and expressed these concerns, I was able to tell him that we were running beautifully, loading tank cars with the best quality product that we'd ever made. I learned that denial could be quite an awesome thing to experience.

This whole experience taught us the power of teams, freely-flowing information, involvement, and building trust. We learned how important it was to be in this sort of thing together. As a manager, I was in the process and not just standing outside of it in judgment. Control came from everywhere, as different people stepped forward to take the leadership of one thing or another. Several years later, I heard Karen Anne Zien use the phrase "leaderful organizations" at one of the Berkana Dialogues; I immediately understood what she meant.

While we had not set out to do anything more than to save our business in the most effective way we could, we wound up setting a new standard for the whole DuPont Company on those sorts of projects, cutting both the cost and the time in half. We did another 15 of them. We never ran parallel and we never failed. These leadership processes work! Not only had we accomplished a neat business objective, but our people felt wonderful for having accomplished such a thing. The business won and the people won. I like that sort of an outcome! Business success and the success of the people go hand in hand. There was meaning in this for people.

We began to use more and more of the things we'd learned in our organizational effectiveness work more deeply. The big project I just described really illustrated the power of this approach. But, for the most part, the Company had moved away from this approach because of our disappointing experiences in the mid 1980's. There were still about 10 plant managers in the company, however, who were trying to learn more and stayed with it. We met in a group every 6 months or so, and we called it the No Name Network. I learned a lot from these other managers and the Krone consultant, Ken Wessel, who worked with us.

During the summer of 1988, Claire, Christine and I went to Davis and Elkins College in Elkins, WV for a week at the Heritage Arts Workshop. Claire and I took hammered dulcimer lessons with Sam Rizzetta. We really liked the instrument, so we purchased two of them to learn more. I took lessons in St. Albans with Sally Hawley. I practiced every day for 30 minutes from 5:30 to 6 A.M. After a few months, some of the plant people had found out I was learning to play it. One guy, Homer Hunter, a First Line Supervisor (FLS) had the courage to could come over and to play his guitar with me.

This was a real breakthrough for me, because up to then most people avoided social activities with me. Homer risked being called a lot of unkind names for doing this. He came over one evening. We both laugh about what we found. I was picking my way through the tunes quite slowly to get them correct. So when we started, Homer started to laugh and said, "Son, you're going to have to play this thing a lot faster." It was pretty funny because I thought I was doing quite well. I played faster and Homer came over several more times. Then he invited me to come to his home and play with the group he had there. This was a real thrill for me. You'll remember that my first wife and two of my daughters were professional musicians and they generally treated me as being non-musical. Now

L

here was a musical group asking me to join them, wonder of wonders!

There was a fiddler, a banjo player, two guitars, a bass player, and a mandolin player. These guys let me play along in the background with them. Now and then, we'd sip a little moonshine. It felt so good to be included in a group like this and begin to be myself. One of the guys was a coal miner, and in WV, managers and coal miners don't normally mix. He was always courteous to me but never used my name or looked me in the eye. A year of getting together gradually helped people to accept me. One day the coal miner looked at me, said my name and asked if I'd like to come to see his truck. He worked in a strip mine where all the equipment is bigger than anything I'd ever seen. I was thrilled to have this opening, so I agreed to go. Homer and Ray Baisden, Homer's cousin who was a guitar player and operator at the plant, took me out to the mine one Saturday morning. The mine was about 20 miles south of Charleston.

It had rained overnight so things were rather muddy. We got a tour and climbed up into the cab of the huge truck. It could carry 250,000 pounds of stone and dirt. The cab was so high it was like sitting in my second floor bedroom. We saw the huge dragline and I learned a lot about strip mining. After that, the group was closer to me and me to them.

Homer and Cathy Hunter and Ray and Sandy Baisden adopted Claire, Christine and me into their families, which was a wonderful experience for us. We went to family reunions and became part of their extended family. Homer and Ray are like brothers to me.

The dulcimer playing of the mountain dance tunes brought us closer to the community in many ways. We'd play at plant functions and schools. For example, I was invited to play at the local Jr. High School, DuPont Jr. High, for their heritage arts days in the spring, so the kids could hear their own music. At one point, I had about 50 tunes memorized. None of the groups I played with used printed music; it's an oral tradition in the Appalachians.

As we worked with the Belle Coordinating Team, they kept pushing us on our costs. I was also getting huge pressure on this from my own Manager. One of the opportunities that became more visible was the chance to reduce the labor component of our capital projects. In West Virginia, the American Federation of Labor-Congress of Industrial Organizations (AFL/ CIO) Building Trades was in control of the labor market. Because of this, we had the second highest construction costs in the

Company. This made it difficult to compete with other DuPont plant sites for new investment and projects for new products. Over a number of years, DuPont had moved to doing capital work using the merit shop approach, which meant that the lowest bidding contractor with a good safety and quality record would be given the contract whether they used union or non-union people.

This changeover in contracting often created a lot of pushback from the unions, since they didn't want to lose control of their labor market. Picketing often occurred as the changeover was taking place. Because of the great support for unions from the people of West Virginia, everyone felt that a switch like this at Belle would meet serious resistance. The people of West Virginia strongly support the Union Movement for good reasons that stem from the strife in the coalfields in the first half of the 1900s. If we tried to make a change like this at Belle, we'd have to be very credible and open. Communication with just about everyone—from our employees, to our pensioners living in the area, to the unions, to the State and local governments, to the neighbors—would have to be ongoing and intense. We had to help people understand that we weren't anti-union, but rather, we were trying to keep the Plant alive by controlling our costs in this area. Both union and non-union organizations were welcome to bid on our work, but everyone had to be cost competitive and have a good safety record. We also had to keep our customers and other business partners in the loop. If there was a big reaction against this attempt to become more competitive and sustainable, we could face mass picketing and perhaps lose a lot of support and business.

My manufacturing VP (my direct manager) had gone through this in Tennessee when he was plant manager there. They planned everything behind closed doors, and then announced the move. The plan had been to implement the changes there right away. Things got hot. He had 4,000 pickets outside the plant, was on TV and had quite a wild show. They succeeded, but it was quite a fight. We had to find a better way than this approach that had caused so much disruption and concern among so many people.

In early 1991, our capital budget began to drop in one of the Company's cash conservation programs. While this was another disappointment, we saw that this would provide the window of opportunity to make the change in the way we contracted our capital work. As the projects were completed, the amount of work declined, and the number of contractors and their employees needed at the plant declined. We saw that if we moved quickly, we could make the change in June.

We decided to use a process that would be wide open. We involved our mechanics, operators, engineers, the businesses, our vendors and the community-at-large. We began by sitting down with the mechanics to review our capital budget. We decided together which of the projects that remained in our budget they would be able to do. As you might expect, they picked the best projects. We then asked them if they'd like to participate in the process of picking the merit shop contractor who we'd hire to do most of the contracted work. About 30-40 of them wanted to participate, so we taught them how to help prepare bidding packages. They reviewed the bids along with the engineers and were involved in the bidders' visits. When the bids came in, we were able to get the Corporate Engineering Department to let us open the bids and to pick the successful bidder. There were three bids. This part of the process took us through early May. We kept the Plant apprised of their progress in the weekly business meetings. The winning bidder used a non-union shop approach.

In April, we began to meet with the operators to talk about the potential for picketing, and asked them to help us to develop procedures that would enable us to maintain supply to our customers. Many of them came into the process and helped develop the plans to maintain the continuity of our businesses. This took some courage on their part because some of them were called scabs by their families when they went home. One of the concerns was about the potential for picketing. None of us wanted to be in a situation where anyone had to cross a picket line. This is usually very dangerous to do. We said we could put radio messages on the air if there was any picketing. Some felt that wasn't enough and a better way was needed. Someone came up with the idea of putting a big strobe light on top of the Administration Building, which would flash green if there was no picketing and red if there was. This began to flash green in late May; everyone in the Plant and community could see it.

We also developed plans with our major vendors on how they would supply us in the event of picketing. Since the West Virginia State Police won't stop strike activity on private property, we moved our fences right onto the property lines, so that any picketing would be in the roads where the police would have to keep things open for traffic.

We developed an off-site communications center and the plans of how to work with some of us inside the plant while others worked off-site with the lawyers in the event an injunction was needed. Those off-site would also be able to work more closely with our suppliers and shippers.

In May, we began a series of meetings with the neighbors to talk about what we were doing. We talked about the need to be competitive, and that we were not being anti-union. We also addressed the need to have high quality construction work and how we'd maintain that high quality. This was necessary to provide the best levels of safety we could. People had many questions, so we did a lot of talking and listening.

June 7th was the day that the successful bidder would start work. We had had several strangers around our parking lot the week before; we guessed they were from the Building Trades trying to size us up. As June 7th approached, we got our supplies into the plant—enough for us to work for 3 weeks without having to cross picket lines. We had 500 beds, several washing machines and dryers, and three truckloads of food including one refrigerated truck. On the 7th, we all came into work with our suitcases packed and ready to staff the plant. I was praying a lot.

The contractor's people arrived at about 8 A.M. There were no pickets! With all the preparation, I think that some of the Plant people were a bit let down. One of my big disappointments was the reaction by some from Headquarters who'd been on the fringe of the activities; they spread the word that this was easy and we'd overdone things. However, my boss was quite supportive of what we'd accomplished.

Over the next few years we had both union and non-union contractors in the plant, sometimes working right next to each other. We never had any problems with anyone over this. The lessons here were the power of involving everyone, sharing the information, getting very clear on what we needed to do and working as fairly as we could with everyone.

Soon after this, we looked at how to make significant changes in the way we worked. The team that played the major role in this was the shift supervisors' team. I was the team leader. The shift supervisors were a team of 5 guys who'd grown up at the plant and were mature, solid leaders. We talked in our meetings for months about the things we might do. We knew that the plant ran very well during the off-shifts when most of the supervision is not at the plant. One evening during the team meeting, I asked them how many steps (one person talking to another) were needed to fix a pump seal at noon and at midnight. When we looked into this, we found that it took 38 steps during the day and 18 during the night. As the Plant Manager, I found it rather unsettling that the place ran better when we in management weren't there.

We then began to talk about running the plant during the day in the same way that we ran it at night, so the plant would run better with fewer people in the decision process. Those people freed up from the decision-making process could now work on things we needed for the future. We talked and talked as we crept up to this one. Finally, we took the plunge. Everyone became involved in the planning to try to figure out how we could do this. The shift supervisors leading the shifts would report directly to me. This gave them the opening to talk with and to work with everyone in the organization. In a sense, we turned the plant inside out. Our performance took another significant step forward.

The central core process consisted of bringing in raw materials, transforming them into products and shipping them to our customers. The rest of us were gathered around in teams to support those who did this core process. Anyone could be on any of the teams as we moved ahead. We'd worried that people would get on to teams to try to avoid what they considered to be the work. This didn't happen. The plant continued to get better in its performance in all aspects. This work clearly showed us that involving the people and taking the time to talk about things so that we could really understand was an important and vital step in our transformation.

I had very few people to talk to about the reasons for things we were doing and began to wonder if I'd gone off the deep end. But the results kept getting better and the people felt better. At first, the managers of the No Name Network seemed to understand pretty well. However, as time moved on, I began to feel that they were stuck. I'd read James Gleick's book *Chaos*. It really opened my mind to new possibilities. I began to wonder if this sort of stuff applied to social structures like organizations. The other No Name managers weren't interested. I kept exploring this area and gradually moved away from them. Now I had no one to talk to other than Claire who kept me from losing faith. I was talking to Alan Gilburg one day and he mentioned that there was a group looking into this called the Chaos Network. I called Mark Michaels, the leader of the Network, and he understood what I meant. Mark said that the Second Annual Chaos Network Conference was going to be held in Santa Cruz, CA in the fall of 1992. It fit my schedule, so I told my boss that I was going to an organizational development conference. When I got to the hotel, I realized that it was called The Dream Inn. My heart sank; if my management found out that I had gone to a chaos conference at the Dream Inn, they'd know I'd gone nuts. I became increasingly worried that the way I was trying to lead was getting too far afield from the main stream. It felt real and important, but was I headed down the wrong path?

What a wonderful 3 days that was. Everything changed, for I had found about 50 other people at least as far out as I was. I learned that there was an emerging body of science that supported the work I was doing and that there was a vocabulary for me to learn. I also met Margaret Wheatley whose book *Leadership and the New Science* had just been published. I got a copy from her and we had a nice visit. On the way home in the airplane, I read it and felt I'd come Home. I was so taken by her book that I ordered 100 copies and sent them out to people all over DuPont. I never heard a word from anyone to whom I'd sent the book. My enthusiasm had overtaken good sense.

I called her and asked her if she'd be willing to come to the plant to tell me what she saw, not what to do. I also asked her to give a seminar to my staff on her book. She came, and we discovered that I was doing the things she was talking about in her book. It was really exciting to have validation for the work and path I was on after so many years.

She invited me to participate in her Berkana Dialogues at Sundance in Utah. Over the next three years, I went to 13 of them and met many interesting people who were trying to get a better understanding of the chaos theories, self-organization ideas, dissipative structure ideas of Prigogine, and the ideas of autopoiesis from Maturana and Varela. About 25 of us gathered for three days of dialogue; there was no agenda or outcome prescribed. Each time I went I wondered what I'd learn; each time was a rich and rewarding learning experience.

The mix of people changed at each dialogue. Some, like Maggie Moore, Karen Anne Zien and Jill Janov came many times. We became very close friends. Meg and Myron Kellner-Rogers, Meg's partner, were there all the time helping to lead us.

At the first dialogue I attended in early 1993, we looked at the conditions for self-organization. We'd seen a video on boids (computer images simulating birds in a flock) that showed that very complex behavior that mimics flocking behavior could be generated with just three simple rules. We talked in the large group as well as in small groups. All of us gathered around the idea that the three criteria for self-organization were information, relationship and self-reference (I, R, S).

I happened to be staying over the Saturday night to save on airfares, so I decided to see if I could use these ideas to organize a talk on how we'd improved safety at Belle. I was scheduled to give this talk in a couple of months to about 300 plant managers in the Texas Chemical Council, and had been stuck trying to figure out how to share anything this complex in just 20 minutes. When I used the I, R, S ideas to organize the work, it was stunning. Everything we'd done could be brought together in a meaningful and coherent way.

I also realized then that the I, R, S relationship connected with some of the work on the triad in J.G. Bennett's Systematics. When two bodies of knowledge come together like that, I pay a lot of attention. I was really excited about this, so I called Meg after I'd returned to the Plant to tell her. I was really pumped up. She said I had better be careful because these were just theories. I said that it didn't look that way to me; these were real! Later, Meg and Myron decided to change self-reference to identity to make it clearer, so now we call it I, R, I. I think that self-reference may be better in this instance because it implies a self (identity) in relation to some reference like an intention to do something. Since 1993, the importance of the idea of information, relationship and identity has become more and more clear to me. The dialogue groups became a very important support group for me, a place where I could talk about the things we were doing at Belle and keep my perspective. I became very close to Maggie Moore and Karen Anna Zien who were among the few who began to live the processes of self-organization. For us, it was a way of life, not just an intellectual exercise.

As the Belle Plant Leadership Team (BPLT) worked on becoming a more effective team, we began to work on the things that needed to be done to move the entire plant to teams. We visited several sites. The DuPont plant in El Paso, IL was doing a lot with teams under the leadership of Dick Page, the plant manager. In our visit, we noticed that they had a set of principles on the treatment of people that they'd found to be a very important part of their process. We took them home with us and decided that we should use ones like them at Belle.

We worked with the principles until everyone on the BPLT were comfortable with them. We then decided to try a different way to move them into the organization. We'd had various experiences with developing principles by starting at the grass roots level and building them with inputs from everybody. This process was a slow one and as the inputs were aggregated at each successive level, important stuff sometimes fell off the table. By the time the process got to the top of the organization, most people didn't recognize their own input. Furthermore, since management hadn't had much input to them, they didn't accept them. They just hung them on the wall and ignored them.

So, we turned the process upside down. We went out to all the people and said, "These were the principles that we'd like to lead by; will you please help us to live up to them." We felt really exposed in doing this. At first, the people just laughed at us because they didn't think we were serious about trying to do this. After a couple of months, they decided we really were serious, so they helped us. We all got a lot of criticism as we tried to learn to live by them. As people were pointing out our shortcomings, they began to take the principles on as their own. Within 9 months they were deeply imbedded in everything we were doing. We tested all changes against them as well as all discipline cases to be sure we were living up to them. They were posted all over the Plant, and we talked about them in many of the business meetings. We gradually learned about our Plant community and what we wanted to be together. When Meg Wheatley came, she found them very well accepted and wanted to know how we'd done it. The approach was new to her.

Here are the Treatment of People Principles.

1. We want interesting work—work that makes good use of their abilities. Boring jobs de-motivate and alienate.
2. We want opportunity for learning and growth and opportunity to apply the skills.
3. We can be trained (that is, we are able and willing) to do several different jobs.
4. We want equal opportunity to advance and try different work.
5. We want responsibility in our work, some degree of decision-making.
6. We "want in" on decisions that affect us.
7. We expect management to lead, not abdicate. We look to management to make its contribution in those critical areas where employees do not have the requisite orientation, knowledge or resources.
8. We expect a leadership team to be consistent and predictable.
9. We want to be part of a winning team.
10. We want to know what's going on at Belle, in the Departments, and in the Company.
11. We want to be informed about the business and get early feedback on the performance of their part of the operation.
12. We want fair pay and knowledge about how the pay system works.
13. We have a need to relate to others on the job.
14. We want rational rules and a minimum of regimentation. We want a say in the rules.

15. We want to be treated like people—people have ego needs.

Another important learning here was the power of putting yourself into the process and becoming a part of it. These principles became the solid base we could stand on when everything else was changing. We couldn't control much around us, but we could control how we treated each other.

We were moving towards teams. We had a deep belief that people wanted to do good work and were trying to make a good contribution. Some of the Belle people went to see the El Paso people to learn from them about this work. We hired a consultant to come in to teach our people how to be facilitators and team leaders. At first, the First Line Supervisors (FLS) were the team leaders for their natural work group teams. Ad Hoc teams addressing site-wide issues were led by who ever had the skills and interest in the particular issue. Many of the people working in the professional roles were trained to be facilitators. We talked about the move to teams in the weekly business meetings. This was all going smoothly until we bumped into our consultant's strong view that we should begin with only one or two teams to see how it would work.

The BPLT view was that it was likely that one or two teams would be killed off by the existing culture like white blood cells surrounding an infection. We said we wanted to go to about 125 teams over a weekend. The consultant thought we were nuts and left. We were on our own again. We moved on this track and had two Share the Future meetings to kick off the effort. We asked everyone to come to these dinner meetings. We gave each one a share of DuPont stock for attending. About 800 of the 1100 people came to the meetings where we tried to introduce the new approach.

One of the people who helped us to get off to a good start was another consultant named David Richie. He was recommended to us by Dick Page from the El Paso plant. David was the keynote person in the Share the Future meetings. He also helped us to develop training programs for the teams in problem solving, leading meetings and other development activities for the teams. Since he was a Board Member, David later helped us with the Association for Quality and Participation (AQP).

We wanted everyone to be on the teams, but knew that requiring them to be on the team would just turn them off. In our culture, most people don't volunteer for things, so we asked everyone to be on the teams. Those who didn't want to could volunteer to drop off the team. Most people stayed on the teams.

We got off to a ragged start. Some work groups were already functioning pretty well as a team and a few of them felt we'd insulted them by now saying they were going to be a team. At the other extreme was a group of guys who did the first thing they'd ever done as a team, by getting up and walking out of the first meeting together.

Each team was slated to meet about 4 hours a month to work on ways to improve their part of the business. The teams decided when and where to meet; some met on work time and some met on overtime. We never looked back. We stayed on the journey, getting better and better as we went.

I knew we were making good progress when the bullies began to grieve. At the third step of the grievance process, I had a few simple questions:

· what happened to cause the grievance;
· did we violate any of our People Principles or HR rules; and
· did the team make the decision being grieved?

If it was a team decision, I'd ask:

· were you on the team making the decision?

If they said they were not on the blankety-blank team, then I'd deny the grievance. I'd point out that they'd have to abide by the team's decision. If they wanted to influence future decisions, they'd better get onto the team.

One of the really important things we did to help the teams was to join the Association for Quality and Participation (AQP), headquartered in Cincinnati, OH. The AQP helped us to develop a plant chapter for our many teams. David Richie helped us to get set up. The Almost Heaven Chapter was led by Charlie Alsup (a Senior Supervisor), Steve Wilson and Eddie Long (mechanics). We had contests for the Team of the Year. We took teams to the Spring AQP Meetings where they were able to meet others who were trying to develop teams. They found that a lot of people were doing similar things. They also found that some teams were more advanced than our teams were, and that some were not as far along. A number of the teams gave papers at the meetings over the next 4 to 5 years. Several times, we took a whole busload of people to meetings in Baltimore and Cincinnati. I gave a paper with Bob Brown (a BPLT member) at one meeting in Jacksonville, FL to talk about the way the leadership team was developing. Peter Block, author of *The Empowered Manager* was there. We talked a little and I gave him a copy of our paper. He later wrote a beautiful letter to me to encourage us in our progress. This really gave me a lift!

Another thing that really helped people to grow was our involvement in Project Teach. This was a project supported by the Charleston Area Chamber of Commerce to help the Kanawha County School Board. They wanted to get a lot of computer training for the school teachers, but were unable to get the time to release the teachers for the training programs. In Project Teach, the local business community was asked to provide volunteers to substitute teach for a half day so that the teachers could be released for training. Debbie Fisher took the lead for us. She developed a terrific program and was able to get about 80 DuPont Plant people to volunteer. She also got our plant photographer involved to provide a video history of the project. I wasn't paying much attention to all this with all the other stuff that was going on.

Our people were doing a lot of teaching, and I heard great stories about how good they felt being able to tell the school kids about the sort of work they were doing. People came back feeling really proud of themselves for having done this and for being acknowledged by the youngsters. This enthusiasm spilled over into their other work at the plant and really helped to build morale.

Debbie invited me to a Chamber of Commerce Dinner that recognized everyone for his or her fine efforts. There I came to realize how much she'd done and what an inspiration she'd become to the community. The more she and Jack Green, our photographer, were praised the more self-conscious she became because I kept leaning over and asking her "Did you really do all that?" It all got to be quite funny between the two of us. Later she was invited to a National Chamber of Commerce meeting in New Orleans where she had a chance to tell people from all over the country about what we'd done in the Kanawha Valley. Debbie had a very clear picture of our organization and what we were trying to do, so she could function very effectively and freely within the constraints of this without having to check everything with me.

While we'd invested a lot in this Chamber of Commerce effort, I felt that it more than paid off in improved morale and other improvements in the way people tackled their jobs. Taking growth risks with people pays big dividends!

On the BPLT, we built on the learnings from my participation in the Berkana Dialogues with Meg Wheatley, Myron Kellner-Rogers and the others who came to them. We also studied the Systematics of John Bennett and Charles Krone; the Systematics models showed themselves to be the best thinking models for the chaos and complexity we were beginning to live. We began to learn what sensitive dependence to initial conditions and strange attractors looked like on the plant floor. At each dialogue, I'd learn about some new aspect of chaos theory, autopoiesis, dissipative structures and self-organization. Then back at the plant I kept asking myself "So what?" We gradually found out the answer to that persistent question. One important metaphor we used was the "Bowl." One afternoon before one of the Berkana Dialogues, I bought a small bowl and sat on the floor looking at it trying to understand "bowlness." I learned a lot that afternoon. The Bowl is a strange attractor for the organization, consisting of the principles, standards, goals and expectations. Later I realized that we were creating the Bowl in using the Process Enneagram. All the walking around the plant I had been doing (I kept track of this for 5 years and averaged 5 hours a day with people in the plant or community) was contributing to this as well. Debbie's work with the Chamber of Commerce is a good example of working within the Bowl

It was during these years that I invented and developed the Process Enneagram, the Emergence of Meaning and the processes to sustain our work. It was also around this time that Maggie Moore invented the Rhythms of Change model. These are all developed further in future sections of this book.

Part way through the Berkana Dialogues (we held 14 of them and I was at 13 of them), Meg asked me if I'd be willing to speak at a whole system conference she and Myron were planning. I asked, "What are whole systems?" She looked at me in a rather funny way, like some of my teachers used to do when I'd asked a dumb question. She said, "This is what you're doing." I laughed and said I'd be glad to speak.

We eventually had 18 of these conferences including one in Australia in October 1998. I spoke at all of them except the one held in the fall of 1995 when I was recovering from prostate cancer surgery. These were great opportunities to have the time to reflect on all the new theories as I heard Meg, Myron and Fritjof Capra talk about the new thinking. They were three-day conferences held mostly at Sundance, Utah in the beautiful mountains.

As we continued to develop, we started to get involved in the work of Steven Covey. Bob Brown was certified first and then we had two mechanics, Eddie Long and Steve Wilson, also certified as Covey Trainers. They developed a 4-day course and over 300 people at Belle went through it. Covey's work was very helpful in the development of the teams. These two mechanics had more credibility with their peers than I would have had trying to teach the course.

Our experiences with the Days Like Nights work continued to evolve. We learned an immense amount about working in new and different ways. What we learned kept reinforcing the ideas of information, relationship and identity. We finally got to the point where we decided to take all the first line supervisors (FLS) off the operating shifts. We had had around 8 FLS per shift reporting to a shift supervisor for operating guidance during the shifts. These supervisors reported into their business units for their normal instructions for the production schedules and normal supervisory work during the day and reported to the Shift Supervisors in the off-shifts.

In the Days Like Nights plan, each shift of about 85-90 people would have one shift supervisor assisted by two former FLS who would be facilitators for the shift teams to help solve problems. This transition went very smoothly. However, the Shift Supervisors were very nervous about making mistakes as we moved into this way of operating the plant. Finally, I made a commitment to them that I would not punish them if they made a mistake. This was a significant shift for us. They were freed up to do all the things they knew how to do very well and we never made any mistakes of any consequence. Learning from the mistakes we did make was another significant move forward for us.

These sorts of changes were the most difficult for the FLS who had a hard time trying to figure out what their new roles would be. We even had a supervisor's team trying to think this through.

In the early 1990's, the mechanics came to the BPLT to ask us to consider going to 4 ten-hour shifts a week instead of the 5-eight hour shifts they were working. We asked them to do some work sampling and to develop justification for this change. We had to be able to operate the plant, so a change like this had to be cost effective. They developed a team to study this and after a few months came to the BPLT to tell us their findings. They had a thorough, sensible presentation so we agreed to the change of schedule. We moved into this pretty smoothly. In looking back on this, I should have insisted they be more rigorous in their analysis and in developing better ways to measure whether or not we were making progress. I'm not sure this new schedule saved us any money in the long-run.

Over the 8 years I was at Belle, we had one reduction in force after another as we kept trying to make our businesses more effective. By the time I'd left, our work force had dropped from about 1300 in 1987 to about 900 people in 1995. It was a painful process—a struggle for all of us. That sort of stuff makes it very hard to keep the focus on growing the teams. Less than 10 of the 400 or so who left were unable to move directly into another job, retire or return to school. Elbert Price and his HR Team worked very hard to help people find jobs at other DuPont sites and with other employers in the Valley. We also got the Company to extend tuition refunds from one to two years for people being laid-off, so some went on to obtain associate degrees, and begin new careers in other fields. Some people retired for a variety of reasons; I'm sure some retired because they didn't want to make the necessary changes. We never hired any hourly people while I was there. We did hire a few engineers each year to fill the ranks as the more experienced people were transferred to other DuPont sites.

Now and then, the businesses came to us with big manufacturing challenges. Our folks responded to them in beautiful ways. In one case, we had to change the product formulation and the packaging of one of our major products very suddenly. We asked for volunteers to help us make the change. It was gratifying to see people come forth to meet the challenge. We put in a temporary packaging line that required a lot of hand labor to fill and seal the 2 and 5 pound packages. The people on the line had to wear respirators for hours as they worked. It was really impressive to see how they'd saved the business. Mechanics and operators worked together on the line so we could meet the challenge.

In another case, after the Berlin Wall came down, our marketing people discovered that a company in Hungary was producing one of our agricultural chemicals. Their costs were lower than ours were and the marketing folks wanted to buy their material. We got permission to send an engineer over there to inspect their operation. He came home and informed us that their product was as good as ours, their process was better than ours, their environmental performance was very good, and they were paying their people $50/ month. We paid our people $3,000/ month.

This threat to our business really shook us up. We went to our people with the problem, and told them we didn't know how we'd survive in the business. Over the next 8 months or so, the operators, mechanics and engineers worked to figure out how to remain in the business. They came up with all sorts of work practice and other changes, which enabled us to survive.

Both of these examples really showed us what could happen if we just asked our folks for their help. They developed better answers than we'd have come up with, every time. We began to realize that defining the question and the parameters we'd have to operate within were all that was necessary. Later on, I came across Monty Roberts' book, *The Man Who Listens to Horses*, in which he describes the process he uses to train horses to be ridden for the first time. By inviting the horse into the process, the time it takes to ride one the first time is only 30 minutes or less rather than 6 weeks by the traditional process. When we change the process, we change the outcome. This was a nice parallel to our own work.

After we'd taken the FLS off the shifts, the operator teams really began to blossom. They began to work together in new ways like doing cross audits on safety and cost reduction programs. One team discovered that we were paying $800,000/ year on demurrage. Demurrage is the name for the payments we make to companies whose tank cars and tank trucks stay at the plant too long. Normally, we would have a few hours to unload the material we'd receive. After that, we pay them a fee for each hour the tank trucks were at the plant. This was not a very large part of our total costs. But, it was money we were just giving away. I'd pestered the organization unsuccessfully for years to reduce our demurrage costs, but had made no progress. Other priorities were always more important.

One day I noticed that the demurrage costs in our quarterly report had dropped from the rate of $200,000/ quarter to $100,000. I wondered what had happened, and learned from the shift supervisors that one of the shift operating teams had decided to do something about the problem. They were especially frustrated with all the excess equipment sitting around the plant causing congestion in their operating areas. Over the next few months, they reduced the demurrage costs to a rate of only about $100,000/ year, an 88% reduction in just one year! This was more reinforcement for I, R, I.

One of the products we made was a major product in the Japanese market. We were quite proud of this, and had received an award for our quality. One day I heard we'd inadvertently sent the Japanese a lot of out-of-specification material. We were all quite upset and concerned. Some people thought we'd be okay telling them of the error and asking them to send the product back. But, the more we talked, the more it became apparent that we needed to be more proactive in order to protect our market there. We decided to have two engineers from the plant on hand when the ship arrived there so they could physically segregate the out-of-specification product. Our customers were so impressed with our stewardship of the business that they gave us a lot of positive comments. The lesson was to be open and get out to the customer because we could turn a big negative into a positive.

In 1991, we learned that the EPA had issued new permit requirements for wastewater discharge. We had a wastewater treatment plant to treat all our process and sanitary wastewater. It ran quite well, but our studies indicated it would take $10,000,000 of investment to meet the new, much lower discharge requirements. Rather than sitting around for a couple of years until we had to do something, we plunged into trying to meet the discharge requirements without having to spend so much money. The plant environmental group, with a lot of BPLT support, searched every wastewater stream to see if we could find places to eliminate wastes through better process controls. Over a two-year period, we found ways to get the wastes out of the system. As a result, we only had to spend about $800,000 to meet the new discharge requirements. We learned that involving everyone in trying to solve problems really worked. We found that most of the knowledge we needed to solve our problems was already in the organization if only we could tap into it.

By 1993, we were doing much better in our total performance. We'd invented a way to measure the effect of all the changes that really showed that we were doing very well. More and more people came forward and so, more and more, we were becoming leaderful. Many of the operators were on many different teams. Becky Dixon, an operator, was on several environmental teams in addition to her own operating team. One morning Becky called me. She was quite upset because, as she was coming into start her 6 A.M. shift, she'd heard several guys on a radio music/talk show talking about all the pollution from our plant. The night had been clear and the moon was shining. Our steam plumes glistened in the moonlight. These guys had driven past the plant on their way in to do their show. They assumed that these steam plumes were toxic chemicals, so they were telling their listening audience about it. Becky knew differently and was very upset about the bad rap we were getting. Then she went on to tell me that she'd called them and invited them to visit the plant the following Monday. They were scheduled to come at 1 P.M. Becky told me that I was to talk to them for about an hour and then she'd get them to meet other people to talk about what we were already doing to improve our environmental performance. This delighted me because it showed real growth in her. The only thing I had to do in preparation for the visit was to keep my public affairs person from getting into it. Becky did a beautiful job, and the visit was one of the best we'd ever had. Over the next few weeks, these guys told their listeners about the visit and about all the neat people and good work we were doing. Becky was far more credible than I would have been. I knew Becky very well from all the walking around the plant I'd done. I trusted her fully in this effort. Her involvement and initiative really paid off.

We were learning to live with ambiguity, and we found that as long as the Bowl was strong, we were okay. We were learning to trust the process. It took me four years to learn that as long as the Bowl was in good shape, we didn't have to be afraid of what our people would do. They never went outside of the Bowl as far as I knew.

In 1992, the Local Emergency Planning Committee (LEPC), which had been formed under the environmental laws arising from the Love Canal tragedy, asked the plants in the Kanawha Valley to share their worst-case scenarios so that they could do a better planning job for emergency chemical releases and spills. The person on the LEPC who asked for this was Pam Nixon, the Vice-Chairwoman of the environmental group called Citizens Concerned About MIC (methylisocyanate). This was the community group formed after the Aldecarbe® release in 1985.

Under the Clean Air Act of 1990, those who handled some kinds of hazardous chemicals in large quantities would be required to share their worst-case scenarios. But, this part of the Act was not slated to go into place for another 4 years because so much technical work had to be done to develop the protocols. The implementation date actually slipped to June20, 1999. While the LEPC had the right to ask for the information now to prepare emergency response plans, we, in the industry, felt that this was an unreasonable request. Furthermore, we didn't know how to comply with the request, given the complexity of the issues.

The Plant Managers talked and fussed about the request while the newspaper media began to raise the heat. I knew from my previous experiences in Niagara Falls that eventually we'd have to do something. I also knew that if we took the initiative on this we could put our best foot forward. We could talk about all the good work we'd done. But the tensions in the community were so high that we feared that the reaction against us would be very negative and that it would further reduce our ability to operate there. The industry had already lost over half the jobs during the last 20 years as business moved to the Gulf Coast areas. We had to find a way to balance everything for the well being of plants and the community.

The more the managers talked, the more I felt we had to become more proactive so that we wouldn't become victims of the request. Some of us formed a little team and began to plan how to do it. From all I'd learned, I knew that we had to include the public and environmentalists in the process. I knew we'd have to share a lot of information and be open with everyone. I believed that in an interactive process we might possibly succeed in this effort and build community rather than destroy it.

Our little team formed a committee to help develop the technical parameters of the work and a communications committee to figure out how to share all this with the community and the whole country. The Chairperson for each committee had to be someone from the community because the credibility the industry had with the community was so low. If the managers led the effort, it would be seen as self-serving and not be credible. I led this little team and orchestrated this work from Belle. Most of the other Managers were still resisting the idea and not paying much attention to what was going on.

Everything we were doing was totally consistent with the CMA principles of Responsible Care®. I had been talking about this work at the CAER Task Group meetings. I'd also been talking with the DuPont management about it. We all felt it was the right thing to move ahead. One of the best process safety experts in the industry, Art Burke, worked for DuPont. We knew each other well. We worked and planned together that the CMA would form a technical committee to develop the technology and a communications committee to start the communications for the whole industry. Our vision was that these committees would work in parallel at the National level and the local level in the Kanawha Valley. Art would be on both technical committees and I'd be on both communications committees. This way we could provide the guidance to try to keep the work in the Kanawha Valley and the CMA from getting too far apart. Art was also working with the CMA committees helping the EPA develop the rules. Everything was in flux and we were trying to keep everything from breaking apart. We all wanted to have a solid technical basis for the rules and a consistent approach for communications that would be open and inclusive. The process had to be developed by all the stakeholders as we moved forward.

Then there was a change of managers at one of the other major plants in the Valley. The new guy who was very much a command and control manager, looked into the effort and got very upset. He didn't have any of the community experience I'd had and wanted to slow down the process a lot. He wanted to be in control. The processes I was fostering were not what he had in mind. Before one of the monthly Plant Managers Meetings, a monthly get together sponsored by the West Virginia Manufacturers Association where the managers could talk about our shared struggles, this new guy and several others wanted to meet with me to stop the process. It was an intense meeting.

I said at one point that it was so important for the Belle Plant and the DuPont Company to be up front with this issue that we would go ahead alone if we needed to do so. I believed that we could land on our feet if we were up front and honest. The other plants would then have the problem of trying to tell the community why they hadn't gone ahead. I expected there'd be a lot of pressure on us to slow down, but I decided not to give in easily. We were all members of the CMA and breaking ranks with our fellow members was frowned upon. This was an uncomfortable position for me.

The very next morning the new plant manager's plant had an explosion that seriously hurt three men and caused the community to shelter-in-place for several hours. Later, one of the men who was a brother to one of our operators, died from his injuries. All the managers realized that we had to move ahead immediately to address the worst-case scenario request.

I went to NICS to ask that the Board approve the NICS President, Paul Hill, as the leader of the technical committee. As we talked about this, it became obvious to everyone that the work was in keeping with the principles of NICS. Paul stepped into the role professionally, and each of the plants assigned engineers to work on the project. The local environmentalists were also invited to participate. Art Burke was a member of the committee. We knew that we needed further technical help, so I went to the LEPC to get them to take the overall lead in the effort. Their funding and leadership was essential to keep this a community-wide effort. They had no funding, so the plants agreed to put up the funds in proportion to the number of worst-case scenarios we each had to report. The meetings were made more difficult because all of the LEPC people didn't go to every meetings. As a result, it took several months to get everyone on board. The technical committee had to develop the procedures to identify how to select the materials we'd use in the scenarios. They had to decide how to run the computer modeling for the plume maps. They had to develop an agreed upon set of toxicity criteria. They had to decide how to handle potential explosions. The LEPC hired a consultant who was an expert on process safety to help lead the effort. It was now almost 18 months after the LEPC request.

Mary Frances Bleidt from the local community led the communications committee, which included community members, industry people including me and environmentalists. As the technical committee progressed, we began to get a clearer picture of what needed to be done.

At one point, I was talking to Mildred Holt who was a Co-chair of the Citizens Concerned About MIC, as well as a NICS Board member. She was a retired school teacher who wanted the community to be a safe and prosperous place to live. I was feeling rather down at this point, and as I talked Mildred said, "You don't need to be worried about what you're going to tell us about the toxic chemicals. I know you can kill me. I want to know what you're doing about it." She about blew my mind. This opened up the whole picture for me. The industry people had been doing a lot to improve the safety of our operations. We were all trying to live up to the CMA Responsible Care® Principles and Practices. We were all working to comply with the Occupational Health and Safety Administration (OSHA) process safety guidelines and rules. I realized that we could talk about hypothetical worst-case scenarios and the more plausible ones in the framework of all we were doing to prevent them. That was what Mildred was telling me. I was so internally focused on all this that I'd lost sight of the context.

I went to the Belle CAC to ask them about Mildred's insight. They almost laughed at my naiveté. I knew we were finally on the right track. At one point, the EPA people, who were trying to develop the rules for sharing the worst-case scenarios for the whole US, came to our meetings. They didn't know any more than we did on how to do this stuff; we were creating our own future.

At about this time I went to the Hospital Association to tell them about the event and that they'd need to be ready to answer questions about how they'd respond in the event of a major emergency. There were 6 hospitals in the region. All of them had their own emergency plans, but they had not done the work to develop a joint plan. They immediately moved ahead to do this.

I had decided to invite the local DuPont Jr. High School kids into the communications effort. I'd learned a year earlier that having youngsters involved was important. Adults behave better when kids are watching! I met with the school principal and social studies teacher to talk about the idea. They liked it, so I talked to the class one day and invited them into the project. For every meeting, I'd call the school and 2-3 kids would be on the front steps waiting for me. The class did a big project on the history of the industry in the area and about the work we were doing. They were involved in history as it was being made. They won first place in the State Social Studies Fair with their project. One of their most active leaders was Nikki Smith. Nikki graduated from Ohio State University in 2001 and is now working in public affairs for Dow Chemical Company.

The Communications Committee moved ahead—building on this insight. We decided it was time to set the dates for the sharing process, and picked June 3rd and 4th, 1994 as the dates. We rented the Charleston Convention Center, which had a big auditorium, as well as a big hall for our displays. We decided to have a series of presentations about the background of the work and a talk by the EPA people to tell about their work to support what we were doing. The first responders (LEPC) talked about their role in the effort, and the hospitals talked about their plans. Then we all moved from the auditorium to the convention hall where each plant had a display table. Every manager was with his experts to tell people about their scenarios and their prevention efforts. The local environmental groups had their displays as well.

We at Belle put together a 4-page booklet for each chemical that had a dispersion plume map for the worst-case and more plausible-case scenarios. The booklet also had a summary of the preventive efforts and the history of previous releases. At Belle, we had booklets for anhydrous ammonia, butylisocyanate and the methylamines. All the plants agreed to have booklets similar to them. In the convention center, we gave them to people as we talked.

About 5 weeks before the big date (late April), Mary Frances and several other women on the Committee pointed out that if we had both June 3rd (Friday) and 4th (Saturday) in the Convention Center that people wouldn't come on Saturday. A bunch of dull plant managers wouldn't attract many people on a nice Saturday in June. She said we needed to do the second day in the Charleston Town Center Mall, the biggest shopping mall in the area. I swallowed hard and agreed that it was a good idea. When I went to the plant managers, and told them we should go to the shopping mall, they really struggled. But, after talking with their wives, most of them felt it was the right thing to do.

The DuPont management was terrifically supportive in this whole effort; they trusted what we were doing and didn't try to second-guess us at all. Others in the industry, however, were very nervous about the whole thing. Some critics labeled it as Knowles' Scare Fair. We had no chance for a dress rehearsal, and we knew that whatever we did would impact the rest of the chemical industry.

On Friday, June 4th, about 700 people gathered in the Convention Center Auditorium. About a third were from the local industry, a third from the community and a third from the rest of the chemical industry across the country who wanted to get a first-hand look at what we were doing. Reporters from CNN, The New York Times and the London Times were there as well. At the end of the Auditorium session, I shared the ammonia scenarios and Van Long, the Rhone-Poulenc Manager shared the MIC scenario as examples of how the information would be displayed.

I was sitting by myself at the front of the hall hoping and praying that everything would come off okay. I was worried about the ammonia scenario. I would be the first one to share specific plume information. I would be telling the people that the worst-case release could cause, after an hour's exposure, irreversible health effects 32 miles from the plant and that within 25 miles, people would be killed. Trying to put things into perspective, I would also tell them that never in the 75 year history of the plant had anyone been hurt because of a release from the plant.

I was really nervous. Claire was there in the crowd to support me. At one point, I looked up and there came Nikki and her classmates to sit with me. The school administration had postponed the final examinations so they could come. I still get tears in my eyes when I think about the lift they gave me.

When I stood up to share the ammonia scenarios, the hall became very quiet. When I got to the point where I showed the plume maps, people jumped into the isles taking pictures. I almost laughed at the way this happened. Van's presentation also went well.

After this part of the process, we all moved into the Convention Center hall. We had a light lunch for everyone and we shared all the information. We talked with many people. The first responders had display booths, the hospitals had a booth and the local environmentalists had their booth to talk about the whole thing as well. They told the people we were trying to do the right thing. They didn't want us in the chemical industry to leave the Valley, but they wanted us to get greener and cleaner. CNN and the New York Times had positive stories about the effort. They told their readers about a community that had struggled and was now coming together.

The next day (Saturday) in the Charleston Town Center Mall we talked with people from 10 A.M. to 9 P.M. when the mall closed. I don't think that any of the managers had ever spent that long in a mall. We guessed that we talked to over 5000 people directly about the work. As we were leaving the mall, one of the managers pulled me aside and said "We've done something really significant here these last two days, and you dragged us all kicking and screaming. Thanks."

The next week, Van Long, the Rhone-Poulenc Plant Manager, and I went to the CMA Annual Board Meeting at the Greenbriar, which was about 100 miles away, to report on the event. About 75 chemical company CEOs attend these meetings. They are very structured meetings and we were given a specific time to report. I talked for about 10 minutes about the process and then Van talked about 10 minutes on what happened. Then something, I am told, that has never happened before at a Board meeting occurred, we received applause. Then they went into questions, which were really good. We got another round of applause. The schedule for the whole meeting was messed up.

After the meeting one of the CEOs, a big tall guy, pulled me aside and told me that it was good it had gone well because I really had stuck my neck out. I'm glad DuPont supported me as they did. I think that they must have gotten a lot of calls about the concerns in the industry. This process has since been used to share worst-case scenarios in Victoria, TX and Houston, TX as well as in Indianapolis, IN. Involving people, inviting them to help, sharing information and developing a shared future are powerful lessons.

I was invited to speak at many CMA meetings around the country as people began to prepare for the sharing of worst-case scenarios under the Clear Air Act. The final implementation date for the process was June 20, 1999.

In 1993, we decided to develop a new secure landfill for the non-hazardous sludge from our wastewater treatment plant. This would save us over $150,000/month if we could dispose of it this way rather than in a commercial landfill. We'd also have more control over the landfill if we ran it. We filed for the permits and began to construct it. During the construction, we had a number of meetings with the neighbors and several tours so that people could see how it was constructed. They talked to the people building it and got a sense of their dedication to doing a good job with it. When it came to the public hearing, the public notice was posted, but there were no requests for a meeting. We were issued the operating permit without any delays. This also saved us a lot of money and was an environmentally sound decision.

The more people at the plant learned how to live in this world of change, the more they thrived on change. Early in the Belle journey, changes came slowly and we all struggled to adjust. Later in my time there, the rate of change had increased so much that I was actually slowing us down because I feared we'd out-run our technology. In the chemical business, this can cause serious incidents like fires and releases. At first, we were making a significant change every 2 to 3 months. At the end of my time there, we were making 3 or 4 such changes a month. I even realized that I was limiting the organization in my setting of goals. The people not only set more ambitious goals than I did, they realized them!

My transfer from the plant came in January 1995. I was disappointed to leave the plant and the community where we'd all grown so much. Maybe it was the right time to go. Before I left, the Principal of DuPont Jr. High School, Forest Mann, invited me to come over to his office. When I got there, he asked me to come down the hall to the auditorium. There was the whole school gathered there to wish me well and to thank us at DuPont for all the support over the years. Even a member of the School Board was there. I was really touched. It was difficult to keep back the tears.

I love the people there in West Virginia, and Claire, Christine and I go back for reunions and visits. We usually take our dulcimers with us when we go.

I grew up at Belle. It was a tough and often frightening journey. But, with the help of Claire and Debbie as well as many other people at the plant, I was able to grow. Homer and Cathy Hunter, and Ray and Sandy Baisden adopted Claire, Christine and me so we found a place of caring and warmth. Craig Skaggs of DuPont Governmental and External Affairs helped me in both Niagara Falls and in Belle to function effectively in the community. I appreciate the help of Bannie Kennedy who was my Manu-facturing VP when I moved from Niagara Falls. Gary Lewis, Jim Borel, Tom Carpenito, Ken Cook and Elbert Price were also key players on the BPLT who helped to make it all successful. Maggie Moore, Meg Wheatley and Myron Kellner-Rogers and many others in the Berkana Dialogues and Self-Organizing Systems Conferences played an important role in helping to support me as I moved through all the changes. I am thankful for the love and support of my children all through this difficult time. It is clear that I couldn't have done it all by myself. I have always felt the closeness of God helping me to grow and keep going.

Since I left the plant, it has continued to improve. My DuPont management asked me to help select my replacement so that the progress would continue. I give them a lot of credit for trying to keep things going. Several managers have held the post since I left and have tried to help the plant move forward. Their safety performance clearly illustrates this. When I was there, we had gone 454 days without a recordable injury. By 1999, they had more than 1000 days without a recordable injury, thus becoming the safest DuPont Plant in the world.

This is really the story of my growing up. In my search, I read widely. Through some associates of Charles Krone who were working in DuPont I was introduced to the work of people like George Ivanovich Gurdjieff, Peter Demian Ouspensky, John Godolphin Bennett, Maurice Nicoll, Saul Kuchinsky, Anthony G. E. Blake, and, more recently, Ken Wilber and Klausbernd Vollmar. These remarkable teachers revealed many new possibilities. Their work is difficult, deep, and for me, often quite obscure, yet I was drawn by some profound truths I found in their writings. I also read many other books that have taught me and have influenced my thinking as well. A complete listing of my readings is in the Bibliography.

The ideas I'll share in this book weave a network of threads from the Systematics of Gurdjieff, Ouspensky, Bennett, Blake and Kuchinsky with those of Meg and others about chaos and complexity. What I've learned is based on my own experiences, intense observations of a number of organizations within and outside of DuPont, and the theories and ideas I've been able to develop and test first hand. I've tested them in several large manufacturing plants, a transportation organization, an information technology organization, several schools and universities and a city government. Much of this experience is based on my 13 years as a Plant Manager, and, since my retirement, as a guide in a variety of organizations in America, Canada, the United Kingdom, Australia and New Zealand.

My focus is on organizations, on trying to learn why people do the things they do. When I use the word "organization," I intend to encompass all groups of people gathered for a common purpose, from families to communities to large businesses and Government. I've discovered that the deeper patterns and processes are similar everywhere I've been. Everyone seems to struggle with the same sort of problems in how they lead and work with the people in their organizations regardless of the sort of product they produce or work they do. How do they change? How do they sustain themselves and build for the future?

It was during these years that I invented and developed the Process Enneagram, the Emergence of Meaning, the Sustainability Ratios and the processes needed to sustain our work. It was also around this time that Maggie Moore invented the Rhythms of Change model. These are all developed further in sections of this book.

Acknowledgments

People in the DuPont Plants and communities who were particularly helpful were Gary Lewis, Elbert Price, Tom Carpenito, Jim Borel, C. K. Chen, Kathy Reidinger, Ken Cook, John Jeffries, Donnie Parry, Mike Murphy, Denver Paxton, Roger Hess, Homer Hunter and Cathy Hunter, Ray and Sandy Baisden, Martha Mullins (a local science teacher), John and Debbie Fisher, Linda Joyce Cosby, Mary Hastings, Charlie Alsup, Lester Gore, Marty Gresham, Bob Brown, Eddie Long, Steve Wilson, Kelly Kober, Becky Dixon, Dick Sherman, Andy Ceperly, Tim Albert, Sally Hawley (my dulcimer teacher), Mildred Holt, Pam Nixon, Chuck Woody, Paul Hill, Mary Frances Bleidt, Sister Margeen Hofmann, Paul McClennon, Robin Ollis and Craig Skaggs. We also received a lot of support from DuPont corporate management people like Doc Blanchard, Bannie Kennedy, Jack Krol, Archie Dunham, Roger Gregg, Pete Myers, Bill Kirk and Jim Gregg.

Claire Stoelting, who worked at the DuPont Plant in Niagara Falls where I was the manager, saw and understood what I was trying to do. Over the years, our work drew us closer together and we were married on New Year's Eve in 1988. She is my soul mate, and companion on this journey. I couldn't have made it without her support and help.

Alan Gilburg was very helpful in the early stages of this work.

Meg Wheatley, Myron Kellner-Rogers, Maggie Moore, Karen Anne Zien, Tom Hench, Jeraldene Lovell, Jill Janov and others in the Berkana Dialogues (1992-1996) helped in my growth and understanding. Fritjof Capra who worked with Meg, Myron and me in the Self-Organizing Systems Conferences (1994-1998) helped to broaden and deepen my insights as well as giving me a lot of encouragement in this journey.

Tim Dalmau, whom I met in one of the Self-Organizing Systems Conferences, invited me to come to work with him in Australia, New Zealand and the West Coast of the US. He taught me an immense amount, and helped me to develop my thoughts more clearly. His successful use of these processes in Australia, South Africa, New Zealand, Canada, Thailand, Malaysia, Indonesia, Singapore and America has continued to reinforce my own work and development.

Tony Blake and the late Saul Kuchinsky were important in their support of the development of my thinking and in their encouragement for this work.

The help and guidance of Jennifer Glenister, an editor, and David Lovell, a publisher, who live in Melbourne Australia in moving this work towards publication is deeply appreciated.

Andrew Moyer, an editor and publisher and consultant who understands Systematics was an immense help in working with me to help me get clearer in my language, in editing and in getting the final version of the book into shape and ready for printing.

Introduction

My focus in this book is on organizations, on trying to learn why people do the things they do. By focusing on the way people engage in their work, on the ways in which they relate to each other, new patterns and processes were uncovered that can greatly help us to understand what's going on. Building on these patterns and processes, new tools to sustain and enhance the health of our organizations have been developed. I have come to these discoveries through many years of struggle and personal experience. In using these new patterns and processes, both as a plant manager and now as a teacher and guide, I've seen the effectiveness of organizations rise by as much as 30-40%.

Over the last 30 years, I developed a deep sense of dissatisfaction with the way we managed and led our organizations. I was very unhappy about the way I was learning to lead and the way in which I was treating people. I was trying to model my behavior on the more senior and successful managers that I'd met, as well as on some of the teachers and coaches I'd had in school.

As individuals meeting outside of the organization, I found most of these people to be quite kind, doing their best to live good lives. Inside of the organization, these same people seemed to change into someone else, making decisions that were often harsh, uncaring and very tough on the people in the organization. I was doing this too. We engaged in a lot of self-centered behavior and tried to push people around to get our way. We did a lot of fighting, both openly and covertly. Our organizations were not fun places to be, even when the businesses were doing well. Even though we were getting great results, almost everyone felt lousy. Why was this happening? What were we doing? Did we need to behave this way?

One of the things that I've noticed is how much and how rapidly people in organizations change when confronted with a crisis – we change in an instant. In several of the plants where I worked, we'd had a fire or other crisis, which put the business in jeopardy. When the business was suddenly confronted with a crisis that could destroy it, people came together in a different way and achieved extraordinary things. It wasn't that people suddenly became saintly. Rather, we stopped most of the stupid games we were playing and worked together purposefully, to get the business back up and running as quickly as possible. People worked hard and effectively. And then, when we were back in operation, we'd revert to the old ways of doing things with all the sick games and fighting. We often became quite nostalgic about the crisis, and what we'd accomplished, wondering why we couldn't live that way all the time, albeit at a lower level of intensity. We tended to look at this experience in the crisis as the exception, and not as the way an organization could really operate.

While in the normal mode of day-to-day operation, we often felt little energy or creativity; we felt dull and asleep. We did the work to make enough money to take care of our families and ourselves and be able to do the things outside of work that we thought were fun. But in a crisis, this changed and we came alive. In many ways, the crisis was fun, and we gained a deep sense of satisfaction in what we accomplished together. What I see now is that the clues to our future as living organizations are revealed in the lessons we can learn from the crises.

When I use the word "organization," I use it to encompass all groups of people gathered for a common purpose, from families to communities to large businesses and governments. I've discovered that the deeper patterns and processes are similar everywhere I've been. Everyone seems to struggle with the same sort of problems in how they lead and work with the people in their organizations, regardless of the product they produce or the work they do. How do they change? How do they sustain themselves and build for the future?

Our organizations have many of the characteristics of living systems. The patterns and the processes of the living systems discussed in this book underlie the surface of our visible world – they run all the time, whether or not we are conscious of them. Whether we use them or not, they have always been there. When used consciously, they are the tools we can use to make sense of the world and to function in it effectively. These patterns and processes enable us to see more deeply and to function more effectively. With them, we can move joyfully into the living systems model.

In this book, when I refer to organizations as living systems, I am referring to the structures, patterns and processes used by the people in the organizations that make them like living systems. This metaphor is very useful, in that it opens up new and creative ways to see organizations and to understand them more fully. Whether or not organizations are living systems in a deeply philosophical sense is not a concern of this book; the metaphor is very powerful, however.

Change is all around us and the rate of change is certainly increasing. Our times are now fundamentally different from the past. The immense flow of information across the Internet and the rapid increase in the number of interconnections has enabled us to do things more quickly than ever before. We are all more interconnected and have unheard of access to each other. Our banks, businesses and other institutions have moved from a national scale to a global one.

People in more traditional organizations, which usually function according to a machine paradigm, tend to be quite resistant to change. The thinking and behavior of the people in these organizations can be rather incoherent. People in organizations functioning more like living systems, however, proactively and intentionally co-create their future together. The thinking and behavior take on a deeper coherence. Resistance to change almost disappears. With information flowing freely, with strong relationships and trust, with a clear sense of identity and intention, the people in such organizations move into the future together, creating as they go. They embrace the wholeness, variety and chaos, for with their agreements on how they'll be together, they can trust and have confidence in each other.

These patterns and processes work in a variety of cultures. I've seen no differences in how they work in the US, Canada, the UK, Australia and New Zealand. Tim Dalmau, CEO of Dalmau Associates, has also used them successfully in Australia, New Zealand, South Africa, Canada, Malaysia, Thailand, Indonesia and Singapore. C. K. Chen, who studied with me for a year in Belle, West Virginia, took them to Shanghai, China where he was a plant manager, and found they worked beautifully. The visible things we see in each of these cultures are different, but the underlying patterns and deeper processes seem to be the same.

As we live in the complexity and chaos, it's important that our mental models are clear, relevant, internally consistent, and useful. This book presents three such mental models. They are archetypal patterns and processes we can use to help us make sense and meaning out of what is happening. They allow us to navigate through the uncertainty and chaos we experience all around us. Although these patterns and processes are the manifestations of deep archetypes, they are not the archetypes themselves. When the word "archetypal" is used, it refers to these manifestations. Because similar patterns in organizations show up at many levels of scale, these mental models can be very widely used. The term *fractals* is used to denote similar patterns that show up at many levels of scale. The fractal nature of these patterns makes the mental models presented in this book very powerful.

The patterns and processes described in the chapters ahead are largely consistent with Complex Adaptive Systems theories and practices, as I understand them. I have lived and taught this way of becoming and being; it works! Complex Adaptive Systems (CAS) are characterized by having a number of non-linear, dynamical interactions among the members of the system. CAS have emergent properties that cannot be predicted from the parts and arise through the interactions and relationships of all the parts. The CAS approach is based in artificial intelligence work in computers. Consciousness, for example, cannot be predicted from our understanding of neurons. CAS are destroyed when we take them apart. We do not get two cows if we cut one in half; we just get a dead cow. Complex Responsive Processes theories put more focus on how the people in the organization behave and their responsibility for making their organization behave as it behaves.

This book is about *Self-Organizing Leadership*: a way of leading that enables organizations and the people within them to achieve extraordinary results. In organizations using this way of leading, leadership shows up at all levels, all over the place, as people see what needs to be done for the good of the whole and step forward to make it happen. Self-Organizing Leadership employs essential core processes that can be used to increase coherence, to release the energy and to open up the creativity in our organizations. These core processes lie beneath the well-known procedures of operational and strategic leadership.

While self-organization is always occurring in organizations, most do not recognize, value nor use Self-Organizing Leadership processes. Such organizations behave as if they are machines, lacking coherence, energy and creativity. By contrast, organizations behaving like living systems consciously use Self-Organizing Leadership processes to support the operational and strategic work in which they are engaged.

There are three major threads woven into the tapestry of this book, each a major aspect of Self-Organizing Leadership. One thread is the personal story of my own transformation, from a traditional command-and-control manager to one who is more open and able to live, lead and

4

work in a radically new world. The need to embrace chaos and complexity required a deep shift in my state of being. It required me to be a more courageous, open and dedicated person who was willing to put myself at risk for the organization's success. For me, this transformation was the hardest work I've ever done; it's still work in progress. This was not just a change in my behavior, it is a transformation in my way of seeing and being. The extensive Bibliography at the end of this book gives you some sense of the terrain I've covered.

The second thread woven into this book is the discovery of three deep, archetypal, Self-Organizing Leadership patterns and processes that run in all organizations. These are the maps that we can use in our work of Self-Organizing Leadership to see and to help us move through the ever-changing, unpredictable landscape of our personal and organizational lives.

The first of these is the *Process Enneagram*, a model for looking at organizations from nine different perspectives in a highly disciplined and focused way. I developed this particular way of using the enneagram to look at the patterns and processes within organizations. I call this way of using it the Process Enneagram to distinguish it from it's other uses, such as a tool to look at personality types. That use I call the Enneagram of Personality. Using the raw experience of the people in an organization, the Process Enneagram opens up a way to see the patterns and processes that are operating. It works in organizations of any size and kind. As we see these patterns and processes in new ways, we are able to connect complexity science and Ralph Stacey's theories (*Complex Responsive Processes in Organizations 2001*) of complex responsive processes to what is happening in our organizations. We move into the underlying processes mapped on the Process Enneagram almost automatically in a crisis. At a deep level, we know them; we've lived them. The Process Enneagram looks complex at first, but as we become more conscious and learn to use it, we find it flows easily and quickly. This is an intellectual process we can use to understand what's happening. You will find that it meets the criteria of being clear, relevant, internally consistent, fractal and easy to use. This way of seeing and the deeper understanding that flows from it, in turn, open up both the organization and the people within it to new possibilities for transformation and growth.

The second pattern and process relates to the emotional changes that we experience as we move through periods of transition. It is called the *Rhythms of Change*. It maps our process of emotional change and is also one we've lived many times. Emotionally, change and transition feel very bumpy and frightening. No matter how frequently I go through these periods of change, I feel some unease. I expect that you've experienced this as well. When Maggie Moore began to teach me about the Rhythms of Change, I became very conscious of the nature of the flow. I could feel the patterns and learned that I could move through these patterns and not become my fear. As long as I paid attention to the process, I could move through it okay, and land on my feet on the other side of each period of change. It too meets the criteria of being clear, relevant, internally consistent, fractal and easy to use.

The third pattern and process, the *Emergence of Meaning and the Will to Act*, is also one we know. The discovery of meaning in our work brings creativity, energy and a sense of spirit into our work. Becoming more conscious of this process shows us how important it is to purposefully create the conditions in our organizations where meaning can emerge. It releases great energy and creativity.

The last thread woven into this book relates to sustainability. As we're engaged in these patterns and processes of living systems, we need to sustain the work. Tools to help us build more sustainable organizations are introduced in Section 3 of this book. I look through the lens of complex adaptive systems theory, as I understand it, at what it takes to build more sustainable, responsive organizations. Ways of observing, qualitatively measuring and improving sustainability are developed and explored. The Self-Organizing Leadership processes are a key to building sustainability.

All these dynamic processes are grounded in complexity science and complex responsive processes theories. It's critical for people in organizations to bring the key models and tools for Self-Organizing Leadership to the surface and to use these models, patterns and processes consciously. They can then use these models to create the environment where the organization blossoms and grows. I have used them successfully in over 16 years of hands-on experience as a plant manager and now as a guide and consultant for organizations. I call this dynamic way of leading the *Leadership Dance*.

I like pictures to see how things fit together, so I've created one here, which helps me to see all these ideas, and how everything ties together. I call it "Congruence: Criteria for a Living Organization." These are the elements of the Leadership Dance. In this picture, I can see all the elements, as well as get a sense of the dynamic flow of everything. It will begin to have meaning for you as you move through the book.

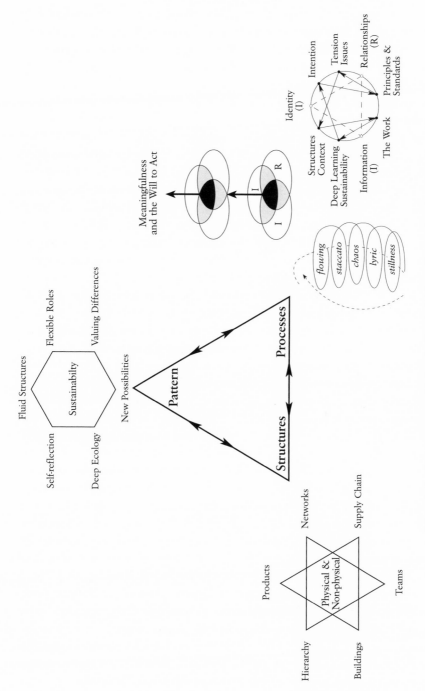

Figure 1 Congruence Criteria for a Living Organization

Introduction

Come join me as I tell a living, vital story of how I came to discover a new way to breathe life into our organizations, discover meaning, free up our creativity and energy, and improve the business results that are so critical for our lives and the success of our people and businesses. From my 36-year journey in the DuPont Company, I'll share the insights I've gained on organizational development and change.

I will focus particularly on the last 13 years of the adventure at the Niagara Falls, NY and Belle, WV Plants where the plant people, the leadership teams and I slowly discovered how to bring our organizations to life. I will tell you of the extraordinary results we achieved for both the business and the people, by learning to live and work in a new way. I'll share how we learned to use the Process Enneagram, the Rhythms of Change and the Emergence of Meaning as maps and guidance, and how we discovered new ways to track and measure the progress of the whole organization towards greater health and sustainability. These are stories and learnings from ordinary people who did extraordinary things together. My hope is that this will be of some help to you as you create your own vibrant, growing and thriving organization.

This invitation is to take a journey that will move us from relating to the world as a machine, a perception most of us have had for most of our lives, to an understanding of ourselves as part of the living world, of its people, its organizations, its communities and its families. We'll move to a place where the things that have been hidden from our awareness can be seen and embraced, a place where we can find meaning. Here, as we encounter each other in new ways, we grow in mutual respect and admiration, and our individual and collective wholeness grows.

Henri Bortoft, in his extraordinary book, *The Wholeness of Nature*, describes the shift as one in which we move from the analytical level of consciousness to the wholeness level of consciousness. At this level of consciousness, everything shifts.

Dee Hock, the Founder of Visa International, wrote in "Thoughts on Change" in the August/September, 1999 issue of *Wired Magazine*,

"Change is not about understanding new things or having new ideas; it's about seeing old things with new eyes from different perspectives. Change is not about re-organizing, re-engineering, re-inventing, re-capitalizing. It is about re-conceiving! When you re-conceive something – a thought, a situation, a corporation, or a product – you create a whole new order. Do that and creativity will flood your mind." (90)

In the Forward, I recounted my personal story, so that you can get a "real life" sense of the transformation I experienced. I hope that this will give hope and confidence to others embarking on or already on their own journey. It is the story of my adventures in discovering understanding and meaning. Sections 1, 2 and 3 look more deeply into what was going on in the Journey. In these sections the deep patterns and processes I discovered are presented.

In Section 1, we'll look at some crises and other leadership challenges to reveal the similarity of the patterns and processes running throughout these events.

In Section 2, we'll go more deeply into the theories and models which help us to understand the nature of the way organizations, and the people in them, tend to behave. We'll also look more deeply at the three archetypal processes of Self-Organizing Leadership: The Process Enneagram, The Rhythms of Change and The Emergence of Meaning. There's also a brief history of our scientific and technological journey of the last 350 years.

In Section 3, we'll look at ways to see and to measure the health and sustainability of our organizations.

The story of this work continues to unfold. To find more examples of how this work is progressing you can go to the web page for the Center for Self-Organizing Leadership.

www.centerforselforganizingleadership.com

SECTION ONE

STORIES

· 1 ·

Some Crises

Introduction

The three crises described and discussed in this chapter replicate to some extent the ones told in The Story of the Journey. They are retold here so that an easier comparison of the patterns can be made. Each of the crises took place over different time periods, yet the patterns are the same.

The Sodium Plant Fire

We'd had a good summer in 1982; it had been one of those that make you like living on the Niagara Frontier. It had been cool with bright skies and gentle breezes. We'd had good rainfall so the corn was tall and ready for the harvest. The apples were coming in, beautiful and crisp. The roadside markets were full of pumpkins, squash, and corn. The shelves were full of the golden clover and dark buckwheat honeys.

The tourist season that year had been a good one. The shows at Niagara-on-the-Lake were outstanding. The shops and restaurants had done well. The re-enactments of the War of 1812 engagements at Fort Niagara were well attended and fun for all.

The towns and villages had completed the pothole repairs and were getting in their winter's supply of road salt. Everyone was getting ready for the winter and enjoying the bountiful harvest and the fine weather.

Chet Kodeski, Union President and electrician, was working at the far end of the Plant repairing the electrical tracing on the pipes when he heard the major emergency alarm sound. Looking towards the sodium plant, he saw black smoke coming out of all the vent stacks. He quickly secured his job, gathered up his tools and headed for the central shops.

13

He knew there would be a lot of work to do. Even before the fires were completely out, he went in with another electrician to begin to assess the damage. The sodium filters were black and covered in debris. Overhead, the cable trays were twisted with burned cables and instrument tubing, broken and hanging down like the Devil's cobwebs. The business was in deep trouble, but fortunately, no one was hurt.

It was clear that we had a major problem and that a lot needed to be done to keep from losing the whole sodium business. Sodium is manufactured by the electrolysis of salt (like table salt only more pure) in electrolytic cells about 6 feet in diameter and 8 feet high. The salt must be melted, so the cells run at very high temperatures and use a lot of electricity. If the cells were to cool too much, the molten salt would crystallize and break up the anodes and cathodes that are critical for their operation. They wear out slowly so we routinely build about 7 or 8 cells a month as part of the operation of the plant. But if the whole sodium shop stopped running and the salts crystallize, there was no way we could rebuild the more than 100 cells fast enough for the business to survive.

Everyone moved into action to assess the extent of the damage, contacting suppliers for parts and assemble the schedules so the work could be done. Close coordination with operations had to be done because the sodium filters that were operable had to run to keep the production high enough to supply our customers and to keep the shop from freezing up.

The union and management agreed to postpone all scheduled grievance and other meetings during the crisis. At that point, there were usually so many grievances that the union was meeting with management twice a week to keep up with them. The service people went to 12-hour shifts and everyone went onto demanding overtime schedules, within the bounds of the contract. A variance was signed to comply with state law on the overtime changes. The craft people began to help each other with the cleanup and dismantling of the damaged equipment, often crossing craft lines to do so. They cleared the way, so the operations people could get the filters up and running again. People worked shoulder-to-shoulder to do what was needed. A sense of family began to develop as the management nitpicking of the craft people stopped. The craft people were recognized for their professionalism and were given a lot of discretion in doing their work in the best way they could. Everyone felt a shared stake in the need to get up and running again.

The first night it rained, and water came in through the holes in the roof. Residual bits of sodium began to catch fire in the area. Sodium reacts with water, and burns with a brilliant, intense fire that is quite frightening. Chet remembered one operator who was nearly in tears over what would happen to them if they couldn't get the shop up quickly.

There were no slackers and no excuses. It was clear what had to be done. Everyone knew that the work had to be done safely and everyone worked together. People were all over the place removing the damaged equipment and beginning to pull the new cables to restore electrical service. With all the cooperation, with all the support from supervision, people made decisions about the work without having to go to the supervisor for each one. Everyone in the shop knew how the work was progressing. They could see it; bulletins were issued on the progress. The suppliers were also closely involved. They were doing their best to keep the plant running as well.

Gradually, the temporary repairs brought the shop back to life. One filter after another was brought back on-line. Within about 10 days, full operation had been restored to the shop. No one had believed it could be done that fast when the initial assessments of the damage were made. The business had been saved. Everyone knew the part they'd played and how their contributions had made a difference. A lot of overtime money was paid. The work had been done safely with no injuries. No grievances were filed.

Over the next few months, the temporary repairs were replaced with permanent ones. The physical facilities were restored. But, the way everyone worked together went back to the old way. People stopped helping each other. The separation among the craft lines hardened. Management was again on people's backs picking about the details of the work. The flow of information shut down again, so most people didn't know what was going on. The grievances started up again. The work had become just more work to be done so folks could be paid and get out of there. Cooperation between operations and the maintenance people fell down.

In the lunchrooms, people talked about the fire and all they'd done. The stories were compelling and exciting to retell. These were also told in the management offices. The fire had brought people together in an exciting way, but that was now in the past, so it was back to business as usual.

Saving the Amines Business

Our DuPont Belle Plant had been built in the hills and valleys of West Virginia in 1927 to make ammonia. The chemical industry had come to

15

West Virginia in those early days because of the abundant supply of good water, coal and salt. Many chemical process operations were first developed in the Kanawha Valley near Charleston in the first half of the twentieth century. After the Second World War, many of the new plants for products like those made in the Valley had gone to the Gulf Coast in Texas and Louisiana where natural gas was cheap and the climate better. Employment in the Valley's chemical industry had dropped by over 50% since the War. During those years, the industry lost the support of much of the community because of the pollution problems.

One of the product families we still made at the DuPont Plant in Belle, near Charleston was called methylamines. We made mono-, di-, and tri-methylamines. All are stored under pressure; two are gases at atmospheric pressure. All of them smell like dead fish at very low concentrations in the air. Our production facilities were over 30 years old and used nitrogen and air pressure to measure temperature and process pressure changes. At the time this equipment was installed, these pneumatic controls were the best around, but now they were obsolete. We were having problems keeping the facilities running and we had quality problems. We were the second largest producer in this business, but with problems like these, we had a difficult time earning enough money to justify staying in the business. Even though it was a sizable business with annual sales of around $50 million, the business team decided that we had to either restore the business or get out of it. Staying where we were was not acceptable. Getting out would have caused the loss of over 100 jobs.

Together with the Business team, we decided to take some risks and upgrade the product and plant to become more competitive. One major change we decided upon was to change the pneumatic control system to an electronic system called a DCS (Distributive Control System). Normally, when an old facility faces a retrofit change like this, a parallel control system is built and brought into operation before the old control system is dismantled. This is the conservative way to do it. Our Engineering Department people said it would take two years and cost around 6 million dollars, but we at the Plant decided that this was too long a time and too expensive.

After much soul searching, we decided to do the job ourselves with our DuPont R&D people helping. We decided we would not run parallel. My older brother Frank was the Manager for this R&D group; we looked forward to this challenge together. The level of trust and respect we had for each other was high. Working under him, Frank had a highly competent and dedicated group of engineers, led by DuPont Senior Engineer Pretop Gohel. They became involved in making this a success. Our goal was to begin the planning in January 1988 and to install the project in our maintenance shutdown, which was scheduled for the following November.

We knew that everyone had to be involved in this if we were to have a chance of being successful, so we began to have project status meetings every week in the control room where the operators, mechanics and engineers could all talk about what was happening. This gave everyone a chance to give their inputs, raise concerns and ask questions. At first, some felt that the operating control room was a poor place to hold the meeting because it was so crowded, with no room to sit down. Actually, it turned out to be the very best place because that is where the people were. Each month, everyone was able to get up to speed as the shift rotations brought folks through the day shift. I stood up during these 1½-hour weekly meetings along with most of the others.

The first meeting was in January 1988, and by June, we were far enough along to have the capital projects ready for authorization by our Business Division VP in Wilmington, Delaware. We had two projects totaling around $3 million, rather than the originally forecasted $6 million. We signed off on the plant level of authorizations for these projects on each other's backs in about 10 minutes during the course of one of the meetings. The normal routing procedure would have taken 6-8 weeks. A person from the business team was there, and she took the projects to the VP the next day.

We continued to meet every week through the summer and fall. The intensity and excitement built as we got closer to the November shutdown. We sent about 15 operators and mechanics to the Honeywell Instrument School in Phoenix for three weeks of training. When they got home, they helped to train all the others. Operators, mechanics and engineers from several organizations within DuPont, as well as engineers from Honeywell were working closely in teams around all the key work. Since people had all the information and knew what to do, they spontaneously formed teams around the work and simply did it.

The operators helped to design the process control graphics. They worked with the engineers to define what sort of information they needed on the screens to be able to run the process safely and easily. The mechanics worked with the engineers and operators on the choice and location of the instrument sensors in the process. The mechanics installed the

17

instruments, pulled the wire and did the loop-checks to be sure everything was connected correctly. The planning and scheduling people worked closely with the teams to build the shutdown schedule and to make sure we hadn't missed anything. In working like this, people were able to overcome the myriad problems that came up because the trust levels had grown much higher. Information was flowing freely and we all knew what needed to be accomplished.

When our two-week November shutdown came, people worked day and night to get everything done. The close coordination and cooperation that took place were really beautiful to see. In addition to the DCS project, we were also doing critical maintenance of all the major pieces of process equipment including, for example, taking the tops off the 100-foot tall distillation columns to do the internal parts inspections. We took out the 100 or so pneumatic process control loops that had to be changed when the whole process was shutdown and put in the new DCS system. After two weeks of beehive-like activity, everything was back together and we started up the process. Within 4 days, we were running at capacity. We achieved all of our goal improvements for product quality, improved productivity and lower environmental emissions.

In my experience with changes like this, where a parallel system is installed by the engineers and then handed over to the operators, it often takes well over a year to get the process running well. The training that is required and imposed on the operators, the mechanical and instrument problems that pop up and the resistance to changing from the old, familiar process are big hurdles that we didn't run into at all.

The deep involvement of everyone, the sharing of all the information, the trusting relationships we'd built in all the project meetings, and the clarity that was there that the business would die unless we were successful, helped to bring all this to a successful conclusion. A seamless team of highly competent engineers from DuPont and Honeywell along with the operators and mechanics from the plant had been formed. Everyone was pleased and proud in having set a new DuPont standard for retrofitting DCS systems into old plants. We'd cut the time and cost in half compared to the more conservative approach of building parallel control processes. After that, the plant did 15 more DCS conversions on other product units, and improved our performance each time. Many of our operators became active in corporation-wide teams to help other plants to do this.

My role as plant manager really shifted. I participated in almost all the project status meetings each week in the control room. I insisted that everyone really listen to each other as the ideas flew around. I encouraged them to make the decisions as we went, right there in the meetings. We were making adjustments and corrections to the process and plan as we went. Mostly I was a cheerleader. At night, I prayed a lot too!

Risk Management Planning: Sharing Worst-Case Scenarios

The Clean Air Act of 1990 required companies that handle hazardous chemicals above certain threshold quantities to develop risk management plans (RMP) and to share these with the Environmental Protection Agency (EPA), the Local Emergency Planning Committees (LEPC), State Regulators and the general public no later than June 20, 1999. Being more open with the public, in general, and plant neighbors, in particular, has been encouraged by the Chemical Manufacturers Association (now known as The American Chemical Council) Responsible Care® Principles and Practices for about 10 years. A good review of the progress of Responsible Care® is in *Chemical Week*, July 1-8, 1998. Responsible Care® is an outstanding initiative that has helped the chemical industry to make significant improvements in operations, environmental and safety standards and practices. The Clean Air Act requirements on the communications of RMPs and worst-case scenarios, however, stretched everyone around the communication issues. It took a lot of effort by the EPA, the industry and the major environmental groups to get us to the June 20, 1999 milestone.

The Superfund Amendment and Reauthorization Act, Title III of 1986 required LEPCs to be established in each state. Most states have designated LEPCs that function at the county or municipal level. The LEPC is charged with developing emergency response plans to deal with chemical disasters in their communities. The LEPCs have the right to ask local industries for information on the chemicals that they handle, so that they can prepare appropriate community emergency response plans.

In order to fulfill its obligation on planning, the Kanawha-Putnam LEPC in West Virginia asked, in January of 1992, some seven years before the due date, for the worst-case scenarios for the three most hazardous chemicals used or manufactured by the eight chemical companies in their 13 chemical plants in the Kanawha Valley. All the plants are located within about 15 miles of Charleston, the State Capital.

While the industry is a major employer and taxpayer, environmental concerns over the years had caused a lot of ill will and distrust between the plants and the communities. One plant handled large quantities of methylisocyanate, the material that was released and which hurt and killed so many people in Bhopal, India. All of the plants handled hazardous materials, and from time to time, one or the other of us would have a small release causing inconvenience and disruption in the communities.

A request to share our worst-case scenarios felt like a huge threat to us in the industry, and we feared being shut down and driven from the Valley. We didn't know if responding to the request would lead to a lot of lawsuits. Would we face some sort of mass community action? Would water and air permits be withdrawn? Would we be able to get new permits? Would the business environment become so difficult in the Valley that our companies would stop the flow of new investment to these plants and build new facilities elsewhere? We didn't know how to do the technical work to comply with the request. We didn't have any agreement among the managers or their companies on how we should respond. The media were all over us, relentlessly insisting that we comply with the request.

The thirteen managers and their home offices struggled with how to meet this request. We were all members of the CMA, and positively responding to this request was in keeping with Responsible Care®. After about 6 months, we began to work with the LEPC to develop plans to share the information. We hoped to do this in a way that would not be a disaster for us in the Valley or for the CMA membership as a whole.

Our credibility was so low that we decided to have lots of community involvement from the beginning. We set up two committees. One addressed the technical issues. We went to the National Institute for Chemical Studies in Charleston and asked that their president, Paul Hill, become the chairperson for this committee. Paul, later the next year, became the head of the National Chemical Safety Board in Washington. At the time we started, there was so little guidance available that we needed to develop definitions of what constituted a worst-case, and a more likely case. We had to determine how to calculate the plume dispersion diagrams and agree on the choice of weather conditions to use in the calculations. We had to develop a methodology for selecting the particular chemicals to study. We had so many issues that trying to develop consensus among the eight companies was difficult and slow.

We felt we also needed a communications committee. We found a lady in the community, Mary Frances Bleidt, who was a strong and excellent chairperson. None of us knew how to do the communications task so that the complicated technology would be understood and the stories would be heard.

Both committees had members from the community, local environmentalists and industry people. As you can imagine, our meetings were often quite lively. Everyone was involved, we openly shared the information on the technology, we listened to each other, and we built trusting relationships. We discovered that we all had a stake in the successful communications of the risk management plans and the scenarios.

The communications committee and the technical committee shared their developments and findings with the CMA so the whole industry could stay connected to what was happening in the Kanawha Valley. Several people from the EPA Chemical Emergency Planning and Preparedness Office in Washington occasionally attended our meetings so they could learn what we were doing as they (the EPA) drafted the RMP Rules. The development work in the Kanawha Valley was running in parallel to, but ahead of the EPA work at the National level.

Mildred Holt, who was co-chair of the Citizens Concerned About Methylisocyanate, and a trusted friend, really helped me one day. I was sharing my worries about the whole effort and wondering how the community would react when they found out about the various scenarios. Her response really opened my eyes. She said, "I know you guys can kill me. What I want to know is what you guys are doing to prevent it." I knew then and there that talking about our progress in Responsible Care® and risk management would be of real interest to the people in our community.

We invited 9th grade social studies students from the DuPont Junior High School near the Belle Plant to come as part of the communications meetings; they attended all 22 of the meetings. One of the students, Nikki Smith, played a key role in keeping their enthusiasm high. Their most important contribution was in observing the meetings: *adults behave better when the kids are watching!* Most of the work of the communications committee took place between September 1993 and June 1994, so the kids were in on all of it.

The whole effort finally culminated in presentations on June 3rd and 4th to the community. We held the first day in the Charleston Convention Center. The meetings were widely advertised in the Charleston newspapers and on TV. The CMA made sure the industry as a whole knew of the events. In the morning, we made technical presentations to the 700 or so attendees in the auditorium, and after lunch each plant had a display set up in the large meeting hall so that anyone who wanted to talk to a

21

manager could do so face-to-face. Attendees came from the local communities, the media, the local business community and from other chemical companies around the country. The next day, at the urging of the women on the committee, we moved the displays to the Charleston Town Center Mall; the ladies told us that was where we would meet people. The managers, all men, would never have come up with this idea, and while we struggled with it, every manager and his team participated fully. The environmental groups had their displays as well and were able to give people their own opinions on what the plants were saying and doing.

Through the openness, the information sharing, the relationship building and the discovery of commonly shared values, we were able to exchange all the information in a way that resulted in the community coming together. The environmentalists were able to tell everyone that we'd made progress, but that there was still more to be done. None of the dire consequences that we'd feared happened. The New York Times, CNN and the London Times were there and saw a community that had come together successfully around a difficult issue.

The work and activities related to being more open, sharing information more effectively, and building relationships were conducted broadly in the chemical industry around the country as others prepared for the June 20, 1999 deadline to publicly share all worst-case scenarios as required under the Clean Air Act. There was a lot of involvement and interaction between the industry and their communities. The EPA built many of the learnings into the Rule they developed as well. A similar process for sharing the RMPs and the various scenarios was done successfully in Victoria, TX in 1995, in the communities around the Houston Ship Channel and in Indianapolis, IN a little later. As people come together around this work and become involved, they develop plans that are appropriate for their communities. While the small details, like whether to go to a Mall or not are different, the deeper processes we used in the Kanawha Valley work wherever they're used.

Some Common Threads and Deeper Processes

Our Traditional Approach to Dealing with Crises

Each of the crises you yourself have experienced or those that were just described can be seen from several different perspectives. In my experience, the way we normally look at them is that they are abnormal events or exceptional happenings. As good stewards of our businesses, our communities and our families, we want to keep fires, explosions and other calamities to a minimum, eliminating them if possible. We don't want to lose our businesses and jobs, or have our communities and families turned upside down. We want them to function as well as they can. When crises like these happen, we see them as a failure of some sort in the way in which we lead, manage and conduct ourselves. We normally take a lot of time and put a lot of effort into preventing these things from happening in the future, which is appropriate. We strive to bring our organizations, families and communities back into control so they'll be more stable, dependable and predictable. We tend to generate more rules and procedures, even new laws and regulations so this won't happen again. We impose them and then build the structures or make the other changes we feel we need to make sure that everyone is doing what's required.

We try to figure out how we got into the problem in the first place. We go after the planning process, or whatever we think it was that caused the problem, and keep revising or fixing it so that it will give us better predictions for the future. We often try to find someone to blame. We try to acquire more information, believing that if we just had more information we'd know what to do. Sometimes these measures work for a while. But are we satisfied with the results of all this effort by all the well-intentioned and committed people? We do see progress, but is it enough?

The chemical industry, as I can attest, has made huge progress over the last 35 years in process safety management and risk reduction. A thoughtful summary of much of this work can be found in the November 9th issue of *The Chemical and Engineering News* (1998) in two articles: "How to Profitably Avoid Doomsday" and "Good Design Heads Off Human Error." The whole thrust of these articles is that if we just have more control, more knowledge, better designs, more reliability and better trained people, we'll have fewer incidents. My experience tells me this is true; we do make progress this way. But are we moving fast enough?

"How to Profitably Avoid Doomsday" (p. 71-84) lists major accidents in the chemical industry at 25 sites worldwide, over the last 25 years. Many were killed, hundreds were injured and thousands were evacuated.

If we shift our attention to business crises, we have a similar story. Every day we read in the business trade press, the newspapers and see on TV stories about companies struggling to overcome the latest crises. CEOs get the axe, reorganizations take place, units are sold off, huge mergers take place and some businesses just disappear. A crisis or threat appears, and the first step usually seems to be some sort of reorganization. Important management strategies like re-engineering are developed. They are implemented vigorously, and people's jobs are changed or eliminated. After all the effort and change, we are often disappointed with the results. Then we do it again to try to get it right. What seems to be the normal way of doing things to address these crises doesn't quite get us to where we want to be.

When a community is facing a crisis like in the one in the Kanawha Valley, the norm seems to be that those in charge at the center of things go behind closed doors and make critical decisions. They often do good work and have the best of intentions for their community. Then they announce their decision and people in the community start to raise all sorts of concerns and questions. There seems to be a feeling that this is just the way it is. Right here where I live in the Niagara Falls, NY community, this was played out right in front of my eyes in 1998 and 1999. The Niagara Falls Memorial Hospital and the St. Mary's Hospital Boards got together to see what they might do to combine forces and develop improved, more cost-effective medical care for our community. They announced the plan that had been developed in private by the Boards with a lot of fanfare, and the community, the nurses and some of the doctors came down on it like a ton of bricks. Months later, they were still having huge arguments. Things were so bogged down that the whole effort was abandoned and each hospital went its separate way. There were many good things our community needed in the proposals. Everyone lost when the proposals were abandoned.

Another Way of Dealing with Crises

There is another way to look at crises. So many times when we successfully come through a crisis like those I just described, we feel pretty darn good and have a lot for which we can be proud. Many times, I've asked myself, "Why can't we live with the sense of togetherness, trust, well-being, and community that we have during a crisis, *all the time*? Why can't we have the sense of fulfillment and meaning that we have then? Why can't we have the high levels of productivity and accomplishment we experience in a crisis?"

When we look more deeply at the things that occur during a crisis, we can see the underlying patterns and processes. In each of these crises our sense of *identity*, who we are right now, is very clear and well understood.

24

In the sodium fire, we were flat on our backs; in the amines case, we were on the verge of shutting down, and in the case of the Risk Management Plans, we were facing a critical, long-term, business survival issue.

In each case, *what we needed to accomplish was clear*. In the sodium fire, we had to get the plant repaired and running as quickly as possible, while maintaining what production we could. In the amines case, we had to improve quality, productivity and environmental performance at lower costs. In the RMP case, we had to do a complex communications task in a way that was innovative, credible and understandable and that would allow us to continue to operate our plants with improved environmental performance. At the beginning, none of us knew how we were going to accomplish and fulfill all these complex demands.

However, we knew we had to do things differently; we needed *new principles and standards of behavior*. We deeply believed that the knowledge was in the system (the people in our organization) and we had to access it. We had to *work interdependently, learning to trust each other*. We had to share all the *information* so we could make good decisions quickly at whatever level in the system they needed to be made. We had to work with the freedom to go and do the sensible things that were needed. In the sodium fire case, the situation evolved quickly because of the nature of the crisis. In the amines case, it evolved more slowly in our weekly project status review meetings. In the RMP case, the situation evolved and emerged over the 2½ years of the work. The principles and standards were there. For example, we agreed that we had to share information, tell the truth and work for the good of the whole Kanawha Valley and the Country as a whole. We talked about these things and, as the needs changed, our principles and standards strengthened and evolved with us. These were always very visible to everyone.

We could address the *dilemmas, tensions, issues* and *questions* that constantly arose because we operated out of these principles and standards of behavior, and we had clarity about who we were and what needed to be done. We had a context for engaging in the crucial conversations, which enabled us *to move and to act*.

All the information was available and shared in each of the crisis cases just described. In the sodium fire, it was there in front of our eyes. In the amines case, we expressly shared all the information in each weekly meeting and set the standard for the continuous, open sharing of information. New information, as it was co-created by the operators, mechanics, engineers and the design team, was shared in each meeting. In the RMP case, all information was shared and the decisions and procedures were co-created by the committees.

Having all the information, being clear on who we were and what we had to do, and operating out of shared principles and standards, enabled the people *to spontaneously self-organize around the work* that needed to be done. Ad hoc teams were formed in some cases around a particular piece of work. In other cases, committees or teams were formed with the flexibility to change and evolve as the needs changed. These tended to be longer-term projects than the ad hoc teams took on.

The *teams then did the work and made many decisions* on their own as they went. They often *saw better ways to do things and did them.* We learned as we went! Sometimes there were mistakes, but there were no penalties. In all these cases, we were in so much trouble that doing something was better than doing nothing. Everyone knew that he or she could ask anyone questions and get the best answers possible. *Everyone had access to everyone.* As we shared the information about our progress, we just kept learning from our mistakes and successes. All the systems were full of *constant feedback*.

As we worked together this way, the things we had to do got increasingly clear as we went along. New issues arose and were addressed. We kept on self-organizing and doing the work and learning. In all these crises, *we co-created our future together. People didn't resist the changes they were helping to create;* they helped to lead the changes we needed to make things better.

In looking at these crises and in thinking about many others I know about, there always seems to be the same recurring processes operating under the surface activities. These deeper processes of how we think and decide how to come together to do the work are there all the time for us to use, if we choose. I now know that we can have the togetherness, trust, well-being and community all the time *if this is what we choose.* We can make a difference and have fulfillment and meaning in our work. We can have high levels of accomplishment and productivity. This doesn't require huge programs, or large capital commitments to gain these things. We simply have to choose to live this way, and put the systems and processes I'm talking about in this book into place to sustain the work.

· 2 ·

Defining the Processes

In this chapter, we explore new ways of understanding how organizations function, and how we can be more effective. By abstracting what we've learned from the crisis examples, we gain new insights about the underlying patterns and processes of living and working together in organizations. The patterns and processes are revealed using a new tool called the Process Enneagram. In using this tool, the choice to live and work in a different way opens up for us.

Using the Process Enneagram to Understand Organizations as Living Systems

The patterns and processes of the Process Enneagram introduced here are grounded in our experiences of organizational life. They emerge quickly in times of crisis. Understanding them will help us to have deeper insights into the way organizations function. We can think of organizations as living systems where all the parts are connected, constantly interacting and adapting to changes in their environment in ways that maintain their identity and sustainability.

All organizations are complex systems where the people are constantly changing as they interact with each other and their environment. Properties emerge from the non-linear, dynamical processes taking place among the people and their environment. We can't predict what these emergent properties will be, merely by knowing all the parts. These properties emerge from the complex patterns and processes that run in the organization. All the organizations that I know about constantly use some mixture of patterns and processes characteristic of living systems. The healthiest organizations are centered in self-organizing processes. There is, however, also a need for operational management and strategic leadership as well.

We begin the development of the Process Enneagram by looking at the organization from 9 different perspectives. I have found this to be a useful and illuminating way to look at organizations. These are the same perspectives I found so useful when talking about the crises in the previous chapter. The attributes of these perspectives are easily seen and felt when we step into any organization, whether a family, a store, a business, a not-for-profit group, a church or a school. We all use some of these, almost automatically, as we step in the front door.

From each of these nine perspectives, we can ask unique, penetrating questions about the people and their organization.

Point 0 (Identity): Who are they? What is their Identity? What is their history, individually and collectively? (As the first cycle is completed, this point becomes point 9.)

Point 1 (Intention): What are they trying to do? What are their Intentions? What is the future potential?

Point 2 (Issues): What are the problems and Issues facing them? What are their dilemmas, paradoxes and questions?

Point 3 (Relationship): What are their Relationships like? How are they connected to others they need in the system? What is the quality of these connections? Are there too many or too few of them?

Point 4 (Principles and Standards): What are their Principles and Standards of behavior? What are their ground-rules, really? What are the undiscussable behaviors that go on, over and over?

Point 5 (Work): What is their Work? On what are they physically working?

Point 6 (Information): Do the people know what's going on? How do they create and handle Information?

Point 7 (Learning): Are they Learning anything? What are their Learning processes? What is the future potential?

Point 8 (Structure and Context): How are they organized? What is their Structure? Where does the energy come from that makes things happen in their organization? Is their hierarchy deep or flat? What's happening in the larger environment, in which they're living and trying to thrive? Who are their competitors and what are they doing? What is the Context or surrounding environment in which they are living and working?

Point 9 (Their New Identity): As they have moved through these questions, how has their Identity changed? Have they expanded and grown? What new things do they now know? What new skills do they now have?

This may seem like a complicated way of looking at organizations, but it is actually a process that we all use unconsciously, at least in part. To make the point, let's use the points of the Process Enneagram to compare two large stores I use. One is a large, mass-merchandiser with a national chain of stores. From the company's name, I know who they are and that they are trying to sell modestly priced clothing and home furnishings. This is their Identity at point 0 and Intention at point 1. One of the Issues (point 2) I see when I step in the door is the clutter in the aisles that makes it difficult to get around the store. Their behavior towards each other and me is not particularly courteous or considerate. They complain about their Company, so I conclude that they don't have much value for their Relationships with each other, with me their customer, or with their employer. The poor relationships show up at point 3, and the lack of values supporting good customer relations shows up at point 4. Their physical Work (point 5) is to sell a lot of merchandise. Whenever I ask help to find something, I get vague answers like "It's over there somewhere," so I must go on a search for what I need. From this, I conclude that the clerks don't know much about what's going on. They are limited in the amount of Information they have, or maybe they just don't care. This shows up at point 6. I also conclude that there isn't much Learning going on here about the business or about ways to improve it since nothing seems to change from one visit to the next. This lack of Learning shows up at point 7. Finally, I also conclude that their Structure (point 8) must be organized in a rigid hierarchy because that's the only way that they can keep things organized, even a little bit. In my experience of organizations behaving like this, most of the employees do as little as possible. I don't feel very good in a place like this, so I try not to go there to shop. Their Context (point 8) is one where there are other stores nearby, so I prefer to shop in those stores.

When I go into a large store of a different company with a national chain of stores, however, the picture is quite different. I know from their name who they are and that they are trying to sell stuff for helping me to keep up my home. This is their Identity and Intention, which show up at points 0 and 1. They have some things in the aisles, but seem to have them well ordered and the housekeeping is quite good. The aisles are more open and easy to move through. They have tried to address the

Issue of inventory supply much better than the store in the first example; this shows up at point 2. Their behavior towards each other and me is helpful and courteous; they are interested in me, the customer. From this, I conclude that they have good working relationships and value the way they treat each other and their customers. These are their Relationships (point 3) and their Principles and Standards (point 4). Their physical Work is to sell stuff, like the first store. This shows up at point 5. Information (point 6) seems to be flow freely because the clerks know the answers to my questions. When I take something back, they talk with me and seem to try to learn how to serve me better and have a more successful business. This Learning shows up at point 7. I conclude that to do the work they are doing and to behave in the way I see them behaving, they must be organized in teams and their Structure must be fairly flat. These observations show up at point 8. I feel vitality in this store and like to shop there. In considering their Context, their competitive environment, I know that the price of the stock for the second Company has gone up while the first one has entered into bankruptcy. I expect that there is a relationship between these observations made at the local level and the things going on at the national level. This is a simple example of the kind of more or less unconscious analyses we all can and do make in a matter of seconds, at least in part, whenever we see and experience an organization.

With these nine perspectives arranged around the circle, their interconnectedness becomes quite clear (Figure 2). This Figure illustrates the "webbiness" of so much that's going on.

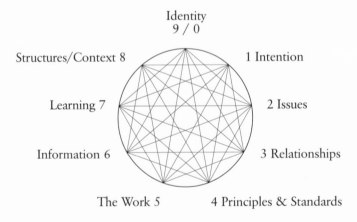

Figure 2 The Enneagram Web

The Web of connections is like a nervous system with each perspective informing all the others. As in a nervous system, some of the connections are stronger than others, and the connections need to function in specific sequences. We can't walk, for example, if our nerves fire in the wrong sequence.

The way that we usually see things happening in organizations, like in the preceding store examples, shows up around the circumference of the circle in Figure 2. These are visible things we see in the physical world.

In order to develop a deeper understanding of what's happening in organizations, however, we need to look into the inner patterns and processes. In the next sections, the command and control patterns and processes and the living systems patterns and processes are explored.

Command and Control Mode: the "Machine" Paradigm

Most leaders and managers desire reliability, stability, predictability and control in their organizations. These are great for machines, but people and organizations are not machines. We all want these attributes in an airplane, computer or a car, but in organizations they can cause serious problems.

The intense desire by many managers for reliability, stability, predictability and control often leads them to try to use excessive control over their organization in order to achieve these results. This leads to many undesirable and unintended consequences.

Over the last year or so, I've had a chance to talk with some TEC[1] Groups. I ran a brief survey in 5 groups from around the USA to see what they thought about these things. Out of twenty-nine CEOs, twenty-eight strongly desired these features. They all felt their employees were not contributing their best. Twenty-eight saw high stress-related problems in their organizations, fourteen had high turnover, twenty-two faced serious resistance to change in their organizations, and twenty-eight of them were unsatisfied with their overall business performance. Yet all of them reported that they were working very hard to improve their results. In their personal lives, sixteen reported that they were not happy with the balance between work and family.

Figure 3 depicts the archetypal, command and control pattern and process.

31

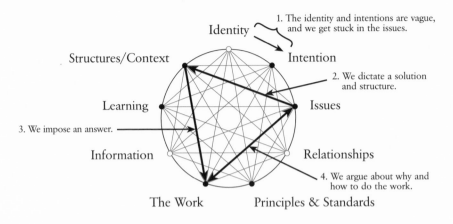

Figure 3 The Command and Control Pattern and Process

Let us now look at these inner patterns and processes. Many times, the leaders in the organization are vague and unclear about who they really are, (Identity) and what they're trying to do (Intention). Normally, they don't engage the organization in conversations about such things, so when they announce a new initiative, no matter how good and well thought out, lots of Issues are raised. This is illustrated in Step 1 in Figure 3. People at the top see all the questions and Issues that people raise about the changes as resistance to change.

Typically, they hurry to move on. They will probably dictate a Structural solution, like a new organizational structure (as in re-engineering) or new rules and procedures. This is illustrated as Step 2 in Figure 3. Then the new Work is imposed, in the belief that this is the answer to the problems. This is illustrated as Step 3 in Figure 3. Those who actually do the physical Work under the imposed Structure try to make sense of what's going on, and become stuck in all the unresolved Issues. This is illustrated as Step 4 in Figure 3.

As the organization's leaders push harder so that they can accomplish their goals, the people doing the work push back just as hard as they struggle to make sense of what's happening and why. Around and around this triangular pattern we go. *Principles* and *Standards, Information, Relationships and Learning* simply aren't discussed. This creates enormous incoherence and waste in the organization and is a source of much of the stress that people experience.

The "Living Systems" Paradigm

In Chapter 1, we looked at the story of saving the amines business. You'll remember that we decided to do the work in a very unusual way. We worked with our R&D and Plant people, as well as the instrument vendor to design the project. Everyone from the mechanics and operators to the top plant management was deeply involved in weekly project meetings in the control room of the existing operation. We did not run a parallel process and we made the needed changes during the scheduled, annual maintenance shutdown. This was about a $50 million/year sales business so these decisions were not inconsequential.

The project was done working out of the living systems paradigm. The net result of working this way was a project costing only about $3 million and we were able to do it in only 10 months. The process started up without incident and ran at full capacity, producing top quality product in only 4 days. We set a new standard for the whole Company in retrofit projects like this, cutting both the cost and the time in half.

As we explore using the living systems paradigm, two patterns and processes will be developed. The first concerns self-organizing patterns and processes, while the other concerns the way that the actual work takes place.

In looking at the pattern in Figure 4, we will now look at the inner patterns and processes at points 0, 3 and 6 which are concerned with

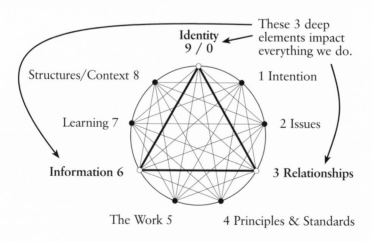

Figure 4 The Domains of Self-Organization

Identity, Relationship and Information respectively. These are the central elements of Self-Organization.

As we did the amines instrument conversion project, everyone in the project was clear about our Identity. We shared all the Information at least weekly and, as we worked together, listened, and talked, trust and interdependence built. Our Relationships became healthier and stronger. Anyone could go to whomever they wanted to get the Information they needed. This was a very deep process. Working in this way improved everything we did, both during the conversion and afterwards. Used consciously together, these are the patterns and processes for developing self-organization.

This process of self-organization goes on continuously in organizations. It is a process that has a timeless quality; it can be seen as operating outside of our normal view of linear time. It applies to everything we do, now and into the future. One of the first things a leader can do to open up his or her organization is to share Information, to help people get clear on their Identity and to help set the environment so that healthy Relationships can develop. When these processes improve they have a positive impact in all future work.

To have our work processes go well we need to begin with a clear, compelling question that relates to the specific work that we wish to do. This question is developed by the people involved and must be compelling in order for us to have the interest and energy to take on the work effectively. For the amines business example, the question was: "How do we make an effective, low cost conversion from pneumatic to distributive control systems?" The scope of the beginning question can vary enormously. It can be very narrow, like "How do I type a report?" or broader like "How do we improve the customer service in our business?" or very broad like "How do we change the entire nature of our business?"

The elements highlighted in Figure 5 all relate to how specific work gets done. For example, if I discover that I need to join two boards (Identity) and I decide to use a nail to join them (my Intention), I must hold the hammer and nail properly (Principles and Standards). I must decide where to put it, and how to hold the work (Issues and Tensions). Then I have to decide how to set up the work place (Structure) and actually drive the nail (Work). Hopefully, I get better at driving nails and building things (Learning). If I write a few notes, I'll have some Information that will help me as I go forward. I'm in a process of Learning and growth.

The questions that the people in the organization address as they

34

consider the 9 attributes all relate to the opening question, and so this opening question must be important and compelling to them.

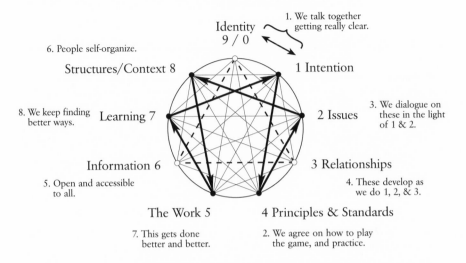

Figure 5 The Living Pattern and Process of How the Work Is Done

All the elements of effective work processes are fractal in nature; that is, they display repeating patterns that are similar at many levels of scale, can be used at any level of scale, and show up throughout the organizations in similar but not identical ways. In my own experience, I've used these patterns and processes to consider questions of my own personal development, for mentoring, for developing my leadership team, for operating a whole plant and for working in the community. We are using them now as we develop the leadership team for the City of Niagara Falls, NY.

When we in the organization are engaged in conversations about Identity and Intentions, we all get clear on what we're about together. This shows up as Step 1 in Figure 5. The double arrows show, that as we move around the Process Enneagram, our intentions at the base level become part of our Identity at the next, upper level. This indicates we're growing and learning. We then agree to work together in new ways (Principles and Standards: the organization's ground rules). This shows up as Step 2 in Figure 5. We can then take on the Issues in a way that deals with them much more effectively. We can move away from an "either/or" debate and explore "both/and" possibilities. This shows up as Step 3 in Figure 5. The Principles and Standards can be seen as analogous to homeostatic processes for a living organization. These homeostatic processes maintain the stable way in which the people in the organization agree to engage each other. I see them like the simple rules that underlie complex behavior in chaotic systems.

In many organizations, management imposes these rules. Typically, in mature organizations, the rules have grown and evolved over the years in such a way that practically no one knows where they all came from or why they were developed in the first place. Such things are usually undiscussed. The fact that they are undiscussed is often undiscussable. Yet these rules exert a powerful influence on the way people in the organization work together. These hidden, powerful forces play a major role in management's efforts to maintain stability, reliability, predictability and control. They often are in conflict with the overt things management is saying about how they want things to be in the organization, so we have incoherence and stress. This mode of operation blocks any real chance for learning and growth.

When people in an organization realize that they need and want to change, then together they must address these undiscussables and develop new Principles and Standards (new homeostatic processes). These must be put into place so the new behavior can be maintained in order to reach the new Intention. The new simple rules should be developed by the people themselves in conversation with, but not imposed by management. In this process, Relationships strengthen. This is difficult work, so everyone must help each other through the process.

As people work together on the Issues, using the new Principles and Standards they've developed, a profound shift in Relationships occurs. Trust and interdependence begin to build as everyone learns to keep their word and commitments, to be willing and able to help each other, to do what they say they will do, to be there when they're needed, and to be dependable and reliable. This shows up at Step 4 in Figure 5.

One of the key things we agree to in our Principles and Standards is to share Information abundantly. This actual sharing of Information shows up in Step 5 in Figure 5. When the Information flows and the necessary work is done on our Identity, Intentions, Principles and Standards and Issues, people spontaneously self-organize around the needed Work. This shows up at Step 6 in Figure 5.

With this preparation, everyone can do the Work much more effectively and efficiently. This shows up at Step 7 of Figure 5. When we reflect on and review our Work, we Learn and find better ways to do things.

New potential and possibilities for the future open up. This shows up as Step 8 in Figure 5. Meaning and creativity emerge and performance improves enormously.

The process by which we do the tasks before us in moving through the 1, 4, 2, 8, 5, 7, 1 sequence, takes place in the here and now. This is the specific work before us that we need to accomplish for the organization to succeed. As we use the Process Enneagram in this way, our work tends to be of a local nature. Our tasks may be quite specific to a particular location and time or they may be of a more global nature in their potential impact. Most of the time, we do our work with only a small number of people, whether we're down deep in an organization or at the top. Most of my work with the Process Enneagram has been with small to medium sized groups. These have ranged from men working to make concrete bridge beams in Kansas City, to the top team of a large steel company in Australia, to the partners of a local accounting firm, to the Mayor and her leadership team in Niagara Falls, NY. In all these cases, the Process Enneagram work unfolds in similar ways with the people they are working most closely with. This is true regardless of whether the potential impact of the work of the group is quite local or quite broad. These patterns and processes apply to all levels of work, and are useful to everyone in the organization. The living systems patterns and processes are running all the time in organizations, whether people in the organizations recognize it or not. They are running in healthy as well as dying organizations. They are running in caring as well as brutal organizations, all the time.

I mentioned earlier that the Process Enneagram should begin with a compelling question of importance to the group and organization. The Process Enneagram does not have much impact with very loose groups of people who do not have important issues in common. Teams and groups of people, like those I mentioned in the proceeding paragraph, have many issues that are important to them. As people work closely with each other, they will have important issues that they share and on which they will want to work.

We can see what happens in a command and control organization when it is confronted with a crisis like those described in the stories in Chapter 1. We can visualize the command and control process, connecting the pattern of points 2, 8 and 5, as running on top of a set of multilayered processes which look something like a layer cake. The deeper, self-organizing processes are often invisible to those at the top. This may be what I've heard some people call "the shadow organization." It's where the grapevines are running. It takes place in the little groups that form deep in the organization where people are trying to find refuge, to make sense of what's going on and do the work that needs to be done. Unfortunately, in many organizations, the command and control process has been pushed so far that many people become cynical, resulting in a shutdown of people's energy and creativity. Even so, the living systems processes are running, but they are weaker and more dysfunctional.

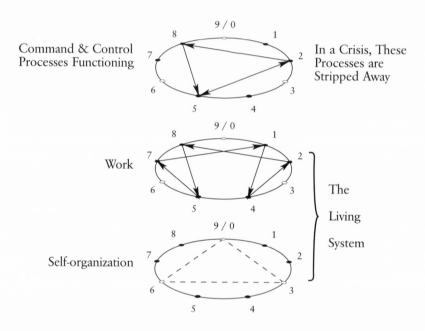

Figure 6 Simultaneous Processes of Living Systems: The Layer Cake

In an emergency, so many things happen so fast that management can no longer control the flow of events. Usually the command and control process is stripped away from the top of the layer cake, and the deeper, living systems patterns and processes emerge spontaneously. This profoundly influences the way people work together; they become much more focused and productive. In a real emergency, everyone knows who they are – we're flat on our backs (Identity at point 0), and what they need to do – get up and running again (Intention at point 1). The need to get up and running transcends their differences and people pull together in ways that no one imagined possible (Principles and Standards at point 4).

38

Everyone plows into all the issues facing him or her (Issues at point 2). Trust and interdependence build quickly (Relationship at point 3). Since all the information about the situation is visible (Information at point 6), people spontaneously self-organize (Structure and Context at point 8), do the work (Work at point 5), learn how to do it better (Learning at point 7) and keep going until the emergency is over (the new Identity at point 9). Everyone feels really good about how the work was done and how everyone came together, but as the flow of the events of the crisis slow down, management reasserts itself and the organization goes back to the old command and control paradigm.

If we can learn how to stay in the living systems processes, we don't have to go back to the old way. The shift away from command and control systems into living systems is illustrated in Figure 6.

With living systems patterns and processes, we can achieve superior results and people will feel better at the same time. We can have it all. These processes open up the flow of energy and creativity. The system (the people and the processes in the organization) becomes more coherent. Figure 7 shows the combined patterns of all 9 parts for both the processes of Self-Organization and for doing the Work. This is called the Process Enneagram; it describes the processes for living systems.

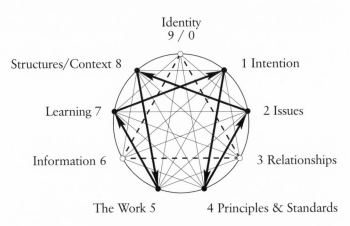

**Figure 7 The Living Systems Patterns and Processes:
The Process Enneagram**

As we look at these figures, other important patterns emerge and inform us about what's happening in our organizations. These patterns are summarized in Figure 8 which shows the Self-Organizing Leadership processes that lead to coherence in the central column. It also shows the necessary balance between, and the interplay with operational management processes on the left side and the strategic leadership processes on the right side. These patterns and processes are all within the Web. The Web is a way of seeing organizations as a whole. In the unity of the Web, we can see all the multiplicity of the leadership processes.

In this book, the term operational management speaks to working with specific things and events whether they are happening now or in the future. Strategic leadership relates to working on future possibilities. When I decide to work on one of the many possibilities and select one or two, I move from strategic leadership process into operational management and implementation. For example, when I'm playing around with the idea of traveling to new places, that would be strategic leadership. When I decide on a particular trip and begin the detailed planning, I've moved into operational management.

In actual practice, strategic and operational distinctions become blurred because of their endless interaction in the constantly changing world in which we live. Complexity theory teaches us that the old ways of strategic planning break down because of these complex interactions. Operational management, that is working with things and events to make sure that things get done, and operational leadership, stepping out and taking the initiative to get things done (just get up, get going and do it) are intertwined. In this book, it's best to keep both these ideas in mind because operational work requires that both of them happen.

The Leadership Dance

In the complexity in which we live and work, it is necessary to constantly use both operational management and strategic leadership processes in dynamical balance with the central Self-Organizing Leadership processes for the organization to be coherent and to function well. In the center column of Figure 8 is the pattern for Self-Organization, Work and the Process Enneagram. If we overuse either the operational management or the strategic leadership processes, however, or fail to connect the self-organizing processes to real work of importance to the organization, we begin to create problems and drive the organization into incoherence.

Incoherence, caused by command and control or imposed processes usually emerges around the Issues. It happens when what the management is saying doesn't make sense to those doing the Work. Incoherence

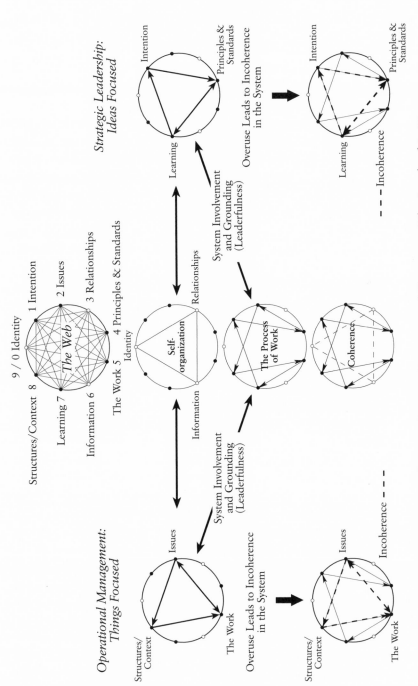

Figure 8 Overview of Living Systems Patterns and Processes: The Leadership Dance

in strategic leadership processes occurs when the leaders are restrictive, closed and exclusive. It shows up around Learning when the new Principles and Standards the leaders are preaching don't make sense to the people actually living in the system and trying to do the Work. The failure to connect self-organizing processes to work important to the organization leads to an excessive amount of time being spent going ever more deeply into the esoteric aspects of Identity, Relationship and Information. People take their eye off what the organization needs to do, so the work of the organization starts to degrade.

In these situations, the espoused values and principles of behavior the leaders preach, and those actually in use – the invisible undiscussables – are in deep conflict. This is the Management Trap as Chris Argyris describes it in his book, *Flawed Advice and the Management Trap*. The defective practices described above show up in what he calls Model I organizations, and they are filled with all the problems and incoherence he describes.

Some of the characteristics of Model I organizations identified by Argyris are:
- management issues injunctions (the basic guidelines);
- they define goals and try to achieve them;
- they try to maximize winning and minimize losing;
- they want to minimize the generation or expression of negative feelings; and
- they want to be rational, objective and intellectual, suppressing feelings.

The managers in the organization seek to:
- design and manage the environment unilaterally;
- own and control the task;
- unilaterally protect themselves;
- unilaterally protect others from being hurt; and
- control others and prevent being controlled by them.

This results in managers:
- running the risk of being seen as defensive and willing to have relationships with others colored by mistrust and rigidity; and
- having an organization where long-term learning and effectiveness are reduced.

Many managers move into defensive routines where:
- they craft messages that contain ambiguities and/or inconsistencies;

- they act as if the messages are not inconsistent;
- they make ambiguity and inconsistency in the message undiscussable; and
- they make the undiscussability undiscussable.

So, as a result:

- it's impossible for the people in the organization to deal effectively with any subject;
- the people feel it's unrealistic or dangerous to confront these patterns and do much about them; so
- many people become cynical.

A dynamic, healthy balance of the Strategic Leadership and Operational Management patterns and processes, centered on the Self-Organizing Leadership patterns and processes needs to be our goal. The use of this dynamic, healthy interplay of these processes is what I've called the *Leadership Dance*.

The use of the Process Enneagram, as discussed here, is an effective way for the organization to become coherent. We begin to be more like what Argyris would describe as Model II organizations where the espoused theory and the theories-in-use are more nearly the same. Model II organizations are characterized by having:

- valid information,
- informed choice,
- internal commitment,
- public testing of theories-in-use,
- clarity and the invitation to confront views and emotions,
- learning through confronting assumptions,
- respect,
- help and support,
- honesty – public verification, and
- integrity – the courage to invite the testing of ideas.

In order for the systems in our organizations to be healthy and vibrant, they must be centered in the Self-Organizing Leadership processes while simultaneously using the operational management and strategic leadership processes as the dynamic situations demand. In this way of leading, the organization is alive, vibrant and far from equilibrium with energy and creativity bubbling forth. Moving among Self-Organizing, Operational and Strategic modes of leadership is a dance. As our conditions and environmental context keep changing, the balance keeps shifting; it's the Leadership Dance. This places a demand on the leaders and all the other people in the organization to be more conscious and to pay careful attention to what's happening around them, both inside and outside the organization. Effective leaders engage the people in the organization to address the challenges they face, so this is not a case of dancing around the serious issues they face. Highly effective leaders know the Leadership Dance.

Notes

1 TEC is an international organization with several thousand chapters consisting of a facilitator and 10-15 CEOs of small to modest size companies who meet monthly to support each other and to learn about new ideas.

2 Information, Relationship and Identity were recognized as the Domains of Self-Organization in the Berkana Dialogue in February, 1993. There were 14 Dialogues held by Meg Wheatley and Myron Kellner-Rogers from 1993 to 1996 in Sundance, Utah. In each Dialogue 25-30 people gathered to consider and reflect upon the new developments in the thinking about self-organization and chaos as it applied to organizations. Most participants attended only one or two sessions. Maggie Moore, who developed the Rhythms of Change Process discussed later in the book, and I participated in 13 of the 14 dialogues. We both participated in the February, 1993 Dialogue. The experiences at the dialogues were critical to the personal transformation of our understanding for both Maggie and me.

· 3 ·

Practical Applications
of the Process Enneagram and the
Successful Implementation of Change

The examples used in this chapter illustrate how the Process Enneagram can be used to see the whole system, as well as the parts and the connections within the organization. You will see it used as a tool for:
· thinking,
· seeing,
· planning,
· analysis and problem solving,
· facilitating personal and organizational change, and
· responding to changes from the external environment.

In these examples, you'll see how the emotional and meaning aspects are played out as well. Because it is fractal, you will see that the Process Enneagram can be used on both broad and narrow issues: it can be used at all levels of scale. The nature and scope of the opening question sets the stage for the work to unfold. As I have noted before, it's critical that this question is both relevant and important to the organization and the people involved. You'll see again, how its patterns emerge spontaneously in crisis situations. You will probably notice that you've had personal experience yourself with these patterns when you've been through a crisis.

You'll also see the Process Enneagram used to look at other situations of a longer-term nature. Let's begin by looking at the crises described in Chapter 1, building on the common threads and deeper processes described there. As you read and study these examples, be mindful of the progression through the inner patterns demonstrated in Chapter 2.

45

Stories

Seeing the Processes During Crises

The Sodium Plant Fire

Below in Figure 9, you will find the Process Enneagram that I constructed to help us see what was happening and how people naturally
followed the process. They didn't know about this tool at the time, they
just did what they knew needed to be done to rescue the business. On
reflecting about the fire, I constructed this Process Enneagram for the
analysis. The central question was "How do we get back up and running
quickly?"

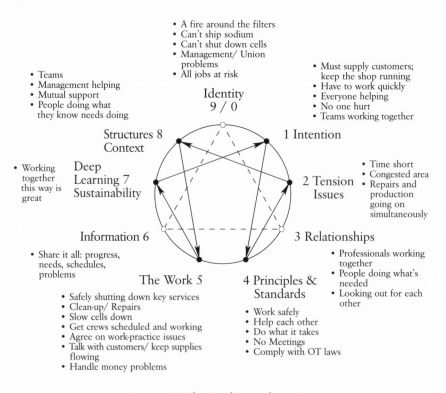

Figure 9 The Sodium Plant Fire:
How do we get back up and running quickly?

You can see the whole picture of what happened as they set about to
repair the damage and restore the business. Using this Process Enneagram
as a map, we can quickly scan the scene to see if there are any major holes

46

or flaws. You can see from the story in Chapter 1 how clear they were about their Identity and their Intention shown at points 0 and 1, and how quickly they moved through Principles and Standards at point 4, the Tensions at point 2, the Structure at point 8 and the Work that needed to be done at point 5. By the time they got into the Work, they were flying with high alignment, purpose and coherence.

This map is a view, from say, 10,000 feet. As each particular task in the Work is taken on, other Process Enneagram maps with more detail could be constructed. Each of these would also begin with an important question about the particular challenge to be addressed. For example, we could look at the specific tasks involved in clean-up, repairs, re-wiring, slowing down the cells, maintaining production work, changes in work-practices, customer supply and the appropriation of project money. Each would have its own map, going as deep as necessary. Process Enneagrams exist at every level of scale we want to go into; it's Process Enneagrams all the way down.

The agreed upon Principles and Standards shown at point 4, provided the basis for us all to live in the Tension at point 2, and deal with the anxiety as we moved through the change process. The realization that everyone was making a difference helped meaning to emerge. There was little worry about making mistakes, because almost anything was better than where we were. Everyone worked safely. All the information was available to everyone because we could all see the damage and the progress of the repairs. People quickly learned to work together and make the decisions they needed to get the work done. As the crisis came under control, however, we in management reasserted ourselves in such a way that the opportunity to learn a new way of working from this experience could not be taken.

In reflecting on the experiences we'd had during this period, the feeling was that this way of working together was good but that it was the exception in our working lives. We have things backwards; this can be the normal way of working! The command and control mode should be the exception not the rule.

Saving the Amines Business

It was clear that the amines crisis, introduced in Chapter 1, was going to span a number of months. The patterns and processes, however, are identical to those in the Sodium Plant Fire example; only the time frame is extended. We set out with a deep belief that our people were capable of saving the business, providing that we had a free and open flow of information and we worked together. We had to share the business information carefully, so everyone could really understand what we were up against. Everything was done openly and we learned as we went.

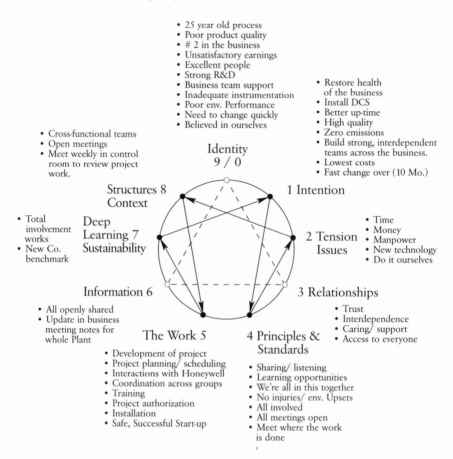

- 25 year old process
- Poor product quality
- # 2 in the business
- Unsatisfactory earnings
- Excellent people
- Strong R&D
- Business team support
- Inadequate instrumentation
- Poor env. Performance
- Need to change quickly
- Believed in ourselves

- Restore health of the business
- Install DCS
- Better up-time
- High quality
- Zero emissions
- Build strong, interdependent teams across the business.
- Lowest costs
- Fast change over (10 Mo.)

- Cross-functional teams
- Open meetings
- Meet weekly in control room to review project work.

Identity
9 / 0

Structures 8
Context

1 Intention

- Total involvement works
- New Co. benchmark

Deep
Learning 7
Sustainability

2 Tension
Issues

- Time
- Money
- Manpower
- New technology
- Do it ourselves

Information 6

3 Relationships

- All openly shared
- Update in business meeting notes for whole Plant

The Work 5

4 Principles &
Standards

- Trust
- Interdependence
- Caring/ support
- Access to everyone

- Development of project
- Project planning/ scheduling
- Interactions with Honeywell
- Coordination across groups
- Training
- Project authorization
- Installation
- Safe, Successful Start-up

- Sharing/ listening
- Learning opportunities
- We're all in this together
- No injuries/ env. Upsets
- All involved
- All meetings open
- Meet where the work is done

Figure 10 Saving the Amines Business:
How do we put the new DCS in as quickly and cost-effectively as possible to help restore and save the business?

My principal role was to try to keep all the connections open. Information had to flow freely. Everyone had to have access to anyone they needed to talk with to get information. Decisions had to be made quickly. We really had to listen to each other, and develop the best understandings we could. I helped to resolve the communications misunderstandings that came up. I had virtually no technical contribution to make, but that wasn't necessary because the knowledge was in the Plant people, the R & D people and the Honeywell people who'd come together for this project. I just had to help create the conditions and keep the situation open.

We learned to help each other through the anxious places time and again. We lived through the Rhythms of Change process (see Chapter 8) many times. The Emergence of Meaning process (also see Chapter 8) functioned as well, since everyone knew what had to be done and just moved into the project. Our commitment to being in a learning process helped to free people up to do their best. As people connected through the work more and more deeply, meaning was discovered and energy and creativity poured forth.

Risk Management Planning: Sharing Worst-Case Scenarios

This crisis, as you saw from Chapter 1, was one that persisted over a much longer period than the Amines Conversion project. Here again, the patterns and processes are the same as in the Sodium Fire and Amines Business examples. It was also much more complex, in that eight companies, 13 plants, the Chemical Manufacturers Association (CMA, now know as the American Chemical Council), local environmentalists and a community of 300,000 people living along 25 miles of the Kanawha River in West Virginia were involved. At this time, I was consciously using the Process Enneagram.

The whole process was very difficult and required endless conversations before we were able to develop a shared Identity and Intention. We went through the Rhythms of Change process many times as we struggled to come together with all our different points of view. In this process, our Relationships deepened and trust developed as we supported each other in the Tension and anxiety.

We realized that we must have a high level of credibility for us to be successful. We needed a committee to develop the technology we'd all use, and another committee to develop the communications content, processes and methods. We saw that both of these committees should be chaired by a community person. We also realized that an independent, third party hired by the Local Emergency Planning Committee, was needed to help build the credibility of the process.

We worked relentlessly to develop the information together and to share it among the various constituencies. We struggled to develop a communications plan that would engage the community, be understandable and credible, and would involve all parties (community members, hospitals, first responders like the fire and ambulance services, environmentalists and plant people). All the voices needed to be heard. We wanted to be as available to the community as possible.

There were times when I felt like I was on an emotional roller coaster, but we knew that staying in the process was where we had to be. In all these conversations and meetings, we began to develop the shared understanding that we all had a vital stake in the success of this whole process. We discovered that we all needed each other. A shared Identity and meaning developed through the connections and the contributions that we made to each other and the community.

When the Risk Management Plans (RMPs) and the worst-case scenarios were shared on June 3 and 4, 1994, we all knew that we had built new strength into our community. We had come together around this, rather than becoming more divided and broken. When the New York Times and CNN came to cover the story, they reported that they'd found a community growing and working together.

This same process was used successfully in Victoria, Texas, where 6 plants shared their RMPs and scenarios in October 1995. The process they used for sharing the Information, building Relationships and developing a shared Identity was very similar to the one we used in the Kanawha Valley. What the Victoria people actually did on the surface, like sharing their stories over 5 nights in different parts of the community was different, but the deeper process was the same.

This same process was also used in the Houston Texas Ship Channel area where 7-8 communities, and about 90 plants worked with about 300 volunteers to co-create their sharing experience. These communications were successfully carried in the early spring and summer of 1999.

Figure 11 maps the Kanawha Valley experience. As you can see if you compare them, the underlying processes are the same as in the Sodium Fire and Amines business examples, even though the day-to-day events are quite different. The issue was, how do we share worst-case scenarios with a community of 300,000 people in a way that will bring the community together and they won't try to drive us out of the Kanawha Valley?

The underlying processes in these three crises are fractal, working at all the levels of scale. In each case, the people in the system (the plants and communities) are deeply involved. By looking at these examples of

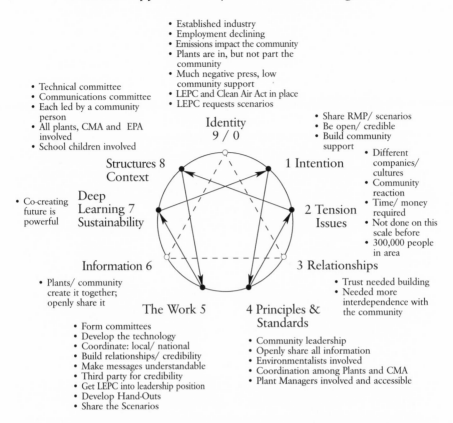

Figure 11 Risk Management Planning – Sharing Worst-Case Scenarios:
How do we share worst-case scenarios with a community of 300,000 people?

crises, and comparing the related points, a deeper understanding of the fractal nature of the process and the similarity of the nature of the attributes at the various points can be gained. For example, the Identity at point 0 in each example informs us about the people who are working on the particular question. It is also clear that similar ideas show up regardless of the size of the group, the nature of the question and the differences in time frame.

You can see the same phenomena when the Relationships at point 3 are compared. Ideas about caring, interdependence, access to everyone, respect and trust are present. You can see this again at Information at point 6 where the need for open sharing is identified in all three examples. Similar phenomena show up when all the other points are compared as well.

51

Shifting the Process

Here's a very simple example that illustrates the way to make the shift from the Machine (command and control) to the Living Systems paradigm. Please keep in mind that the processes are generic and fractal. The processes modeled in the example apply to making shifts like this at any level of scale in an organization. The example involves a problem faced by one of the groups I worked with in Australia. Both the plant management and some of the union officers were present in a Leading Organizational Change (LOC) program Tim Dalmau and I led in October, 1997 at Bateman's Bay, New South Wales.

In Figure 3, the Command and Control process was illustrated. The process described here unfolded in exactly the same manner. The plant was trying to improve its safety performance, and a safety consultant advised that they should use hard hats to prevent head injuries in their manufacturing area. Management decided that this was a good idea and began to implement the change. They required everyone to wear hard hats in the manufacturing area. With all good intentions, the management announced the change without involving the union (Step 1 in Figure 3). The workforce, led by the union leaders, got all worked up about this new rule imposed by management. Here was another inconvenience being imposed, one which made their lives more difficult. Arguments arose about the color and style, about improper fitting, about the exact places they had to wear them, and even when to wear them. Did they have to wear them from the moment they entered a manufacturing area, even if it was not running? Did they have to wear them before they reported to work, or if they had to pass through a work area on the way to their lockers? If so, where would they store them? Did they have to have their names on them? Could they put union stickers on them? Could they wear them backwards? What did the law require? Why waste the money on hats when things are so tight? It went on and on.

People became increasingly polarized as the issue was used as a way to build further opposition to management initiatives. Rather than being seen as a way to reduce injuries, the Issues become part of the union/ management power struggle (Step 2 in Figure 3). Management became increasingly irritated over the bargaining time spent to resolve all the seemingly trivial questions. Other, more important issues, like becoming more competitive, languished while everyone battled over hard hats. Management's Intention was to prevent people from being hurt; their

Principles and Standards included the need for the workers to wear the proper personal protective equipment like hard hats and safety glasses to help prevent injuries in the workplace. Getting the workers to actually wear the hard hats falls into the Work. With little involvement and under-standing by the workers, they tried to force the new Work of having to wear hard hats (Step 3 in Figure 3). Everyone was stuck bouncing between the Issues they'd raise and trying to make sense of why the Work required hard hats. The conversation about Principles and Standards had not taken place (Step 4 in Figure 4) and the people involved had not really discussed why the hats were needed. But, to management, who didn't appreciate the need for the conversation about Principles and Standards, it was just another example of people resisting change.

When I became aware of this issue during the LOC program, we stopped the other things we were doing and walked them through the Process Enneagrams in Figures 12 and 13 in about 30 minutes. After seeing the new possibilities that this presented, they quickly resolved the problem when they returned to the plant.

"Machine Systems" Paradigm

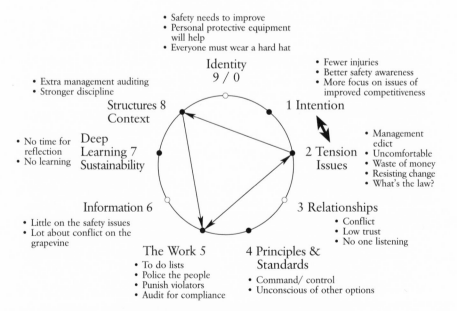

Figure 12 The "Machine Systems" View:
Everyone has to wear hard hats in the manufacturing areas.

In Figure 12, you can see that they were firmly in the machine (command/ control) mode, while in Figure 13 they moved to the living systems mode. The edict that everyone needed to wear hard hats was aimed at introducing this measure quickly and efficiently. It was made with the expectation that everyone would do it immediately because it seemed to management that it made such good sense.

"Living Systems" Paradigm

By moving to the living system process (see Figure 13), the full engagement of everyone resulted in Learning, and a shift in the thinking and reasoning, so that safety became a responsibility of all. Everyone moved through the Change Spiral (see Figure 30). As people connected through the Work, Learning and the evaluation of what they were doing led to the development of deeper meaning. They began to see where this approach could apply to other areas of their work and lives.

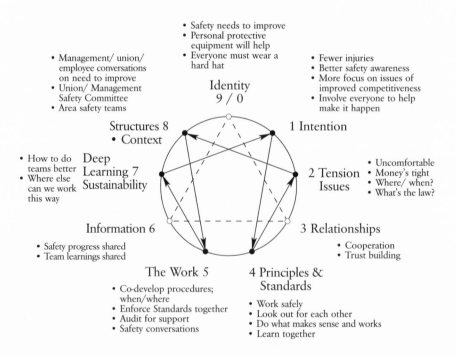

Figure 13 The "Living Systems" View:
How do we improve head protection?

54

Being effective rather than efficient is a key. While being efficient and getting off to a quick start may feel the most expeditious, it often takes much longer to complete the whole task. Being effective is also often more efficient because you don't have to pick up the pieces caused by the poor understandings and confused actions from the start of the project, and try to put them back together again so the task can be accomplished. When working this way, the total time for the project is usually shorter than we normally expect because the people in the organization behave and work much more coherently. A word of caution, however, this approach should not to be used as an excuse to study things forever and to avoid starting the work.

When I visited the same mill about 6 months later, everyone was wearing their hard hats; they were no longer an issue. Furthermore, by building on these insights, the other parts of their safety performance had improved as well. The injury rates were down about 50%. The new way of working together had spread to other areas as well, helping them to improve productivity and customer service.

Using the Process Enneagram to Implement Change

Random, Mandatory Drug Testing

Our plant in Belle handled a number of highly hazardous chemicals. Our core competency was the ability to do this safely and effectively. We in management had heard rumors that illegal drugs were being used on the plant site, but we had no direct evidence, other than that a few people were under the care of our Medical Department for substance abuse. While we surmised that there was probably a problem, we had no other specific information.

Then, in 1989, we were really confronted with the problem. Over a two-week period, we had three serious incidents. The first occurred when a man who was already in drug rehabilitation was found to be on drugs. His job was unloading tank cars of hazardous materials. Then we had another incident where a tank car was moved from a loading spot without the hoses being disconnected. Ripping the hoses apart caused a lot of damage, but fortunately, we were not transferring any material, so there was no spill. We tested the two operators closest to the decision making on releasing and moving the car and found both to be on drugs. Shortly after this, we had a major electrical incident involving a 12,000-volt switch. The men involved were tested and one of them was also on drugs. At this point, we were really alarmed.

We went to the whole plant and told them that we were in trouble. We needed to get drugs out of the workplace because hazardous chemicals and drugs don't belong together. This was a hot issue, which we debated in a number of the manager's weekly business meetings. We invited people to help us figure out who should be involved in the testing, how to select people to test, how often the testing should be done, how many should be tested each time, how to set up the procedures for a legally defensible chain of custody process, how to avoid false positives, how to protect privacy, how to do the sampling in a way that was rigorous yet not offensive, etc., etc.

We engaged everyone in consultations for over 8 months. Procedures were proposed, shared with the whole plant and revised many times during these months of intense conversation and debate. It was like a walking dialogue, day after day, month after month. About half way through this process, someone suggested that we have a voluntary program, so we tried that. About 150 people volunteered. We tested about 5 each week. To select them, each of our social security numbers was put on a card and drawn from a bingo style basket during the business meetings. The entire process was open and visible. When I was first tested as a volunteer, I was nervous about a false positive, even though we had good safeguards. I was relieved when I found that I'd passed. I could really empathize with many of the concerns being raised.

We took people to the labs where the drug testing of the urine would be done as part of the laboratory selection process. In order to avoid any false positives, we decided to use two labs to double-check the results. The journey and the goal were laid out at the start; the specific details and the timing of events evolved as we went. In processes where people are engaged like this, the details emerge in conversations, so it's important to set the goal in a way that shows direction and intent, but does not define things to the point where the details of the outcome are made too specific. The best answers to our questions emerged as we moved through the process.

The use of the Process Enneagram enabled us to keep on course and to stay in balance as we went (Figure 14). As a result, as we dealt with all the details, we were always conscious of the whole system. We cycled through the Process Enneagram many times over the 8 months, as we worked our way together through the process. Figure 14 is a summary of the whole effort. It illustrates the sorts of things we addressed and how they developed.

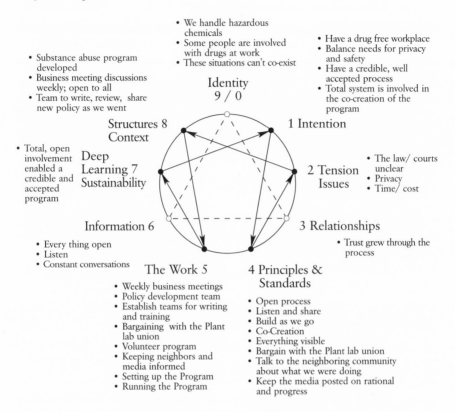

- Substance abuse program developed
- Business meeting discussions weekly; open to all
- Team to write, review, share new policy as we went

- We handle hazardous chemicals
- Some people are involved with drugs at work
- These situations can't co-exist

- Have a drug free workplace
- Balance needs for privacy and safety
- Have a credible, well accepted process
- Total system is involved in the co-creation of the program

Identity
9 / 0

Structures 8
Context

- Total, open involvement enabled a credible and accepted program

Deep
Learning 7
Sustainability

1 Intention

2 Tension
Issues

- The law/ courts unclear
- Privacy
- Time/ cost

Information 6

- Every thing open
- Listen
- Constant conversations

The Work 5

- Weekly business meetings
- Policy development team
- Establish teams for writing and training
- Bargaining with the Plant lab union
- Volunteer program
- Keeping neighbors and media informed
- Setting up the Program
- Running the Program

3 Relationships

- Trust grew through the process

4 Principles & Standards

- Open process
- Listen and share
- Build as we go
- Co-Creation
- Everything visible
- Bargain with the Plant lab union
- Talk to the neighboring community about what we were doing
- Keep the media posted on rational and progress

Figure 14 How Do We Get Mind Altering Drugs Out of the Workplace?

The Union that represented the Belle Plant analytical laboratory people took us to the Federal Court for the Southern District of West Virginia in Charleston because they felt that we were violating people's rights to privacy, which are protected under the US Constitution. The Judge ruled that we'd developed a program that properly balanced the privacy needs of the employees and the safety needs of the plant and community. Only those in safety-critical assignments (about 92% of us) were involved, and the rules were applied equally.

Using the Process Enneagram to implement change worked extremely well with this very difficult issue. If we had not involved everyone, there would have been continuous battles that would have resulted eventually in our losing focus on becoming safer, more competitive and helping the plant to survive. We succeeded in driving drugs out of the workplace. We had no more drug-related incidents and a number of operators and mechanics told me, on the side, that the recreational use of drugs had essentially stopped.

Many of the people at the plant asked whether the contractors working in safety-critical jobs were going to be tested. This set us out on another journey that's beyond the story here. Suffice it to say, that almost all of these contractors are now in drug testing programs, and those few who aren't are escorted while at the plant.

The power and depth of the Process Enneagram was the key to our shared success in planning and implementing this change. The credibility and trust we built in the process spilled over into many other activities in the following years. Everything we do to strengthen the deeper process of getting clear on our Identity and Intention, of building Relationships and sharing Information positively affects all the tasks that follow.

Personal Development and Mentoring

The Process Enneagram has been used in a number of personal development, mentoring and coaching situations (Figure 15). It's critical to spend the time at the beginning to get really clear on the question that will be addressed. With one leader the question was "What leadership style will I use to most effectively free up the talents of the people in my group?" The leader had been a very tight, command and control person who was beginning to see that this approach was blocking the release of energy and creativity in the people in his group. He knew that he was going far too deeply into the details of the work and disempowering people. This meant that he'd really have to have personal commitment to this process in order to have the courage and persistence to carry it through. He needed the caring and support of his people and had to ask for their help to coach him as he went along.

As I worked with this manager, we talked deeply about which things were successful for him, as well as about the things that were causing him problems. We then began to put the ideas onto a Process Enneagram map. His current view of himself showed up in the Identity at point 0. What he wanted to become showed up in his Intention at point 1. We then explored the new Principles and Standards (point 4) that he felt he

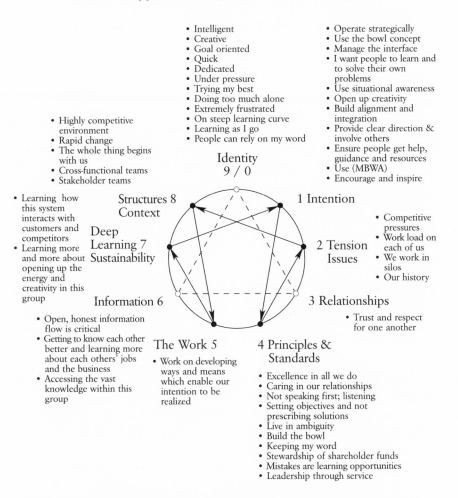

- Intelligent
- Creative
- Goal oriented
- Quick
- Dedicated
- Under pressure
- Trying my best
- Doing too much alone
- Extremely frustrated
- On steep learning curve
- Learning as I go
- People can rely on my word

- Operate strategically
- Use the bowl concept
- Manage the interface
- I want people to learn and to solve their own problems
- Use situational awareness
- Open up creativity
- Build alignment and integration
- Provide clear direction & involve others
- Ensure people get help, guidance and resources
- Use (MBWA)
- Encourage and inspire

- Highly competitive environment
- Rapid change
- The whole thing begins with us
- Cross-functional teams
- Stakeholder teams

Identity
9 / 0

- Learning how this system interacts with customers and competitors
- Learning more and more about opening up the energy and creativity in this group

Structures 8
Context

Deep
Learning 7
Sustainability

Information 6

1 Intention

- Competitive pressures
- Work load on each of us
- We work in silos
- Our history

2 Tension
Issues

3 Relationships

- Trust and respect for one another

- Open, honest information flow is critical
- Getting to know each other better and learning more about each others' jobs and the business
- Accessing the vast knowledge within this group

The Work 5

- Work on developing ways and means which enable our intention to be realized

4 Principles &
Standards

- Excellence in all we do
- Caring in our relationships
- Not speaking first; listening
- Setting objectives and not prescribing solutions
- Live in ambiguity
- Build the bowl
- Keeping my word
- Stewardship of shareholder funds
- Mistakes are learning opportunities
- Leadership through service

Figure 15 What Leadership Style Will Most Effectively Free and Utilize the Talents of These People to Achieve Success?

needed to learn to live by. In operating from these new Principles and Standards, he was able to work on the Issues at point 2 in a new way. He began to see that in the highly competitive environment we were in, that there had to be a structural shift towards working more in teams (point 8). He realized that his major, personal Work effort at point 5 had to be focused on fulfilling his Intention. He realized that there would be a lot of new Learnings (point 7), and he needed to be open to these. He understood that his Relationships at point 3 would become more trusting and that he needed to be sure that Information at point 6 was flowing freely.

59

He posted the map in his office, which enabled him to see it many times each day. He could see his progress and keep his balance. He kept the whole process open to his whole group and asked them for their help.

To stand in front of your group, to let them know that you want to change and will need their help takes a lot of courage. You have to ask them for some feedback on things you need to change, which can be very painful. I have described my own journey for you so you can see that I have a sense of what one can go through. An actual example that we did, modified only to keep it anonymous can be seen in Figure 15.

Solving a Safety Systems Problem

One of the key measurements I kept on myself as Plant Manager was how much time I spent each day (on a monthly average) on Quadrant II safety, health and environmental (SHE) work. Quadrant II time[1] is the time spent on important but not urgent work. These activities included audits, training, talks, reviewing rules, etc. Our safety performance had improved to the point where the entire plant had gone 454 days without an OSHA recordable injury. The Occupational Safety and Health Administration defines such an injury as one that requires any follow-up beyond a first aid, such as one requiring a stitch or treatment for a small second-degree burn. For a group of around 950 people doing the sort of work we were doing, this is a very good record. We then had three relatively minor recordable injuries in a two-month period.

I spent a lot of time trying to understand what had changed. I began to zero in on an observation I'd made a few months earlier. One of the things I'd found in looking at my Quadrant II SHE time was that we had an injury that month when my time involvement dropped below one and a half hours a day on a monthly average. In fact, the 7 months where my time involvement dropped below one and a half hours a day were the only months when we had had an OSHA recordable injuries during the previous five years.

In *Leadership and the New Science*, Margaret Wheatley, develops the idea of the importance of the "energy fields" in organizations. These exert a huge influence on what we do. What I'd observed about my Quadrant II time on SHE and our injury performance is probably related to this is some way.

I was extremely concerned, and had to resist the temptation to revert to a command and control style – remember, this is where I used to live –

to get our safety performance back to where it should be. I used a Process Enneagram (Figure 16) to look at what was going on. I concluded that in terms of safety, we were clear in our Identity, and our Intentions were solid. Our Principles and Standards were okay. There was nothing particularly different in all the Issues we were facing and we had plenty of good Structure to our program.

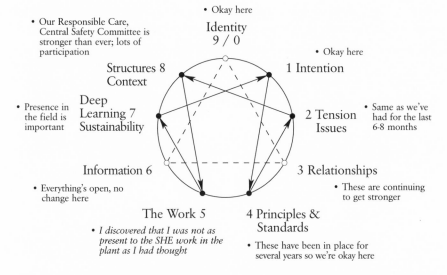

Figure 16 Using the Process Enneagram to Solve a Safety Systems Problem: *What's changed in our environment that may be leading to injuries?*

When I looked at the Work, I realized that while my Quadrant II SHE work had stayed well above the 1-hour and a half per day level, the focus had shifted to being outside the plant. This was during the period when we were working so hard on the RMP and worst-case scenario activities described in Chapter 1. I was spending a lot of time away from the plant. The RMP work took about a third of my time over a 9-month period and I didn't have an assistant plant manager.

When the leadership team looked this over, the conclusion was that we needed to step up the time of all supervisory people in Quadrant II SHE work. So with the involvement of the supervisors, we set a new metric: every supervisor in all the supervisory groups needed to average at least one and a half hours per day on Quadrant II SHE work every week. Many were already doing this, but now we really focused on it.

The Process Enneagram enabled us to look at the whole safety system and see where we needed to change it. After we made this change, we didn't have another OSHA recordable injury for over 9 months.

Mapping a System

Another way to use this tool is to map the current state of an organization. I do this by having a group sit in a circle and begin to tell stories about their organization. As they talk, I capture what I think are the important comments and map them onto the Process Enneagram at the appropriate attribute point. I don't try to identify the comments as being related to any particular person, because I am listening to them as a whole group. In about an hour, a fairly good picture of the group emerges (see Figure 17).

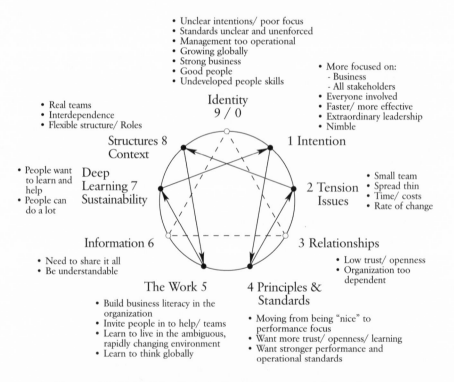

Figure 17 Using the Process Enneagram to Map a System:
Who is this group?

Every time I've used this process and shared the resulting map with the group, they connect to it quite well. Figure 17 is an example of a simple map done with a group of about 10 people who led a modest sized organization. This sort of process is a good way to help a group clarify their Identity and the areas of Work that they feel are important for their development and the effectiveness of their organization. Since Process Enneagrams are fractal, we can use them to go more deeply and develop each point further.

In this chapter, I have illustrated the use of the Process Enneagram to see what is going on in a crisis, and to solve a management/union dispute over hard hats. We have also looked at using the Process Enneagram to implement change at both organizational and personal levels as well as to map a system to understand it better.

The use of the Process Enneagram provides powerful insights into the processes and activities in any kind of organization. The particular nature of the work, whether it's making sugar or governing the City of Niagara Falls, NY does not matter. It illuminates the way that people engage and helps them to see possible solutions to the problems they face.

In the next chapter, two examples illustrate how the combination of mapping and change processes have been used. The first story is about an Australian sugar mill in North Queensland where the challenge was to significantly improve and then sustain safety performance. The second story is about building and sustaining the Leadership Team of the City of Niagara Falls, NY. These are both on-going stories that continue to unfold.

Notes

1   Merrill, in his book *Connections, Quadrant II Time Management* has developed a useful way to look at how we spend our time. He set up a 2 X 2 matrix having 4 quadrants. Quadrant I relates to spending our time on things that are important and urgent, like a crisis. Quadrant II relates to spending time on things that are important but not urgent; this is the most effective place for managers to spend much of their time. Quadrant III relates to work that is urgent but not important like some phone calls. Quadrant IV relates to things that are neither important nor urgent. He believes that managers need to learn to shift a large part of their time from Quadrant I into Quadrant II.

· 4 ·

Using the Process Enneagram
in Organizations

One of the most powerful ways to use this tool is to help organizations see themselves clearly. It helps people to see what's possible, to find out who cares enough to do something about it and then to lay out the path to fulfill their Intention. At the beginning of a workshop, I usually gain the group's permission to work with them by sharing some stories about values that are important. I then guide the organization in a dialogue where they look at themselves from the nine different perspectives of the Process Enneagram. The process is not a lock-step move through nine steps to "the answer." Rather it is an exploration to develop insights in their own words. As we map the nine perspectives together, a comprehensive picture of their own organization emerges. I'll illustrate this with story of CSR's[1] quest for improved safety performance.

The Story of the CSR Safety Improvement Efforts

The Process

This is the process that I've used with the people at several of CSR's sugar mills in North Queensland, Australia. In this process, the group moved through several, very important phases. These phases are illustrated in Figure 18, the Process Workshop Schematic.

As we open up the conversation, the organization often moves into a very unstable, difficult place. Many of the areas of conflict become visible. Many of the undiscussables surface. This is a place that does not feel safe for the group. I've found that every group behaves differently in this space.

Some just open up and talk quite easily. Some pull back and become very quiet. It's often hard to get the conversation going. With some, I just sit down with them and ask for their help to get going; this works. Others explode with pent-up energy and frustration, so I spend a lot of time trying to keep the conversation open and focused. Developing a clear, compelling, shared Intention is a key to doing this successfully. Charting the issues and frustrations using the Process Enneagram also enables us to work through these things.

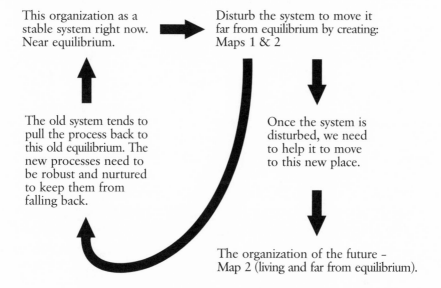

This organization as a stable system right now. Near equilibrium.

Disturb the system to move it far from equilibrium by creating: Maps 1 & 2

The old system tends to pull the process back to this old equilibrium. The new processes need to be robust and nurtured to keep them from falling back.

Once the system is disturbed, we need to help it to move to this new place.

The organization of the future – Map 2 (living and far from equilibrium).

Figure 18 The Workshop Process Schematic

As a guide, being able to dance with the group is critical as it moves out of its old states. By staying with the process, every group I've worked with that really wanted to make the needed changes to improve has made significant progress. They move to a new, far from equilibrium state.

It is critical for the guide to stay with the group once it becomes destabilized. The entropy builds in the group to the point, where all of a sudden, they begin to re-organize their thinking and behaviour to a new state. Professor A. M. de Lange of the University of Pretoria, South Africa, whom I met through the Complexity and Management mailing list of the Institute for the Study of Coherence and Emergence in Boston, MA, has helped me to understand why this happens. As he's explained, entropy and the free energy related to the entropy are self-organizing energies for the system. When the entropy and free energy have increased sufficiently, people reorganize to a new state. This is called the bifurcation point for the system.

In chaos theory, when a system becomes chaotic enough it bifurcates. That is, it splits into either a more highly ordered state or it destroys itself and has to reform. In my experience, if I stay with the group through this uncomfortable condition and use the Process Enneagram map to keep everything visible, the group can and does re-organize to a new, dynamic, far from equilibrium state.

I did have one group, however, revert to their previous, near equilibrium condition when they got stuck on the Principles and Standards. They refused to agree that they would keep their word (their commitments). This was an organization where the management would not take "No, I can't do it." as an answer, so everyone felt compelled to say "Yes" all the time. As a result, everything just fell apart. There was no basis to move forward together.

The Workshop

The workshop described below grew out of many years of my experience in Plant Management, the LOC experiences with Tim Dalmau and from deep studies of the dynamics of the Process Enneagram. Each workshop is a unique experience. I learn in each one and keep trying to improve the next workshop. The workshops I currently run are similar to the one I describe here, even though they continue to evolve.

The first step in the journey was to get general agreement with the CSR Mill Management Team on what we planned to address. That helped us to develop an initial picture of the particular sugar mill, and to consider who needed to be in the initial group. That was step one. Further definition and clarification of the initial question was done for the group by the workshop group itself in our first meeting.

It was best to involve a cross section of people from the Mill. In discussion with the mill management, I recommended that we include management, supervisors and the people doing the hands-on work, like operators and mechanics. We also included others in the system, like union representatives and the people in cane transport who bring the cut cane to the Mill. Each time the people in the workshop gathered, we would ask if everyone was there who needed to be there. It's important to remember that however we defined the initial group, the definition was quite arbitrary. All parts of the mill are interconnected, so an artificial boundary that defined who's in and who's out needed to be considered each time we met. It's necessary to take a first stab at defining the group to get started, but we needed to keep open to the fact that the decision was arbitrary and that we had to keep asking, "Who needs to be here?"

In the preliminary meetings with the Mill Management Team, I asked them to participate in the meetings, since they are a part of the whole of the mill. I also asked them to listen and not to react defensively to things that might be said. We were trying to get all the different perspectives into the room and onto the map. A defensive reaction to something that was said would push us back into Argyris' Model I discussed in Chapter 2 and shut down the conversation.

Sometimes it was difficult for the managers to hear some of the negative comments that surfaced. I did not sit in judgment on these managers. I've been there and know how difficult it is to take criticism. Some negative comments reflected misunderstanding, some reflected history from years ago, some were just hot air and some were quite on target. We needed to let these things out to clear the air, to learn and to be ready to move on.

In a typical mill, the workforce ranges from 200-350 people, but I can work effectively in the sessions only with 30-35 people. I spent 2 to 3 days working with each team. After introducing myself and opening things up to any questions anyone might have about my credentials and experiences, I explained of the Process Enneagram and described it as a web (see Figure 2). It was very important for everyone to make a personal connection to the Process Enneagram, based on his or her own experience, since this helped to open up the process. To help the participants do this, I developed a simple map of a local fast-food store.

Then we co-developed the opening question for the people in the workshop to consider. All through the process, my role was to facilitate the conversations and encourage people to get their thoughts out. I constantly pushed them to go deeper into what they were saying so that they became more clear and precise. I scribed their comments onto the map as accurately as I could, stopping often to check if what I had written accurately reflected their comments (Figure 19).

The first question for the sugar mills was "What is safety like here at this Mill?" Always keeping this question before us, I began the development of the map showing their current state. I call this Map 1. In this first phase of the process, I proceeded around the circumference of the Process Enneagram. I did this, beginning with their Identity (point 0) and then defined their Intention regarding their desired safety goals (point 1). They were usually quite open, and their Intentions of having everyone go home in one piece were very strong. Next I talked about the Issues confronting them (point 2). A lot of negative comments about all the problems and issues they faced came out. I then asked how they are with each other (their Relationships at point 3).

First, I talked about their relationships and their connections with each other that help them to work more safely. I talked about their relationships when they were in their organizational roles, as well as when they were operating in personal roles like at a picnic. Then I moved on to the Principles and Standards *actually in use*, not the stated ones (point 4). This was often a difficult place for the managers to keep from becoming defensive. Then I moved on, and asked them to tell me about the Work (point 5) they were doing to improve their safety performance. In all cases, they were doing a lot of Work to improve their performance. At this point in the process, it became obvious that the Work they were doing was not supported by well grounded and accepted Principles and Standards, but I didn't comment on this at that point.

The safety Work (point 5) they were already doing was usually focused on making the physical plant and conditions safer, as well as on improving their written job procedures. These are two important legs of the safety Work. The third leg of the safety Work focuses on the way people choose to work. I found that there wasn't usually much effort that focused on reducing or eliminating the unsafe, at-risk behaviors, yet these were the cause of 90 or 95% of the injuries. Most organizations I've worked with have fairly good procedures and have addressed the major facilities problems. This is a necessary, but not sufficient base for their safety. It's by taking risks and cutting corners that most injuries occur.

The next questions related to how they create, use and share Information (point 6). This was followed by questions on how they use the Information and other's experiences to Learn (point 7) and make improvements in their safety performance. Finally, I asked them about their Structure and about their Context, that is, their coupling to their external environment (point 8).

Typically, Structure questions focused a group internally on the way they are organized, around identifying who initiates and drives the Work, around finding the source of ideas and to where they look for leadership. Context questions related to the external environment in which they were living and working. Here the questions were related to identifying the competitors, understanding the nature of their business environment, finding out what their costs and earnings pictures are like, and developing an understanding of their regulatory environment and the social changes that might impact them.

I used questions like, How does the safety process flow? Is it top-down driven? Do you use teams? I also asked them about their competitive environment, both locally and globally. Many people within the organizations were quite unaware of their external environment. This brought an opportunity to bring some competitive reality into the conversation. Many people thought that they could just throw money at a problem, not realizing the intense nature of the competitive environment. I told a story about one place where I've worked where a manager fell down the steps in the factory. They spent about $100,000 to replace the steps, and then the manager fell down them again. Stair-climbing lessons would have been less expensive and would probably have solved the problem. In moving through the process, participants began to see more clearly that the number and severity of most of the injuries could be reduced by simply reducing the at-risk behaviors.

The whole process is a bit like focused brain storming. Ideas were jotted down in the appropriate place on Map 1 in the order they came up. There was no attempt to put them into any particular order in the various categories or to coalesce them. During the mapping process, if we decided that I'd put one of the ideas into the wrong place, we simply moved it. After completing the first cycle, we had a comprehensive map that described about 80% of their current state – *in their own words*.

It is important to have the major features and insights of the organization on the map, but having all the detail is not needed. The process is cyclical, so we could always add things later if the group felt they were important. It's a very forgiving process in this way. The map was there on the wall in front of them for all to see and to reflect upon. I asked them to see if the whole picture made sense to them and if we needed to add anything to it.

This work normally required the whole morning of the first day of the workshop. The map looked like the one below (see Figure 19 p. 70), which I call Map 1. It's a composite from three mills that were very similar. Map 1 is a description of their current state.

It was clear from the map that:
· they had a good sense of their Identity around safety issues;

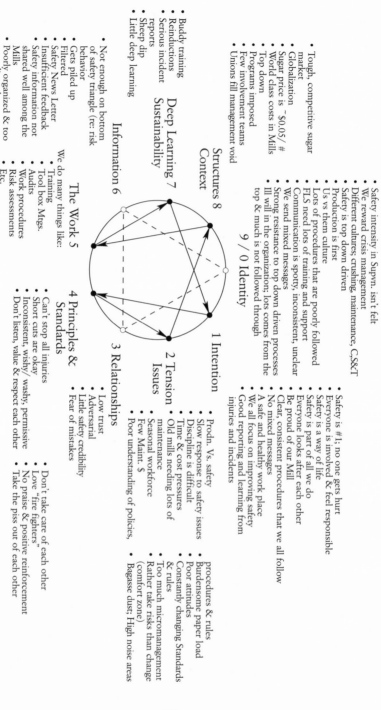

Structures 8
Context

- Tough, competitive sugar market
- Globalization
- Sugar price is ~ $0.05/ #
- World class costs in Mills
- Top down
- Programs imposed
- Few involvement teams
- Unions fill management void

Deep Learning 7
Sustainability

- Buddy training
- Reinductions
- Serious incident reports
- Sheep dip
- Little deep learning

Information 6

- Not enough on bottom of safety triangle (re: risk behavior)
- Gets piled up
- Filtered
- Safety News Letter
- Insufficient feedback
- Safety information not shared well among the Mills
- Poorly organized & too complicated

The Work 5

We do many things like:
- Training
- Tool box Mtgs.
- Audits
- Work procedures
- Risk assessments
- Etc.

4 Principles & Standards

- Can't stop all inquiries
- Short cuts are okay
- Inconsistent, wishy/ washy; permissive
- Don't listen, value & respect each other

- Don't take care of each other
- Love "fire fighters"
- No praise & positive reinforcement
- Take the piss out of each other

3 Relationships

- Low trust
- Adversarial
- Little safety credibility
- Fear of mistakes

2 Tension Issues

- Prodn. Vs. safety
- Slow response to safety issues
- Discipline is difficult
- Time & cost pressures
- Old mills needing lots of maintenance
- Seasonal workforce
- Few Maint. $
- Poor understanding of policies,

procedures & rules
- Burdensome paper load
- Poor attitudes
- Constantly changing Standards & rules
- Too much micromanagement
- Rather take risks than change (comfort zone)
- Bagasse dust; High noise areas

1 Intention

- Safety is #1; no one gets hurt
- Everyone is involved & feel responsible
- Safety is a way of life
- Safety is part of all we do
- Everyone looks after each other
- Be proud of our Mill
- Clear, consistent procedures that we all follow
- No mixed messages
- A safe and healthy work place
- We all focus on improving safety
- Good reporting and learning from injuries and incidents

9 / 0 Identity

- Safety intensity in Suyn. isn't felt
- We reward crisis management
- Different cultures; crushing, maintenance, C.S&T
- Safety is top down driven
- Production is first
- Us vs them culture
- Lots of procedures that are poorly followed
- FLS need lots of training and support
- Communication is spotty, inconsistent, unclear
- We send mixed messages
- Strong resistance to top down processes
- Ill will in the organization; lots comes from the top & much is not followed through

Figure 19 Map 1 – What's Safety Like in CSR Mills?

- they clearly Intended to have a place to work where everyone goes home in one piece;
- the Issues were pretty negative;
- the Relationships were not supportive of interdependent work;
- the Principles and Standards didn't support improvement;
- the Work was not well focused on reducing the eye, hand and back injuries, which was where they were having most of their injuries;
- the Information was weak and not well focused;
- the Learnings were not well focused or organized, and
- the Structure of the management process was top-down driven.

They also had a much clearer idea of their Context and the constraints of the tough competitive environment they were living in.

At this point, it was clear to everyone that the things they were doing were not going to get them to being a world class safety organization as their Intention said they wanted to be. Their own words told them of the need to change. No one had to come in and tell them they needed to change. They now saw they had a choice. If they were really serious about their Intention, then *they had to do things differently*. This point of insight and recognition was a critical step in the workshop process.

After lunch, I began to look at the changes that were needed in order for them to achieve their Intention. For this cycle of the Process Enneagram, the question changed to "What can safety be like at this Mill?" In this part of the process, we talked again about their Identity and Intention as we had developed them in the morning, being sure that everyone was clear and that they still agreed on these. We didn't usually need to make any changes.

The next step was another critical shift. In the normal command and control process mode, the focus automatically goes to the Issues next. When this is done the process gets stuck. The Issues generally show up as some sort of a polarity like "We can't do this until we get some more money." Resolving Issues at this level by brute force or compromise means that everyone achieves less than they had hoped. If the transition is made by brute force, there's resentment. If it's made by compromise, there is always an unfinished agenda where someone owes someone else for having given in; there's an expectation that the score will be settled somewhere down the road. At the Issues level, we see things as either/or and tend to become stuck.

Instead, at this point we began to follow the inner path of the Process

Enneagram as was discussed in Chapter 2. We moved from point 1 (Intentions) to point 4 (Principles and Standards). *Going from point 1 to point 4 rather than to point 2 breaks the command and control process.* We could move to a higher level in dealing with the Issues at point 2 *after* we came to agreement on the Principles and Standards by which everyone agreed how to work together. Principles and Standards are an organization's ground rules. It needed to be very clear that these were the group's rules, which they had developed themselves in the workshop. Since the managers were part of the process, their ideas were there as well, along with everyone else's.

The Principles and Standards act as the homeostatic processes for a living organization. If we desire to move from where we are now to a new place (our Intention), we need new homeostatic processes. I think that many change efforts fail because the ground rules (the Principles and Standards) are not addressed. These unaddressed processes act to pull us back to the old way of operating before the change process was initiated.

It was critical, therefore, that we came to an agreement on the new Principles and Standards before we engaged the Issues at point 2. I took the group back to the Identity and Intentions and asked, "If this is where you are (Identity) and this is where you want to go (Intentions), what Principles and Standards do you need in order to work together without anyone getting hurt?"

In my workshops, I often erase the Principles and Standards developed in Map 1 and create new ones. This part of the workshop process must take enough time for the group to come together and make significant agreements. This is where the deep shift that they must make starts to happen. A new Intention like "no one getting hurt" has to be important and compelling enough to the group that they will be willing to rise above their old Principles and Standards and move to the new ones. In the Principles and Standards, there is a hard edge because there must be an agreement that discipline will be used if necessary if someone persists in engaging in unsafe behaviors.

With an agreed upon set of Principles and Standards, we then looked at the Issues that were developed in the first session. They saw that if they lived up to these new Principles and Standards, some Issues, like poor attitudes, putting production before safety, and not addressing discipline problems just dropped away. The remaining Issues were then engaged in the light of the new Principles and Standards. Some were resolved and others remained as challenges they all agreed to work on together. The

Issues that still needed more work showed up again when we came to look at the Work itself (point 5). None of them was a show-stopper. We also saw that their Relationships would start to shift and become more interdependent; trust would begin to build. Everyone began to see the connections with others that were needed in the organization to help develop safer ways to work.

One of the key agreements on the Principles and Standards was how they were going to create, use and share information. Information (point 6) must flow freely and abundantly, so the system as a whole knows what is going on.

Once we'd agreed upon the Issues still facing us, we moved on to how they should be Structured (point 8) in order to move towards a new Intention. Here we talked about the teams, for example, and how the effort would be led. As the participants opened up, the organization became more leaderful. Often, a mix of both self-organizing and operational leadership processes resulted, with the recognition that there would be a transition towards more self-management. Normally, the Context factors didn't change much because of the new Principles and Standards.

Next, the Work (point 5) was addressed. The items now were focused more on dealing with how injuries actually happen, and we moved away from being so focused on physical conditions and procedures. We looked at the sorts of at-risk behaviors that were occurring and looked at reducing and/or eliminating them. We also looked at the Issues and selected some that we needed to work on. And finally, we addressed the conditions that they needed to put into place, so that the organization could learn and develop.

All this took place in the afternoon of the first day with the group. The resulting map (se Figure 20 p. 74) is called Map 2. It is the map of their future state.

Typically, at the end of the first day, a group I work with feels very unsettled and frustrated. It was so at the mills. They could see the new possibilities and felt a strong desire to move into this new place, but they also knew it would be hard. They had experienced new programs before and had seen most of them fail to live up to expectations. Often the cynicism was deeply felt.

I then sent them home to reflect on this overnight without attempting to soften or reduce the significance of the work before them. I asked them to think about the barriers they'll be facing as they tried to bring this into reality, and to come up with ways to overcome these barriers. Many

Structures 8 — Context

- Tough, competitive sugar market
- Globalization
- Sugar price is ~ $0.05/ #
- World class costs in Mills
- Be proactive in making a safer workplace
- Management sets goals and drives the process
- Teams develop and use safety processes to achieve superior performance
- Be proactive in making a safer workplace

Deep Learning 7 — Sustainability

- Walk the talk
- Post and review the map:
  - (how are we playing each week?)
  - (are we living by our principles and standards?)
- Safe Acts Index
- Spend time with our people
- We can work together so lets keep going

Information 6

- Sharing all safety information
- More feed back
- More about the bottom of the triangle

The Work 5

- In addition to all the safety work we are doing:
  - Safe Acts Index
  - Reduce hand, back and eye injury teams
  - Work Permits Team
  - Risk Assessment Team
- Identify unsafe behavior
- Praise good performance

9 / 0 Identity

- Different cultures; crushing, maintenance, C,S&T
- Production is first; Safety is top down driven
- Us vs. them culture
- Lots of procedures that are poorly followed
- FLS need lots of training and support
- Communication is spotty, inconsistent, often unclear
- We send mixed messages
- Strong resistance to top down driven processes
- Ill will in the organization; lots comes from the top & much is not followed through

1 Intention

- Safety is #1; no one gets hurt
- Everyone is involved & feel responsible
- Safety is a way of life
- Safety is part of all we do
- Everyone looks after each other
- Be proud of our Mill
- Clear, consistent procedures that we all follow
- No mixed messages
- A safe and healthy work place
- We all focus on improving safety
- Good reporting and learning from injuries and incidents

2 Tension Issues

- Production versus safety – but less intense
- Lack of maintenance $'s
- Old Mills
- Paper work
- New and changing standards
- Need for training development
- Bagasse
- Noise
- Seasonal workforce
- Time and cost pressures

3 Relationships

- Trust is building
- Becoming interdependent
- Help each other

4 Principles & Standards

- Safety is #1.
- Agreed,consulted set of rules with consequences (+ &-)
- Persistence
- Be honest, consistent and fair
- Measure & track progress
- Sustain the work
- Use discipline when/ where needed

- Everyone personally responsible
- Listen and be respectful
- Reinduction, retrain, develop (all levels)
- Seek understanding & share
- Live and apply safety
- Promote participation
- Commitment
- Help each other through culture change

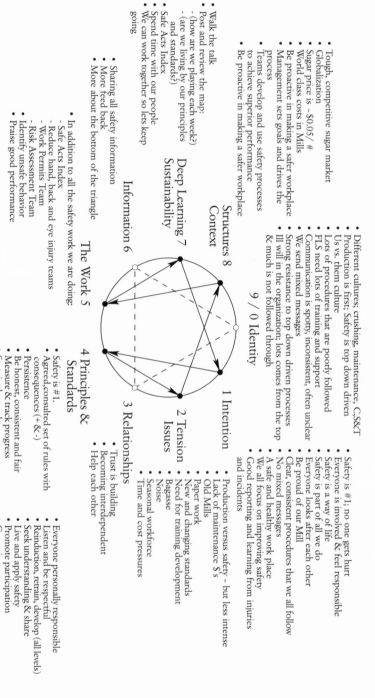

Figure 20 Map 2 – What's Can Safety Be Like in CSR mills?

went home feeling like this was all unlikely and maybe impossible.

The entropy in the system is usually very high; this is the place in the process where the group experiences considerable instability. Having time for people to struggle and reflect is critical for the shift to take place. It does not work to try to do the workshop in one day. People need the overnight time to process things.

The next morning, we created a list of all the barriers they'd identified. We talked about them to get as clear as we could and to understand them more deeply. Then, we talked about what needed to be in place to overcome them. This conversation took some time and went very deep. Somehow, overnight they experienced a deep shift away from the cynicism and frustration of the night before. They moved to a place of new possibilities, expectations and energy. In the language of chaos theory, this is called a bifurcation; they came to a fork in the road and chose to move to a new place.

We spent most of the morning in conversation about how to put this into place. We also spent some time talking about what some of the new Principles and Standards would be like from an operational point of view. For example, when it was agreed that safety would be Number 1, what would that look like? It showed up in things like thinking about the safety requirements before jumping into a piece of equipment to fix it. That might mean shutting the production line down.

By the afternoon, we had a good sense of what needed to be done, and the group had developed some hope that they could do this important work. What was different from their previous experiences was that they had developed this together. Because they all could see themselves in the picture and had a stake in it, they were committed to its success.

In order to sustain the learnings and to begin the actual work of reducing injuries and addressing key Issues, I invited people to self-organize into cross-functional, multi-level teams around the specific areas where the injuries were happening. In developing Map 1, we identified that eye, hand and back injuries were the most common. We had also seen that stronger procedures were needed before breaking into equipment to repair it. Teams gathered around this Work and laid their plans to address the problems. I then taught them some audit procedures, so that they could tell where they were and whether progress was being made as they went forward. Focusing on the ongoing work of these teams was one of the key elements for them to learn how to function in the new way and to sustain the processes.

Another key part of the learning and sustaining process as they went forward was to post Map 2 in their meeting room. It was there for all to see and to talk about as they went forward. At the start of each meeting, they spent some time asking themselves how they were doing. The map serves as evergreen guidance for the group. As work is completed and conditions change, the map is updated.

Each person involved in such a process needs to reflect on the previous week and comment about their own experience. They need to be open and to help each other as they develop and learn. Map 2 holds the space open for these conversations. If Map 2 is not posted, reviewed and tested at least weekly, they will quickly fall back into Map 1 behaviors.

A key leadership role for the manager is to help hold everyone accountable for living up to the Principles and Standards they've made together. People must learn to live and work together in a new way. This is where the operational management part of the Leadership Dance comes into play (see Chapter 2). The manager has to take the position that the agreements on the Principles and Standards that they've made together are serious, valid and real. Now she or he must insist that everyone learn to live them and to grow. Going back to the old ways (the Principles and Standards of Map 1) is unacceptable. The manager must make every effort him or herself to live and model these new behaviors. Mistakes will be made, so it's good to ask the group for their help in living up to them. When people see the manager moving, they come along as well. This is a process of constant feedback and learning to live and work differently.

Without this discipline to sustain the system, it's quite easy to slip back into the old ways. After a few weeks or months, everyone will see that they are growing and that they need to develop a new map (Map 3, etc.) to reflect their learning and growth. In holding the space open by posting Map 2, in being in conversation about their experience and in helping each other, they and the organization blossom and develop. By doing this, the whole process gets stronger and sustainability builds.

At the end of the workshop, we spent some time talking about how to involve the others who were unable to participate in the workshop. The next step was to talk with the others about what the workshop meant and the way everyone had a part in developing Map 2. The workshop participants asked people to talk with them about Map 2 and to offer any insights about what might be missing. They invited the people who were interested to join the teams that were looking at solving some of the problems they had identified. They asked the others for their help in making the whole thing work. It was a slow process, but one that moved throughout the mill as everyone saw management's commitment to the process, as well as the commitment of the other workshop participants. It was also extremely important that they were seen as trying to live up to the new Principles and Standards. Union support was critical; they were in the workshop and helped to develop Map 2, so this was not a problem.

In the mills where this process was used to address safety problems, they saw over a 50% drop in their injury frequency rates in less than 6 months. As they continue to use this process to work on safety improvements, they are also seeing opportunities to use this same process to begin to address other challenges facing their organization. In one mill, the recordable injury frequency rate dropped from over 30 injuries/ 1,000,000 exposure hours to 0 in just 3 months. Eight months later, it was still zero. By the end of the year, they'd had only two small injuries.

As of mid 2002, I've run about 40 workshops in Australia and the US similar to the one described here. In nearly every case, I started with a group of disorganized, somewhat disgruntled people and came out a couple of days later with an excited group that had come together with tremendous creativity, coherence and energy flowing. They'd come alive. They were ready to make the changes they knew were necessary.

The Niagara Falls, NY Leadership Team

Another powerful use for the Process Enneagram is to help a newly formed group establish, right from the start, how they'll function together. After gaining their permission to work together and telling some stories, I guide them through the 9 aspects and map their inputs. We then agree on how we'll use the map in the future to hold the space open for the group to talk, to learn and to grow together. I'll illustrate this use with stories of how the new Mayor and her leadership team in the city of Niagara Falls, NY, used it in 2000 to help set the City on a new path towards a more sustainable future.

In November of 1999, Dr. Irene Elia was the first woman in the history of Niagara Falls, NY to be elected as Mayor. She campaigned to help bring Niagara Falls out of its decline and to restore economic health and vitality to the City, the home of one of the great wonders of the world.

As I listened to her campaign, it became obvious to me that the sorts of processes built around the Process Enneagram could be very helpful in this work. She was campaigning for openness and inclusion, for bringing the whole community together to help make the transformation. I also developed a sense during the campaign that Mayor Elia would be drawn to the approach I had to offer. So after the election, I called her. We connected in the first five minutes.

In the first transition team meeting, we developed a Process Enneagram on how we wanted to work and about what we wanted to accomplish. The Process Enneagram developed here was like Map 2 in the Sugar Mill example. This was a new group of people, so Map 1 (their current state) was not relevant. The team members said that this was the clearest and most open process that any of them had experienced. It set the basis for our work, which was completed in only 5 meetings. We identified all the

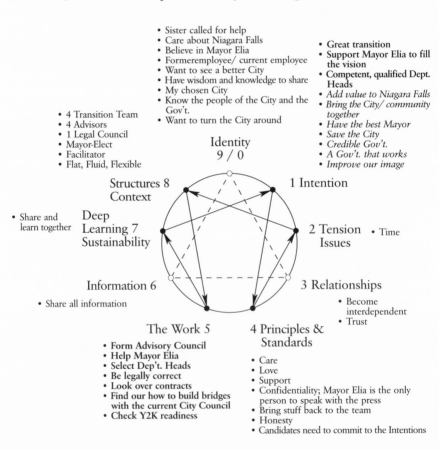

**Figure 21 How Can We Build the Best Leadership Team
Possible for Our City?**

openings in the new administration, identified the leading candidates after a lot of dialogue and determined the process for selecting those in the new administration. Figure 21 is the map the Transition Team developed and used. Every piece of Work aimed at fulfilling their Intentions was completed. The phrases in bold in Figure 21 describe Work that was completed during the 5 week process. The remaining items associated with their Intention (marked in italics) were Work left to be addressed by the Mayor's new leadership team. We did all we had set out to accomplish.

At the end of the Transition Team Process, the reflections from the Team were very positive. They accomplished more work, faster and with better quality than they thought possible. They felt really good about their accomplishments. Mayor Elia felt they were off to a good start. In all the interviews for the Department Heads, I reviewed the work of the Transition Team so the candidates could see the process and to see how Mayor Elia wanted to lead the City into the future. We asked each candidate to consider if he or she could be part of a team that worked this way. We put all the cards on the table.

On December 21st, when the Leadership Team was almost complete, and just before they all were to take office on January 1st, 2000, we had a three-hour meeting with all of them. Since we were modeling being open and putting all the cards on the table, Mayor Elia invited Joann Scelsa, the Buffalo News reporter for Niagara County to join us, so she could see what we were trying to do. There were about 20 people involved in this meeting; everyone participated. Most of the people had never worked together before, so we had to start at the beginning. Figure 22 is the Process Enneagram we developed. This is like Map 2 (the future state) in the Sugar Mill example.

At the end of the meeting, we reflected on the work. Everyone felt we were off to a good start, and the job now was to sustain the effort. The map was copied onto a large chart made up of six sheets of newsprint mounted on poster board for support.

We held a meeting for the Leadership Team almost every week. These largely consisted of each person talking about how they were working and interacting with the others. During the first 12 months, a strong team developed that functioned very well. The Team has had its difficulties, but it is still moving together. As this is being written in 2002, they have opened up their processes so the City Council members and the public can interact with them effectively. After only the first month, Mayor Elia

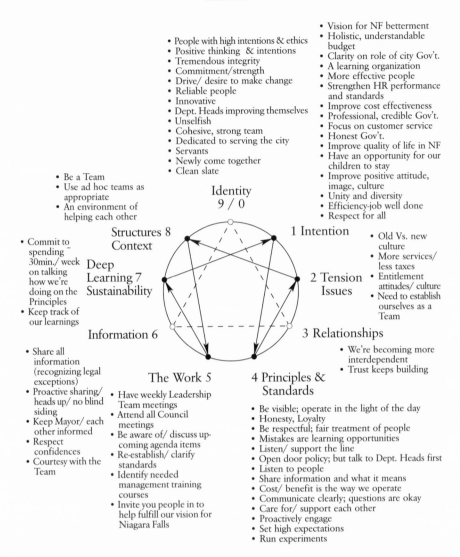

Figure 22 Developing The Niagara Falls City Leadership Team

got a letter from one of the leading businessmen in town commending her for having accomplished more already than the previous administrations had done in 15 years.

Most of the Team members value the Model, so much so in fact, that a number have asked me to bring it into their own departments. People like how it feels and works. Many in the government, as well as in the City itself report how positively things are changing.

After 5 months, the Team had grown so much that another iteration of their Process Enneagram was done, and a few months later they did another cycle on the Map. They wanted the Map to reflect their thinking and agreements more deeply. Al Joseph, the City Administrator, led them through the process. During the first year, about an hour each week was devoted to looking more deeply at each point on the Process Enneagram.

Since they are making progress in the City's transformation, the old establishment is beginning to attack them. Rumors and unkind comments are floated in the press, in the halls behind people's backs and in other ways, in an attempt to undermine the Team. The Team recognizes that if they succumb to these attacks, their efforts to build a revitalized, healthier City will fail. The weekly conversations about the Map (which they call "The Model") and their process are vital to helping them stay together.

They accomplished much of what they had set out to do in the first year, so they could see how much they'd grown. Keeping the Model in front of everyone at each Team meeting and using it as a way to keep the conversation open and healthy is really paying off for the Mayor, the Team and the City. The Governor of New York promised to bring real help to the development of the City in his January, 2001 State of the State Address. The City had its first realistic budget in years, which included a significant painful tax increase the first year.

In the second year, the old culture attacked every step of the way, but the Team stayed together. They developed a 2002 budget with no tax increase. The City has signed contracts with all the City's Public Safety Unions; we have been told that Niagara Falls is the only City in the State of New York to have done so. The City finished up their 2001 year with a modest surplus – the first in many years. While 2001 was a very tough year, real progress was made and overall the Leadership Team functioned quite well. At a Leadership Team meeting in July 2002, one of the Department heads commented that in his 20 years with the City government, this is by far the most effective City leadership he's seen. Integrity is at the heart of their Model.

The Team is continuing to review their Map as they move through 2002. The task ahead remains very difficult.

In a Nutshell

The Process Enneagram is a tool for understanding how organizations operate. We can use this tool to map where we are now, develop a path for where we want to go, and plan how to get there. Map 2 that we develop allows us to see whether we are getting to where we want to be, and if we aren't, why we aren't. It helps us figure out what to do about it when we get off track. The Map helps to pull us into a future we co-create together.

The Process Enneagram has wide application. It is now used successfully in organizations on both sides of the Pacific and Atlantic Oceans. A primary strength of the Process Enneagram is that its use connects people at all levels of the organization. Everybody has a voice. People feel at home with it because it speaks to their own experience and makes sense to them. In opening up the relationships, sharing the information and being clear on who we are, remarkable things happen.

The examples used in this Chapter are just two from among many we have experienced. The more we use the Process Enneagram with groups in conversation, the more we see its power to bring people together around an important question or issue facing them. The Process Enneagram can be used in a vast number of situations to discover and resolve problems before a crisis arises. It's a way to get ahead of things and make a significant, positive difference.

Notes

1   CSR is a large Australian sugar and building materials company with growing operations in building materials in both Australia and the US. They are the largest producer of concrete pipe in the US and are known in the US as Rinker Materials.

UNDERSTANDING THE PROCESS ENNEAGRAM: A TOOL TO LOOK AT PATTERNS AND PROCESSES

• 5 •

The Historical Journey

What sort of a choice do we really have to make? The patterns and processes of the Process Enneagram that are revealed in the proceeding chapters don't look all that profound on the surface; it seems like all we have to do is to come together in a different way. The choices do look simple, yet for me, it was far from simple. The decision to live in this new way called everything I was doing into question. Many of my beliefs and assumptions had to change. The way I saw myself as a manager, a leader, a husband, a father, a community member all shifted. Why?

The view that we've held for hundreds of years, that the world and all that's in it is basically a machine that we can dominate, manipulate and control, is no longer valid as an organizational model. Using the machine paradigm as we work with machines is appropriate, but an error occurs when we extrapolate this idea to people, families, communities, organizations and all of life. While seeing the world as a machine has enabled us to do a lot of positive things, it has cost us dearly. We have lost much of our sense of spirit, life and meaning. We use each other and the environment in ways that are not sustainable. We are tearing our world and ourselves apart. Like Humpty Dumpty, "all the Kings Horses and all the King's Men" may not be able to put us together again.

The crisis examples of the Sodium Plant Fire, the saving of the Amines Business and Risk Management Planning illustrate the differences between organizations that see themselves as machines, and those that utilize the living systems metaphor. Under normal conditions, when we try to maintain rigid control to have stability, dependability and predictability, our organizations are near death. We want equilibrium, yet for any living system, equilibrium is death.

When the organization is in crisis, however, the people in it come alive and creativity and energy flow. We are far from equilibrium and

85

everything is in motion. Information flows freely, interdependence grows, the parts are valued, and we have clarity about who we are and what we need to do together. We co-create our future and have fun doing it. Spirit, life, creativity and meaning come back into our lives.

Most of us have experienced a crisis where we have had a taste of what it would be like to come alive again, to be able to live in exciting, meaningful and sustainable ways. This is something we've known and can do again and again.

As I moved into seeing the way we can communicate, live, love and work together as if we are engaged in living processes, I came to see my family, my community, my organizations and myself in a very new way. I am a whole. I am also part of a family, which is a larger whole. I see and define myself in this relationship and develop a deeper understanding of who I am. My family is part of a community, which is a still larger whole and here too I see and define myself in this relationship and develop an even deeper understanding of who I am. When I step into an organization, my understanding of who I am broadens even further. I see we're all connected in these ever widening wholes.

This is very much like what we've learned in physics: everything is connected at the deepest levels. My world changed! This was a challenge and a struggle. I was a Ph. D. organic chemist, more than half way through my career, manager of a fairly large chemical plant, and now I had to change. Wow!

Why are we confronted with this dilemma and this journey to find meaning and sustainability that is so critical to our rediscovering ourselves? Perhaps, if we consider our collective journey to where we now find ourselves, we can get some understanding of the scientific and technological events that have shaped our life and times.

Almost all of us have been brought up in a world dominated by the machine metaphor. The roots of this go all the way back to the Greeks. Pythagoras (582-500 BC) and Aristotle (384-322 BC), for instance, were trying to understand what things were made of, and the concept of quantity. By the end of the Age of Faith, in the sixteenth century, people like Nicholas Copernicus (1473-1543), Galileo Galilei (1564-1642), Tycho Brahe (1546-1601), Johannes Kepler (1571-1630), René Descartes (1596-1650) and Isaac Newton (1642-1727) turned the way people thought about their world and their solar system upside down. Newton's successes were astounding and informed the materialism of the Enlightenment. Julien Offroy de La Mettrié, in his book *L'Homme Machine* published in 1747, proposed: "man himself is nothing but matter and motion" (see Silver 1998: 57). In this materialistic worldview, if you can't touch and feel something, it doesn't count or perhaps even exist. Spirit and our inner selves are not considered. Descartes split the mind and the body apart.

The scientists of the Enlightenment produced astonishing results. Their approach to the world was reductionist: if you could take a machine like a telescope apart and understand the parts, then you could understand the whole machine. Scientists like Antoine-Laurent Lavoisier (chemistry; 1743-1794), Charles Darwin (evolution; 1809-1882), Gregor Mendel (genetics; 1822-1884), James Maxwell (electromagnetics; 1831-1879), Louis Pasteur (biology; 1822-1895), Marie Curie (radioactivity; 1867-1934), Pierre Curie (radioactivity; 1859-1906), Niels Bohr (physics; 1885-1962), Albert Einstein (physics; 1879-1955), Werner Heisenberg (physics; 1901-1976) and many others vastly changed the way we understand and see the world.

Right on the heels of the scientific revolution in the 16th century came the industrial revolution. Huge changes occurred. Our ability to transform the world exploded. Experimenters and engineers, like Benjamin Franklin (electricity; 1706-1790), Benjamin Thompson, also known as, Count Rumford, (ballistics; 1753-1814), Sadi Carnot (thermodynamics; the Second Law; 1796-1832), James Watt (steam engine; 1736-1819), Oliver Evans (first automatic grain mills; 1755-1819), Robert Fulton (steam powered submarines and boats; 1765-1815), Eli Whitney (cotton gin; 1765-1825), Francis C. Lowell (first machinery powered cotton cloth mills; 1775-1817), Joseph Henry (induction, electromagnetism, electric motors; 1797-1878), Samuel F. B. Morse (telegraph; 1791-1872), Cyrus McCormick (reaper; 1809-1884), George Eastman (photography; 1854-1932), Josiah Willard Gibbs (physical chemistry; 1839-1903), Alexander Graham Bell (telephone; 1847-1922), Thomas Edison (light bulb; 1847-1931), Wilbur Wright (airplane; 1867-1912), Orville Wright (airplane; 1871-1948), Lee de Forest (radio; 1873-1961), Wallace H. Carothers (nylon; 1896-1937), Alexander Fleming (penicillin; 1881-1955), Alan Turing (computing theory, Turing Machine; 1912-1954), William Shockley (semiconductors and transistors; 1910-1989) and many, many others transformed the way we can shape the world (see Wilson, 1954). Everything was swept along before this gigantic wave.

For a long time, science and engineering operated in what was thought to be a stable and predictable world. But then, Henri Poincaré (1854-1912) discovered dynamic sensitivities in the fundamental equations governing the motion of three bodies. "A small difference in initial conditions produces very great ones in the final phenomena" (Peterson 1993: 167). This work, published, in 1889 and 1890, was the winning paper submitted by Poincaré in the mathematical contest that was a part of the celebration of the birthday of Oscar II, King of Sweden. The question posed in the contest was to try to prove the stability of the universe. Poincaré had the first glimpse of chaos, and the stability question remained unresolved.

In the 1920s, physicists were making discoveries that were very unsettling. Heisenberg's uncertainty principle, for instance, threw many things up in the air. You can't know both the momentum and the position of a particle at the same time. The fact that light behaves as a particle or a wave, depending on how you choose to measure it was another challenge.

With the invention of the transistor and high-speed electronic computers, the math that had been so cumbersome for Poincaré became much more accessible. In 1961, Edward Lorenz, a mathematician working at MIT, was studying simultaneous equations to see if they could develop ways to make long-range weather predictions (1995: 137). He was using differential equations to map the flow of weather and discovered that very small changes in the input to these equations resulted in very large changes to the output. Since Newton, science had operated under the assumption that with "approximate knowledge of a system's initial conditions and with an understanding of natural law, one can calculate the approximate behavior of the system. This assumption lay at the philosophical heart of science" (Gleick 1987: 15). Lorenz's discovery changed all this.

Lorenz saw more than randomness in his equations and found a geometrical structure that later became known as the "Butterfly Attractor" (Lorenz 1995: 14-15). Lorenz discovered that long-range weather forecasting was impossible, and the science of chaos was born.

In the 1960s and 70s, Benoit Mandelbrot, a mathematician at IBM, studied complex shapes beyond the scope of Euclidean geometry. He studied things like the degree of roughness of a surface or the twistiness of a coastline, and developed a way to use fractional dimensions. In 1975, fractal geometry was born. A key feature of this was self-similarity: the irregular patterns of nature are similar at many levels of scale. A head of broccoli, for example, is a fractal. If we pull it apart, each smaller piece looks like a whole head, only smaller: it is not the same, but it is similar.

In the 1970s, mathematicians like Stephen Smale, Mitchell J. Feigenbaum, and the Dynamical Systems Collective (Robert S. Shaw, Doyne Farmer, Norman Packard, and James Crutchfield) developed chaos theory.

In the 1980s and 1990s John Holland, Brian Arthur, Murray Gell-Mann, Stuart Kauffman and others at the Santa Fe Institute developed the theory of complex adaptive systems. Christopher G. Langton and others were studying artificial life on computers.

Ilya Prigogine was awarded the Nobel Prize in 1977 for his discoveries in non-equilibrium thermodynamics. In studying chemical systems under non-equilibrium conditions, he found that open systems became ordered when they are in dynamic equilibrium with their environment, drawing energy and raw materials from it. He called these dissipative structures because they exported entropy to the systems around them. In closed systems, like the universe a whole, the Second Law of Thermodynamics indicates that entropy increases. One manifestation of this is that there can be increasing disorder. But open systems that operate within these larger systems can become more ordered. Thus, we can have a beautiful rose, a stately tree or a human form because these open systems self-organize.

Stuart Kauffman, a theoretical biologist, who worked at the Santa Fe Institute and now is Chief Scientific Officer and Chairman of the Board of Biosgroup, continues to develop the thinking around self-organization as a natural property of complex living systems. As he notes, there is a spontaneous ordering of complex systems: "There is order for free" (Kauffman 1995: 71-92).

In the 1960's Humberto R. Maturana and the late Francisco J. Varela in Chile, began to "conceive of living systems in terms of the processes that realized them, and not in terms of the relationship with an environment" (Maturana & Varela 1992: 12). This was a radical departure from traditional biology. Maturana and Varela studied cognition and how living systems are structurally coupled to their environment. By the mid-80s, they'd developed the idea of *autopoiesis,* that "living beings are characterized in that, literally, they are continually self-producing" and must be "dynamically related in a network of ongoing interactions" (ibid.: 43). "The most striking feature of an autopoietic system is that it pulls itself up by its own bootstraps and becomes distinct from its environment through its own dynamics in such a way that both things are inseparable" (ibid.: 46-47). "Conservation of autopoiesis and conservation of adaptation are necessary conditions for the existence of living beings" (ibid.: 103). The living system maintains its identity while it interacts with the environment in selective ways to continually adapt to maintain itself. The ability to continually adapt is more important than the adaptation itself.

Fritjof Capra in his book *The Web of Life* identified the "mind, or cognition, with the process of life, which is a radically new idea in science" (264). This brings back together the mind-body split that began with René Descartes back in the sixteenth century.

In the last 30 or so years, there has been a profound shift in the way we see the deeper patterns and processes of our world. The old model of the world as a machine no longer holds up to scrutiny. The coming together of physics, chemistry and biology has changed everything.

Many people are trying to extend the ideas of biological, living systems to organizations, communities and families in order to open our minds to new possibilities and ways of thinking. Margaret Wheatley who wrote *Leadership and the New Science* and Myron Kellner-Rogers who co-authored *A Simpler Way* with Wheatley are leaders in this work. Thomas Petzinger wrote many thought provoking articles intended to push open our thinking. These were published every Friday for years in the Market Place column he wrote for the Wall Street Journal. He also wrote *The New Pioneers,* which shares stories of people working in this new way. Jeffrey Goldstein who wrote *The Unshackled Organization* and Mark D. Youngblood, the author of *Life at the Edge of Chaos* have also written about this new way. Renate Nummela Caine and Geoffrey Caine have written about working this way in education (*Education on the Edge of Possibility*). Ken Baskin makes a strong case for seeing organizations as living systems in *Corporate DNA*. He shares a number of real-life examples illustrating the wisdom and effectiveness of this approach. Tom Heuerman (http://www.amorenaturalway.com) has published a series of very instructive pamphlets on the Internet. Roger Lewin and Birute Regine in *The Soul at Work* have written beautifully about complex adaptive systems and shared stories of people and organizations living this way. Tim Dalmau and the Dalmau Network (http://www.dalmau.net) are teaching these principles in Australia, South Africa, New Zealand and in the Western United States. Ralph Stacey and his colleagues have developed the thinking about complex responsive processes. Richard N. Knowles and Associates, Inc. and the *Center for Self-Organizing Leadership* are building on these ideas as well, using many years of study and practical application as students and managers in their own work across Canada, the US and the UK.

· 6 ·

Two Metaphors of Organizations: Machine and Living Systems

In this chapter, I will share with you my insights about the characteristics of organizations seen as if they are machines and living systems. I will describe the typical behaviors we see in each type of organization.

The observations and insights developed in this Chapter came out of my experience in DuPont and other organizations, as well as from my association with Margaret Wheatley (Meg) and Myron Kellner-Rogers. I worked with Meg and Myron in the Berkana Dialogues and Self-Organizing Systems Conferences in Sundance, Utah from February 1993 through October 1997. During this time, I participated in thirteen Dialogues and seventeen Conferences. Nancy Margulies and Fritjof Capra joined us part way through the Conference series.

Many other people who participated contributed to my learning as well. I especially remember the contributions of Maggie Moore and Karen Anne Zien who really grasped and understood the transformation in our thinking.

I gave presentations at all the Self-Organizing Systems Conferences, except one that I was unable to attend. I shared the experiences from my work at the DuPont Belle, WV plant where we were applying and using these living systems ideas.

I had begun to use these ideas, largely on an intuitive basis, in Niagara Falls in 1983 and had developed them further in Belle after 1987. It was a great relief when I met Meg and about 50 other people at the Second Annual Chaos Network Conference in Santa Cruz in June of 1992. I discovered that what I was doing was supported by this emerging body of knowledge. Meg, Myron, Maggie, Karen Anne, Nancy, Fritjof, and many others whom I met at the Dialogues and Conferences, became a vital support group for me as I continued to expand my thinking and tried to understand and apply the new ideas. For example, the way in which we deliberately approached the RMP crisis discussed in Chapter 1 was grounded in self-organizing systems work.

In another example of support, I had the good fortune to meet Tim Dalmau in 1995. He leads a consulting network centered in Australia. He quickly grasped the ideas and models I'd developed and invited me to work with him from time-to-time in Australia. I've learned an immense amount from Tim during our relationship.

I expect that many of you reading this book have used some of these self-organizing systems ideas on an intuitive basis, just as I did. The ideas about living systems initially felt strange and foreign to me as I worked deep within a large successful organization that used the machine model. By using the living systems metaphor during my 8 years at Belle, we made tremendous progress. *Our injury frequency rate had dropped by 95%, our emissions were down 87%, our productivity was up by about 45% and our earnings had tripled.*

While these results were good, I felt quite alone, for there were very few people within the Company who understood or acknowledged what we were doing. I had to become increasingly confident, follow my own intuition and build on what I was learning with Meg and the others. I hope that as you see the picture developing in this book, you will also have more confidence in your own intuitive nature.

Now let's take a deeper look at organizations using the machine and living systems metaphors. The scenarios I've developed here are purpose-fully extreme to illustrate the contrasts as clearly as I can. In my actual experience, I have found most people and organizations to be somewhat more moderate.

The step from "organizations as machines" to "organizations as living systems" is a very big one since the beliefs underlying these two views of the world are fundamentally different. As I took that step, it felt like I was jumping into mid-air and only then discovering I could fly. Taking the leap felt extremely risky at the time, but as I look back, I sometimes say to myself, "What was the big deal?" But I know it was a big deal, and that, while many talk about organizations as living systems, few have learned to fly.

The Organization as a Machine Metaphor

Beliefs About People

The majority of the management people I've met don't believe that the people deep within in their organization really want to work. They believe that most of the people don't care about the business or the purpose of the organization, and that they don't understand it. Management people have convinced themselves, "We have to organize people the way we want, and tell them what to do." Some believe that the higher someone is in the hierarchy, the smarter they are and so they have a right and obligation to do this. Those at the top don't trust other people with assets and information for fear they'll misuse them. The carrot and stick approach is what gets people moving and so we have to apply external motivation, like pay for performance systems. Our books of rules and procedures must be comprehensive. We need to build elaborate and extensive human resource systems to be sure that we can keep the personnel issues under control. The only behavior that is approved is what management expressly sanctions. We need detailed job and position descriptions to be sure that people know what they should do. People need to be kept busy to help maintain order because having too much freedom is a problem. Whenever we see people talking together in little clusters or groups, we worry that they are trying to do something to thwart management. Unfortunately, this is sometimes justifiable.

As Meg Wheatley put it, "Change is treated as a problem and we try to avoid it; we want to have things at equilibrium. When change is inevitable, we believe that people will resist it so we need to do all sorts of things to get them to buy in and do what we want them to do. Any time we need to make a major change, we need a major change effort to get it going."[1] The people in the organization often don't trust what management is saying and doing. They often feel that management doesn't trust them enough to share the real information. There are constant fears that management will manipulate them into something that is not in their best interests.

Hierarchies, Boundaries and Boxes

Hierarchy of some variety exists in all human societies and organizations. In our organizations, we want stability, reliability, predictability and control. Hierarchy is a structure that enables a few people to control many people, and to try to get the stability and predictability leaders want. When we operate from the kind of beliefs mentioned in the preceding section, we build many layers into the hierarchal pyramid to be able to keep people in line, and to check that they are doing what we want them to be doing. Everyone is in his or her own organizational box. Each of these layers creates a communication problem because some information gets lost or distorted at each interface as it moves up or down from one layer to the next. The amount of information that gets lost or changed, going from the bottom of the organization to the top and then back down again, is large. It is amazing that the people at the top make as good decisions as they do with such poor information, or that the people at the bottom can make sense of the decisions that management makes. Many times, neither the decision nor the understanding is very good.

In addition to the vertical divisions in the hierarchy, there are horizontal separations among the major functions as well. These are built around specialized expertise and manifest in groupings like finance, legal, manufacturing, sales and marketing, human resources, engineering, research and purchasing. Sometimes we call these "silos" or "stove pipes." There are informational barriers among these silos as well. Information has to flow up the silo, cross to the next silo and then flow down to the people doing the work. The idea of chains of command becomes very important. Turf battles develop quite easily.

Let me illustrate this with a story from my Belle experiences. Our Plant made many products for different Business Divisions in DuPont. Each Division, located 500 miles away in our Wilmington, DE Headquarters, would do their its forecasting, planning and scheduling in isolation from each other. Each Business Division scheduled things like production, maintenance and shutdown activities by themselves. Our Safety Division, also located in Headquarters, would schedule their audits independently from the work of the Business Divisions. Everyone wanted their work done with top priority, which frequently created conflicts at the Plant in terms of manpower and equipment allocations. These conflicts were often resolved by using overtime, hiring outside contractors and renting the special equipment that was needed – all at increased costs. At the same time, we were under a lot of pressure from our Manufacturing Division Management to cut costs. These conflicts were quite difficult to resolve and caused a lot of unnecessary stress among us at the Plant.

Many managers believe that most organizational problems can be solved by restructuring the hierarchy. So when there's a problem, we reorganize. We move people around among the boxes like interchangeable parts of a machine. We re-engineer organizations just like we would a complex machine. Many times the stress, created by the way we did our work became severe enough that the Business Units or my Manufacturing Management wanted to remove people from their jobs. When the new person arrived, they had to struggle with the same issues, since we really hadn't solved the deeper problem; we just moved the chairs around.

We tend to look at things in a linear way: A to B to C, etc. We want sameness and interchangeable parts. We believe that if we have enough information, we can predict the future and control it. When our plans don't work out, we try to gather more information so we can do it better the next time. Sometimes it gets even worse, and we build change processes like the one from the managers of a major company that Meg described at the Conferences.

"Changing a Machine:
Assign a manager;
Set a goal: bigger and better;
Define direct outcomes;
Decide on measures;
Decompose the problem;
Redesign the machine;
Implement the adaptation;
Test the results;
Assess blame."

Basically, this hierarchical model is the only one most of us know. It's in our schools, our governments, our churches, our businesses, our volunteer organizations; it's just about everywhere.

The behavior in a hierarchy can also be a serious problem. Egos can get all puffed up when we come to believe that those higher in the organization are the smartest and those further down are not so smart. We can also get caught up in the power of the positions. Power plays can occur in all parts of an organization – in management, between organizational silos, in special groups and so forth. Behaviors that result from inflated egos and power can become immensely destructive to the organization.

We invest a lot of energy in maintaining boundaries between and among the silos and layers in an effort to control and bring more order to the work. We also do this with the boundaries between ourselves and the outside world by limiting who can talk with customers, the media and the community. Strong boundaries help us to maintain the stability and control we crave. Perhaps, being isolated like this was more workable when the world was changing more slowly than it is right now.

At one point at Belle, some of my Staff wanted me to prioritize everything coming into the Plant, so they could have a more ordered life. From my experience, I felt this was a useless activity. Priorities changed everyday and we couldn't stop the flow of things coming in. At one point, I asked them "How do you prioritize an avalanche?"

In most organizations, only those at the top interact with the outside world. All the information and the interpretation of it must flow through those at the top to those below. There is so much happening that the top becomes a bottleneck. This is like everything flowing through an upside down funnel. It just can't get through fast enough. This restriction of the flow of interactions and information with the outside world is making our organizations less and less able to be nimble and competitive. As a matter of fact, there is often so much trying to come in through the funnel that we put a lot of effort into trying to push it back to keep from being overwhelmed.

The organization is trying to do so much already that the new information causes a lot of disturbance and anguish. The boundary of the organization becomes like an eggshell and we invest a lot of precious energy trying to keep the outside world from penetrating it.

As people are kept in their organizational boxes and isolated from what happens around them, it is very difficult for them to build relationships, make the connections with others in the organization or to make sense of what's going on meaningful. When there's no sense of meaning, when we're isolated and told what to do and how to think, there is little energy and creativity flowing into and around the organization.

A basic mind-set for those managers operating out of the machine metaphor is that the organization and the people within it are things to be acted on and manipulated the way an auto mechanic works on our car or a computer expert works on the autonomous agents in a computer simulation of a living system. The manager sees herself or himself as acting from outside the system. Many organizational development practitioners also operate from this mindset as they work with organizations. With this approach, people feel used and manipulated, and there is often strong resistance to having someone try to change them.

The Organization as a Living Systems Metaphor

Beliefs About People

Other managers I've met believe that most people are trying to do a good job and want to take pride in their work. They believe that people are intelligent, creative and adaptive, that people seek meaning in their work and lives.

When we believe that organizations behave as if they are living systems, we realize that the people in them tend to self-organize around the work, forming patterns and networks. In the Berkana Dialogue in February 1993, we found three conditions were needed for self-organization to emerge. People need:

- a free flow of information,
- to build relationships, develop connections, interdependence and trust, and
- to have a clear sense of identity as individuals and as an organization.

When these conditions are present, we will spontaneously self-organize around the work and energy and creativity will begin to flow. Because we have access to each other and the information, we discover that intelligence is everywhere. Answers to almost all the questions facing an organization already exist within it; we merely need to open up and access them. All behavior is okay except what we, together, have agreed to expressly prohibit. A lot of effort is invested in caring for and supporting each other.

We define ourselves through our relationships. It's through others and our environment that we can see ourselves. As we go deeper, it seems that relationship is all there is. Our connectedness makes us more available to each other, channels open, information flows and learning occurs.

Change is always present, so rather than resisting it, we embrace it. It's as if we are in the River of Life with all its twists and turns, the fast places and the smooth places. We learn to read the water and draw our energy from it. We pay close attention to our environment, sensing the changes. We respond to those changes that we believe are important to us, adapting continually to maintain our identity as we learn and adjust to the changes we feel are critical for our survival.

Chaos theory provides some powerful and useful insights. Living systems are chaotic systems, and organizations are chaotic systems as well.

The word "chaos" is used here in the way defined by Lorenz. Chaos is defined as, "processes that appear to proceed according to chance even though their behavior is in fact determined by precise laws" (Lorenz 1993: 4). These are bounded, deterministic systems that do not appear to be deterministic (Ibid.: 8). These systems are sensitively dependent on initial conditions. The mathematical tool for mapping the state of a system is the difference equation. For simple systems, one can be set up and solve differential equations, but for more complex systems, the equations are difficult to identify and most of the ones that can be identified cannot be solved.

A useful way of analyzing simple, chaotic systems is to draw graphs or patterns of the state of the system in a hypothetical space that has as many dimensions as the system itself. The equations are treated iteratively and the answers are plotted as points in a hypothetical space called "phase space." Iterations of the mathematical equations produce new graphs or patterns that are quite striking in their shape. Lorenz called these patterns "strange attractors" (Ibid.: 39-55). In these systems, each iteration of the differential equations will produce answers that will fall somewhere within the pattern. While the precise locations are not predictable, we can be sure that the answers will fall within the attractor or pattern.

The implications of attractors for organizations are quite profound. Organizations have attractors but they are probably too complex to map in detail. It is useful to picture them as a basin, or a bowl that holds the organization. The bowl may be deep or shallow; it may be floppy or rigid. I like to picture the bowl as a sort of floppy with some permeability like a cell membrane. I call the organization's attractor the Bowl. The Bowl is made up of our vision, strategic intent, principles, standards of performance, values and expectations. This Bowl provides the order, focus and freedom for us in the organization.

When I was Manager at Belle, we built our Bowl together, through many, many conversations and cycles of the Process Enneagram, gaining clarity as we went. As long as we had a good sense of the Bowl, people could operate with great freedom in doing their jobs. I discovered that I could back away from giving detailed directions; people could do almost everything themselves. I was never aware of anyone going outside of the Bowl. *Freedom and order were able to exist simultaneously in the organization.* As we operated with more freedom to do our jobs in the best way we knew how, better ways of doing things emerged, and as we found that we could make a difference, meaning began to emerge in our work. As we began to discover meaning, great energy and creativity began to flow.

The stories of Debbie Fisher's work with the Chamber of Commerce and Becky Dixon's invitation to the talk-show hosts related in the Story of the Journey are examples of people working responsibly in the Bowl. We co-create our future when we share all the information, build the relationships and connections, are very clear on who we are and our intent, and mutually develop and live by behavioral principles and standards.

Hierarchies, the Bowl and Boundaries

When we treat organizations as living systems, the people in them do self-organize and become more leaderful.[2] Nevertheless, I have a hard time envisioning one without some sort of hierarchy, but that may be my own limitation. I do see hierarchies becoming much flatter. This has happened already in many organizations. More importantly, the behavior of people in flatter hierarchies is necessarily based on some of the principles found in the living systems metaphor discussed in the previous section. Leaders become servant leaders (see Block 1987, 1993, Greenleaf 1977 and Depree 1989).

As the organization becomes more leaderful, it's critical that everyone has a good sense of the Bowl. The Bowl consists of agreements that we develop together in ongoing conversations and iterations of the Process Enneagram. These include:
- a clear sense of our shared identity, knowing who "we" are;
- a clear sense of our shared intention, of what we're trying to do and become;
- operational behavioral principles and standards of performance that are co-developed and based on our shared values;
- knowing what our key issues are;
- improving our relationships and interdependence;
- using teams more in our work and knowing our competitive environment much better;
- being sure that our work is focused on fulfilling our intentions;
- keeping the information flowing freely and openly;
- being in a continuous learning mode;
- being clear on the expectations that we have for each other and the business.

If we have a really good sense of these things, then the Bowl provides the order, focus and freedom for us within the Bowl to do what we see needs to be done. We discover that we can make a difference and meaning begins to flow into our work, releasing energy and creativity. We call this discretionary energy.[3] It is the energy a person can choose to put into his or her work. It varies from the minimum required to just keep from losing their job, to the maximum that a person has available (see Figure 23).

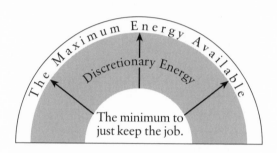

Figure 23 Discretionary Energy

Discretionary energy is a gift that people will give, providing the conditions we've created in our work environment support the emergence of meaning. We can't force people to give this energy, and if we try, they will move towards the minimum, which is what they tend to do in organizations run as machines. Nor can we buy this energy. Based on my experience in plant situations, for example, most pay for performance systems don't work very well. They are hard to set up so that they are perceived as fair, they are hard to administer, and they often become entitlement systems in a couple of years.

As an organization becomes more leaderful, the nature of the external boundary changes. As more people function on the boundary, interacting with external stakeholders, the boundary changes from being like a hard, impervious egg shell to one that is soft, porous and pliable, more like a cell membrane. Rather than trying to keep information out, it provides appropriate pathways for information to flow into and out of the organization. When a very strong sense of the Bowl has developed, it enables everyone to be more responsive, nimble and competitive. As people learn to function in the Bowl, decisions are made faster and we become much more effective in meeting the needs of all the stakeholders.

The basic mind-set for leaders operating from the living systems metaphor is that they are operating inside the organization with the people.

They do not sit outside of it to try to fix it. Rather, they engage people so that information is shared, relationships are built and identity constantly unfolds. They are with the people co-creating their future together. These leaders look for the questions and don't come in with the answers. With this approach, resistance to change almost melts away.

The Changing Role of the Leader

My role as the plant manager had to change from being a command and control driver to becoming a leader who continually tried to raise the consciousness of both the organization and myself. I moved away from being outside and sitting in judgment on the people to becoming a part of them and our work together. I paid a lot of attention to the patterns and processes and to the dynamic balance (not equilibrium). I looked constantly for opportunities for synergy and new possibilities, and tried to keep the connections among us strong and open. In our organizations, we generally have competent people. The people are not what usually need fixing; it's the relationships and connections.

One of the best initiatives we started was the Belle Coordinating Team. It was a new way for us to bring the Business Units, our Manufacturing Management and others together to help us do our jobs at a lower cost and with less stress. We invited them to come in and to be a part of the process. This was a big step away from the machine paradigm where they made decisions from the outside. We changed the patterns and processes we were using and the outcome changed dramatically. We were no longer just moving the chairs around.

One of the metrics I kept on myself was how much time I spent with people who were not direct reports. Over the 5 years that I kept track of this, I averaged around 5 hours a day with people in the plant who were

Primary Value	Decision Making	Logic	Heroes
My relationship to material things	Objectivity vs. Emotional Attachments	Either/Or Yes/No	John Wayne Vince Lombardi

Table 1 Where I Was

not direct reports or with the businesses and the community. I came to realize that the time I spent that way helped to build the Bowl and strengthen the relationships and connections.

I found this transition in my own way of leading to be my most difficult task. The late Richard Orange, a diversity consultant who was working with us in DuPont, shared a picture that fit me quite well in my early days (Table 1).

With a lot of help from my wife, Claire, the Plant people, and a consultant, Alan Gilburg, I was able to move to a different place (Table 2). I prayed a lot as well.

Primary Value	Decision Making	Logic	Heroes

Balance
• Materialism &
  Relationship
• People &
  Environment
• Objectivity &
  Spirituality
• Reconciliation
• Caring &
  Feeling
	Set Direction
	• Vision
	• Mission
	• Principles
	• Standards
	• Expectations
	Be Visible
	• Create the
	  Environment
	  Where People
	  Can Become
	  Empowered
		Ambiguity Is Okay
		Be Effective
		Set Out for the
		Vision
		Co-create It,
		Everyone
		Participating
			Alexander the
			Great (as a
			young man)
			Max DePree
			(Herman Miller
			Inc.)
			Ghandi
			Mother Teresa

Table 2 To Where I Moved

As I undertook this journey, the view shifted enormously (Table 3). I began to experience being in the Plant processes rather than being outside of them. New energy, insights and creativity were released in me. In Table 3, the "Before" column illustrates where I was as I tried to use command and control processes to try to force the organization to achieve my desired outcomes. The "After" column illustrates where I was as I functioned in the living systems processes. The views from the "Inside" are what I thought and experienced. The views from the "Outside" are what people told me. In my command and control mode, I worked hard and tried my best. When the folks told me what they saw before the change, I was crushed. This was a lousy performance review!

The move to the living systems processes was very hard for me - it felt

Two Metaphors of Organizations

	Before	**After**
From the Inside	Strong and Resolute Loner/Lonely Try to Know Everything Controlling Yes/No Center of Things Frustrated	Stronger, yet more Vulnerable Less Sense of Control Learning to Live with Ambiguity Feel Better; More Fun More Conscious of Process Part of the System Connected
From the Outside	Egocentric Don't Ask for Help Confused: Words Don't Match the Behavior One Man Show; No Team	More Effective Organization Lots of Help Coming In More Focused, More Happening More Creative, Relaxed, Fun Cheerleader and Coach

Table 3 The Shifting View

like I was trying to jump across the Grand Canyon. Then I found that leading using the living systems approach was easier, more fun, more effective and more creative. The organization performed a whole lot better too.

When we are *in the system* as participants and co-creators, we experience the sort of synchronicity that Joseph Jaworski talked about (1996). We set out on the path together towards fulfilling our intention. We can continually adjust our path on the way as we bump into one roadblock after another, help each other, and we notice synchronicity. Synchronicity is always happening when we're in the system. For example, I suddenly meet just the right person I need for the next step in my journey, or some event suddenly happens that helps me to solve the problem I am facing. These things seem to happen out of the blue. But we need to be conscious enough to notice them. Without that commitment, without having put ourselves at risk, our consciousness is not high enough, so we miss the experience of synchronicity. Rather, we have to set out on the journey, and be open to what presents itself. If we're engaged *in* the system, this happens.

While we need a clear sense of our shared intention on this journey, we should not try to define it too closely. A tight picture locks us in to a particular outcome and we'll miss some really important achievements.

103

For example, at the Belle plant, I finally learned to quit setting specific goals because I never made them tough enough. This was not a lack of leadership, because we were very clear that we had to do things better to meet the business needs. While I helped to keep everyone focused on the goal and context, their creativity and energy took us much farther than we had imagined we could go. This is quite different from operating on the organization as a machine where the manager sits outside the system in judgment.

Summary

The attributes of organizations in the two systems I have described above are very different. Table 4[4] lists of some of the attributes we ascribe to both kinds of organizations. When organizations operate within the perspective of the machine paradigm, we notice characteristics like those in the left-hand column. When they operate within the perspective of the living systems paradigm, we notice different characteristics like those listed in the right-hand column.

In the next two chapters, we will explore three archetypal processes that open us to the deeper mysteries of the way people and organizations live and behave. These processes are maps for us to use to navigate in the larger systems in which we participate. They enable us to see, understand and feel what's happening and how we are engaged in these systems.

Initially, we will go more deeply into the *Process Enneagram* (see also Bennett 1983, Blake 1996 and Vollmar 1997). As we've already seen in the earlier chapters it is a pattern and process that allows us to map the way we see and think about the system as a whole, as well as the connections, flow and dynamics within the system. The second, *The Rhythms of Change*, is a map of the emotional flow we experience as we move through the process. The third, *The Emergence of Meaning* is a map of the way meaning can emerge and how it releases energy and stimulates the will for creativity and action. With these three processes we can simultaneously hold in our awareness both the intellectual and emotional dimensions of our being as we move into action and function in the living system. With these processes consciously held in mind and body, we can engage, plan, work and live together in a more sustainable world. All of these dynamic processes are fractal; they operate at all levels of scale. All three operate all the time. As we expand our levels of consciousness, we can use them increasingly effectively.

Two Metaphors of Organizations

As a Machine	As a Living System
• Knowledge is structured in pieces	• Knowledge is seamless
• Organizations are structured in functions	• Organizations are a whole system
• Work is structured as roles	• Work is flexible and without boundaries
• People are narrowly skilled	• People are multi-skilled and continuously learning
• Motivation is based on external forces	• Motivation is based on links to the whole
• Change is a troubling exception	• Change is always present
• Information is shared on a need to know basis	• Information flows openly and freely; people decide what they need
• Information flows up and down the organization	• Information flows up, down across and around the organization
• Information from the outside world is often ignored	• Information from the outside world is valued and used
• People work in prescribed roles	• People work beyond their roles
• Organizational barriers inhibit cross-functional interactions	• Interactions across roles and functions are extensive
• People see only their part of the work	• People see their work in relation to the whole, knowing and doing what needs to be done

Table 4 A Comparison of Organizational Paradigms

I have taken a reductionist approach in describing these three processes separately, since this is a useful way to get a clear if partial picture of each one. Since they do operate simultaneously, however, we usually experience them together. It's best, therefore, to keep the parts and the whole in our minds at the same time. As we live out our lives, each of us will create our unique experiences as the processes interact with each other. It's in the sharing in our conversations that the richness of our journey towards a more sustainable future emerges.

Notes

1 Meg Wheatley during one of the Self-Organizing systems conferences.
2 A phrase I first heard from Karen Anne Zien at one of the early Dialogues.
3 A phrase I heard several years ago at an Association for Quality and Participation Conference.
4 Table 4 is derived from conversations at conferences and in working together with Tim Dalmau, Meg Wheatley, Myron Kellner-Rogers, Maggie Moore and others.

• 7 •

The Process Enneagram: An Archetypal Process

The Significance of the Process Enneagram

The Process Enneagram (see also Bennett 1983, 1993, Blake 1996 and Vollmar 1997) developed in Chapter 2 maps the patterns and processes of the way people interact and behave in organizations. John Bennett, Tony Blake and Klausbernd Vollmar provide important information and deep insights about the enneagram. Vollmar reports that Gurdjieff who introduced the enneagram looked on it as a tool to help people make decisions and plan for the future. The way the enneagram is developed and used in this book comes from my own study of these and other authors, my experience and my work. I've spent many hours with Tony Blake who enthusiastically supports the way I've developed it for practical application to our lives and work. One of my goals is to develop this rather esoteric tool in ways that make it accessible and useful to many more of us. It is a tool that provides a way of thinking about and a language for the patterns and processes that have helped me to live and lead successfully in this turbulent, chaotic world.

The rigorous and disciplined use of the Process Enneagram enables us to see and understand, from nine different viewpoints, the interactions and dynamics of people in organizations of all sizes and see them *from the perspective of living systems*. We become healthier when our organizations move into the living systems mode by sharing information, building relationships and becoming clear, together, on our identity and intentions. Although this may look and feel chaotic, we need not worry because the use of the Process Enneagram provides a way to see the order beneath the apparent chaos and confusion that fills everyday life at the surface level. The order, focus and dynamic balance that it reveals, enables us to live in the ambiguity and paradox we find at the edge of chaos. This place at the edge of chaos is where people and businesses can grow and flourish and become maximally effective. It can be used to address questions of any scale and scope. With a little practice, it is rigorous, quick and easy to use.

Some Background and History

I was first introduced to the Enneagram in 1984 by Kenneth Wessel, an Associate of Charles Krone, who was then working in the DuPont Company. I found myself curious, although it was introduced briefly and with little explanation. As I read some of the work of George Ivanovich Gurdjieff (1974), Peter Demian(ovich) Ouspensky (1974) and John Godolphin Bennett (1983, 1989, 1990 and 1992), I came across other references to the enneagram. In our work at the DuPont plant in Belle, WV, we studied it and tried to make sense of it. Something kept pulling us towards it.

One evening in the early 1990's, Robert Brown, who was on the Belle Plant Leadership Team with me, and I were playing around with the enneagram in the USAir Club in Charlotte, NC. We started to put other things we were learning from Bennett's Systematics (see Bennett 1993) around the circumference of the circle. This gave me some important clues for the work that, much later, led me to the development of the Process Enneagram.

Systematics is a conceptual tool that Bennett, a student of Gurdjieff, developed. It seeks to understand the world by investigating the underlying patterns revealed by looking at systems from a variety of perspectives. Put very simply, this is the idea that we can identify significant qualitative distinctions that are intrinsically associated with different numbers and the systems represented by those numbers. He called these numbers "terms," and developed a series of tools that use an ever-increasing number of terms to look more and more deeply into the issues of life. This provides a profound way to see and to understand our world. The one-term system, for instance, he called the *monad*. In the monad we try to get very clear on what it is we're talking about. If we think of the world as a blank sheet of paper, for example, and then draw a circle on the paper, we can ask what's inside the circle and what's outside of it. This is the work of the monad. By using this approach to address a particular subject, we come to a better understanding of it.

As we talk about what is inside and what is outside of the monad, we encounter either/or questions about polarity and tension. We can see these as two-term systems he called *dyads*. True dyads, like male/female, are unresolvable, and we must learn to live and work in their paradox and ambiguity. To do this easily, we need to view what we are doing from a different perspective, so we move to the three-term system called the *triad*.

In the triad, Bennett points out that there is a dynamic struggle we must engage in to find reciprocity, difference and reconciliation. Bennett believed that without this struggle, no real change could be made in the world. It's in our exploration of the triad that we can learn to live and work together, even though there are unresolved dyads.

When we begin to ask ourselves about what's really happening in a particular situation, we must move into looking at the purposeful activity needed to address the problem facing us. To do this we move to the *tetrad*.

These first four systems help us to clarify our thinking and our activities. When we begin to ask about the significance and potentiality of what we are doing, we come to the five-term system called the *pentad*. For meaning to emerge, our work must be more than just an end in itself.

When we move to making our thinking and activities more concrete and to identify the field of action for our work, we move to the six-term system called the *hexad*. This is where the potential of what we're talking about comes into reality. There are higher term systems such as the *heptad*, *octad* and so forth that are even more complex, but they are beyond the scope of my work in this book.

In an enneagram, each point can be explored more deeply using any one of or all the Systems to do this. Earlier, I mentioned that we can find enneagrams "all the way down." We can also say it's monads and dyads, etc. all the way down. The way I've chosen to look at each point on the Process Enneagram is to identify points 1, 2, 4, 5, 7 and 8 with the monad, dyad, triad, tetrad, pentad and hexad respectively. I then go on to relate these systems to Identity, Intention, Issues, Principles and Standards, Work, Learning and Structure and Context, respectively. In doing this, I developed an integrated progression of systems that brings great clarity to our work in organizations and enables us to engage in and to make real change in our world.

The more I played with the Process Enneagram, the more deeply I understood it. I discovered just how powerful it is as a tool to look at how both we, as individuals, and as groups of people in organizations work. I discovered that I could integrate all the human activities that I know using it. It became alive and dynamic. We can use it for planning, for analysis, for problem solving and for taking action. In all these ways, we can see the whole, the parts, the connections and the flow of what is happening simultaneously. The Process Enneagram is there all the time, whether we're conscious of it or not. When we are in a crisis like one of those described in Chapter 1, we naturally flow through it.

The more I work with it, the more inclined I am to see that this may be an important, missing link between the theoretical work of chaos and complexity and the practical applications of these theories to the way we function and behave in our organizations. This is because Systematics and the Process Enneagram provide the models and language we need to bridge the two. Through using these patterns and processes, we become more coherent, produce more effective results, and begin to recover our spirit and soul at work.

But I'm getting ahead of myself, so I'll back up to some of the history of the enneagram and then go more deeply into its use. The historical perspective is drawn from Klausbernd Vollmar (1997) and Anthony G. E. Blake (1996). What I know of the history of the enneagram is shown in Figure 24.

Gurdjieff first introduced the enneagram to small groups in Moscow and St. Petersburg in 1916. I know of no facts strong enough to really establish its history before that time. It was little known until John Bennett, one of Gurdjieff's students, published *The Enneagram* in 1974. (His book *Enneagram Studies* is a revised and expanded edition of this book). The enneagram was seen by Gurdjieff to represent all life processes. One path of the evolution of its use since 1916 is through Peter Demian(ovich) Ouspensky, John Bennett and Anthony (Tony) G. E. Blake.[1] This path leads to the work I describe here. It uses the enneagram as a tool to represent the dynamic, flowing processes of life.

The other path is based on the work of Oscar Ichazo and Claudio Naranjo. Ichazo was introduced to the enneagram by a teacher in La Paz, Bolivia. After 15 years of studying the use of the enneagram to understand personality type, he founded the Arica School in Chile in 1968. Naranjo further developed Ichazo's ideas there in 1969. In 1971 the ARICA Institute, Inc. was founded in New York. From there, this use of the enneagram moved to the Esalen Institute in California. The Jesuits became aware of it there, and developed it further. Helen Palmer, Kathy Hurley, Ted Dob-

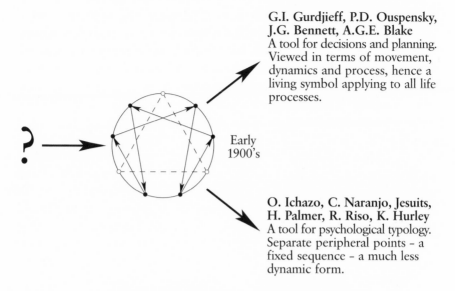

G.I. Gurdjieff, P.D. Ouspensky, J.G. Bennett, A.G.E. Blake
A tool for decisions and planning. Viewed in terms of movement, dynamics and process, hence a living symbol applying to all life processes.

Early 1900's

O. Ichazo, C. Naranjo, Jesuits, H. Palmer, R. Riso, K. Hurley
A tool for psychological typology. Separate peripheral points – a fixed sequence – a much less dynamic form.

Figure 24 History of the Enneagram

son, Don Riso, Russ Hudson and many others using the enneagram in this way have published additional developments. Andrea Isaacs and Jack Labanauskas in Troy, New York publish the Enneagram Monthly. I call this path the Enneagram of Personality.

Each of these paths continues to develop quite independently. The path flowing through Bennett and Blake is the one on which the work in this book is based. Of the two paths, it is the one least traveled.

The Process Enneagram as a Tool

Revealing the Dynamic, Flowing Patterns and Processes of Life

The Process Enneagram shown in Figures 7 and 8 shows how it can be used to map many interacting patterns and processes. When using the Process Enneagram to reveal the dynamic flowing patterns and processes of life, we begin with a question that is very important to us. This is what we did in Chapter 4 with the sugar mill and the Niagara Falls Leadership Team examples. As we frame the question, we focus and begin to learn. It's important that we engage as much of the organization as possible from the very beginning in this process. Since the process is a cyclical one, we always return to ask ourselves who else needs to be present as we become clearer on just what it is we're trying to do. Throughout the process, people in the organization must be engaged. It's important to understand that the initial determination of who needs to be involved in the meetings is rather arbitrary, but we need to start some place and be open to including others as we go. In each cycle, we need to ask "What is going on now and who needs to be here with us?"

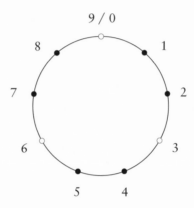

Figure 25 The Nine Points of the Enneagram

The Process Enneagram consists of three sub-systems, all moving and functioning simultaneously. The first is the circle, which is the most obvious of the three systems. There are nine points located around the circle,

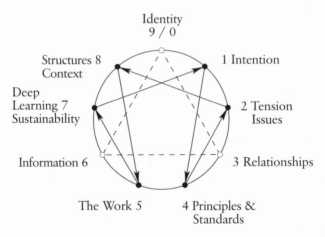

Figure 26 The Nine Attributes on the Process Enneagram

each describing a unique attribute of the whole system (see Figure 25). In using the Process Enneagram, we can see the nine attributes as they reveal themselves in the world around us.

The flow around the circle in Figure 25 proceeds in numerical order beginning with zero. If the first cycle is completed well, the flow continues to point 9 rather than returning to point 0. One can see that metaphorically, point 9 is above the plane of the paper. It is like a helix or spiral staircase rising out of the paper towards you as you read this. The attributes of the Process Enneagram are shown in Figure 26.

Mapping the Machine System

The Process Enneagram can be used to map the many patterns and processes of interaction of people in an organization. These patterns and processes run all the time, even in dysfunctional organizations that operate like machines and are quite close to death. The mapping process will reveal the difference between organizations functioning in the machine mode and those with strong living systems processes.

If you step into an organization that is operating like a machine, for example, like the large mass-merchandiser I mentioned early in Chapter 2, you'll notice that your attention normally follows the sequence shown in Figure 25 with the attributes shown in Figure 26. You'll see that it moves from what people think is their Identity (point 0) towards what they think they want to become (point 1). You'll notice that most people in the organization are not particularly involved in defining these first two items. In all probability, a few people at the top have done this without their involvement. Then you'll notice that the employees are mired in ambiguous and paradoxical issues that cause Tension in the organization (point 2). The Relationships (point 3) are often fairly poor and trust is low. The Principles and Standards (point 4) that govern operation tend to be of a carrot and stick nature and are often undiscussable. Management has to watch workers pretty closely to be sure the Work gets done and people aren't loafing around. The Work (point 5) they're doing does not flow well – it has little energy and creativity in it. Almost certainly, the Information flow (point 6) in the organization is restricted to a need-to-know basis. Little time is spent on Learning (point 7) from their successes and failures. You'll notice that the organization is pretty rigidly Structured (point 8) and people are very "boss oriented." The connections among the various parts and functions in the organization are poor and made with difficulty.

The organization that operates in the machine mode will normally follow the sequence of the outer circle, but without an awareness of that flow. There is usually an unconscious acceptance of the unexamined underlying beliefs. Such organizations go round and round the processes mapped on the circumference, always returning to point 0 because the transformations that could move the organization to point 9 have not occurred. These organizations are near equilibrium and in danger of dying.

Mapping the Living System

If you step into an organization that operates more like a living system, you will see something quite different. It will remind you of the second store that I mentioned in Chapter 2. They will have spent time reflecting on their own processes and on questions like those presented below. These questions can be used intentionally to reveal the real situation associated with each attribute and provide the stimulus to make any needed changes. As you reflect on these questions, please pay attention to the quality and nature of each question since this will help you to get a better understanding of the nature of the attributes. Please also remember that the attributes at points 0, 3, and 6 relate to the self-organizing process while those at points 1, 2, 4, 5, 7, and 8 relate to the specific work under consideration.

As you will recall, Process Enneagram work begins with a compelling question that is important to the group. As we consider the questions for each attribute, remember that these are always related to this initial question.

Here are some questions to consider when examining Identity at point 0.
- Do we agree that the question we've framed is the one we should be working on?
- Who are we, individually and collectively?
- What is the group of people or part of the business we're dealing with?
- What's our history?
- What's our story?
- Where have we come from?
- What are the facts, really?

Here are some questions to consider when examining Intention at point 1.
- What are we trying to do?
- What are we about?
- What do we really want to become?
- What's our vision?
- What value are we trying to create for our stakeholders?
- What is our strategic intent?
- What's possible and who cares enough to do something about it?

Here are some questions to consider when examining the Tensions and Issues at point 2.
- What are the constraints and barriers in moving from 1 to 2?
- How do our values need to change?
- What old behavior do we need to drop?
- What new behavior do we need to adopt to accomplish what we want to do?
- What are the issues impacting us from outside the system?
- How much time do we have?
- How much will it cost?
- Where do we get the people we need to do the work?
- What's happening in the world around us?
- What are people's attitudes like?

Here are some questions to consider when examining Relationship at point 3.
- How do we choose to be together around this?
- How can we become available to each other?
- How do we open up the hierarchy so we can reduce or eliminate the barriers among us?
- How do we learn to trust each other more?
- Are we interdependent?
- How do we connect with those who are critical to the success of our work?
- Do we have about the right number of connections?
- Who needs to know about my work?
- Who's work do I need to know about?

Here are some questions to consider when examining Principles and Standards at point 4.

- What changes in behavior do we need to agree to so we can move from 1 to 2?
- What are we going to do to open up the free flow of information?
- How do we help people become more accessible to each other?
- How are we going to deal with mistakes?
- How are we going to deal with deliberate deviations from the principles and standards?
- How are we going to deal with good news?
- How are we going to deal with bad news?
- How do we celebrate?
- How do we learn to have fun?
- How do we become leaderful?
- Are we willing to keep our word?
- How are we going to bring new people into our group or organization?
- What are we going to do more of, less of, to stop doing and to start doing?
- Do we tell the truth?
- Did we help create the performance standards for things like safety, costs, customer service, business achievements, etc.?

Here are some questions to consider when examining Work at point 5.
- What specifically are we going to do?
- What specific issues are we going to work on?
- When will we do it?
- Who's going to do it?
- What behaviors do we reinforce?
- What behaviors do we try to eliminate?
- How do we create the feedback loops that are necessary?
- How do we make sure we're listening to each other?
- How do we make sure that the information is flowing freely?
- How do we build the Bowl?
- What key measurements will we use?
- How do we stay connected to each other in the system?
- How do we stay connected to the environment: the larger systems in which we're embedded?
- Is our work aimed at helping us to fulfill our Intention?

Here are some questions to consider when examining Information at

point 6.
- What information is in the system?
- What additional information do we need?
- How do we create information?
- Does everyone have access to the information?
- Are we talking with and listening to each other?
- Is there a lot of feedback in the system?
- Are we all in conversations about all this?
- Do people know how to use the information we're already using or creating?
- Can everyone read?
- What languages do we need to be able to communicate?
- Is the information understandable?
- Do people have the skills and knowledge to use and act on the information?
- Is it available in a timely way?
- Do we know the performance goals? Did we help to create these goals?
- Are we gathering information from the outside world, engaging it and deciding what we should be doing next?

Here are some questions to consider when examining Deep Learning, Potential and Sustainability at point 7.
- What are we creating for the future? What's the significance of our work?
- What are we learning?
- Do we really know what's going on?
- How do we capture and build on our learnings?
- Is meaning flowing from our work?
- How are we impacting the environment, the larger systems, around us?
- What is the organization we are in now? Has it changed? Do we need to redefine it?
- What new questions does the organization need to confront now?
- How do we get below the surface to see what's happening?
- How do we sustain this work? Are we using the Sustainability Ratios?[2]
- Are we using Map 2 (our picture of what we want to become) and reflecting on it each time that we meet?

- Do we take time to reflect and learn after every significant event?
- What new potential is opening up for us?
- Are we developing our new performance goals?

Here are some questions to consider when examining Structure and Context at point 8.

Structure:
- Are the people in the system self-organizing around the work?
- Are our structures flexible and fluid enough to constantly adapt to the changing environment and the nature of the work we have to do?
- Are we becoming too rigid?
- Who decides on the appropriate structure?
- Where does the energy come from in our organization to make things happen?

Context:
- Do we know our competitors and the competitive environment?
- What is the context we're co-creating?
- What is the external environment we're living in?
- Who is our community?
- Who are our stakeholders?
- How are we connected and coupled to our external environment?
- What are the governmental regulations or other regulations relating to us?
- How are we sure that we know what's going on in the world around us?
- How do we know this?

Here are some questions to consider when examining the new Identity at point 9.
- Having moved through this process, who are we now?
- What's our group and organization now?
- What are the new questions and challenges we face?
- Is it time to move into the next cycle around the Process Enneagram on the issue we've been dealing with or do we move to a new question?
- Do we need to narrow or broaden the scope of our work either going more deeply into a point or expanding the scale of one?
- What do we know now that we didn't know when we started?

· Who else needs to be involved now?

As we develop answers to these and other questions, it's important to plot them around the Process Enneagram Map immediately. In this way, you can keep the whole picture in mind as you work on the specific parts. Keeping them associated with the Process Enneagram Map keeps us mindful of the system as a whole with all its relationships and interconnections. If this is not done, your work tends to come undone. One group I knew, for instance, listed all the answers on separate sheets of paper. This resulted in their losing the sense of the whole and the interconnectedness, which were critical for their success. They began to get lost until they put them back onto the Process Enneagram Map.

As we move from looking at the circumference of the Process Enneagram, we see two other systems inside the circle. The two are shown in Figure 27. These are critical to an organization's ability to operate as a

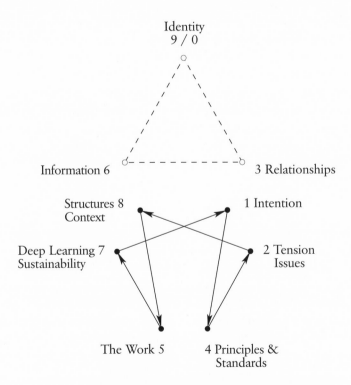

Figure 27 Three-Attribute and Six-Attribute Systems in the Process Enneagram

living system. One of these systems has six attributes and the other has three. The six-attribute system is related to the specific work called for in the opening question, while the three-attribute system is related to the process of self-organization. Self-organization is the deepest process in the organization, and runs to some extent in all organizations, all the time.

When we intentionally make use of the six-attribute system, we break the pattern of the machine paradigm. As always, we begin by helping the people in the organization to focus on their Identity (point 0) and Intention (point 1). Without using the enneagram, organizations operating from the machine paradigm would then begin to talk about the problems and barriers (the Issues at point 2) that prevent them from fulfilling their Intention (point 1). By using the living systems approach, we break this pattern and follow the inner lines of the Process Enneagram. As we follow the inner six-attribute process, we move from Intention (point 1) to point 4 and develop the Principles and Standards that are needed to enable us to constructively move from point 0 to point 1. The revised Principles and Standards also enable us to address the Issues and Tensions (point 2) from an entirely new perspective. Some of the Issues can then be resolved. Even though some simply must be lived with, they too will be understood differently. These Tensions are created partially by moving from Identity (point 0) to Intention (point 1), but they are also created as the organization bumps into the outside world (the Context at point 8) and notices what the environment requires. It's important to notice that each point in the Process Enneagram is informed by two other points. In this case, the Issues at point 2 are informed by the Principles and Standards at point 4 as well as the Structure and Context at point 8.

The main thing is that we don't get stuck at point 2 and waste a lot of energy arguing over these items. The work around points 0, 1, 4 and 2 is where the major work of leadership takes place. *This is where leadership emerges and creates value in an organization.* When people have the Information, have clarity about who they are (point 0) and what they want to become (their Intention at point 1), and know that they are operating with a co-created, operational set of Principles and Standards (point 4), they will spontaneously self-organize around the tasks (point 8). They will do whatever is required (point 5), see better ways to actually do it (point 7), and keep moving on. *This is where an organization realizes the value created on the right side of the Process Enneagram.*

The deeper, three-attribute system connects Identity (point 0) with Relationship (point 3) and Information (point 6). It is always operating regardless of the specific work taking place in the six-attribute system. This is where the role of Information, Relationship and Identity that we identified in the early Berkana Dialogues becomes important. Functionality at these points provides the conditions that must be present for self-organization to occur. Transformation of the organization will not occur unless the difficulties at these points are addressed.

These three points can also be seen as points of hazard. If we're too unconscious to know who we are and what's happening (point 0), we won't even start to change; we'll simply drift. If we are unable to develop the relationships and learn to trust each other and become interdependent (point 3), we will remain stuck in the machine mode. If we do not share the information that enables us to act (point 6), nothing will happen regardless of all the work we've done; we'll just stay in the darkness.

In an organization where the patterns and processes of interaction are vibrant and full of energy, the nine, six and three-attribute systems are all operating consciously at the same time on multiple levels. They are moving and dynamic. Paying attention to them enables us to keep the whole in mind, as we deal with the detail and challenges of the various points.

Figure 28 summarizes many of the points I've been making. The Process Enneagram is fractal in nature. Depending on the question it's being

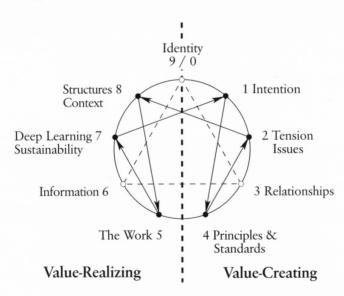

Figure 28 Value-Creating and Value-Realizing Attributes on the Process Enneagram

used to address, it can be used on any level of scale. I have used it in my own personal development, the development of the Belle Leadership Team, the Belle Plant as a whole and in a community of 300,000 people as we did the RMP work discussed in Chapter 1.

When we in our organizations use the tool in this way, it is dynamic and alive. Since the process is cyclical, we can begin to use it without having each step complete or perfect. As we move through it, we'll come back to each point in the next cycle and can modify and/or expand it as we learn and grow.

We can move into action quickly without having to study everything to death. If we create an environment where we constantly engage in experiments, we can free people to be their best. We know that experiments will have to be revised and adjusted as we learn more, since experiments are, above all, learning opportunities. There are two keys to operating successfully in the experimental mode. First, we must think about the experiment itself and pay attention to the boundaries of the Bowl. The Bowl, which was already developed in earlier conversations, provides a good sense of the field of play. As long as we're in the Bowl, we're okay.

The second key is that anyone in the experiment can stop the experiment if he or she believes there is a need to do so for the good of the organization. In the days when we talked about taking prudent risks, I found that people would come up with the most unlikely scenarios that had to be investigated before we could do the risk taking. This seemed like a good way to avoid having to take the risk because each time more research and analysis was needed. This caused endless delays. So when we made the change to "running an experiment," unlikely scenarios would be raised, but rather than studying them to death, we just asked the person who came up with the scenario to keep an eye open for this and stop the experiment if they saw it was becoming a problem. Then we did the experiment without the endless delays. Of course, our Principles and Standards included that we would learn from mistakes and that we would not use them as punishment opportunities.

We can visualize the processes of learning, growing and moving towards our goal as one Process Enneagram feeds into another one with each succeeding revolution. In the story about the Risk Management Plan in Chapter 1, for example, you can see how we moved through many cycles as our thinking and the development of both the technical and communications processes evolved, clarified and grew. This idea is illustrated in Figure 29.

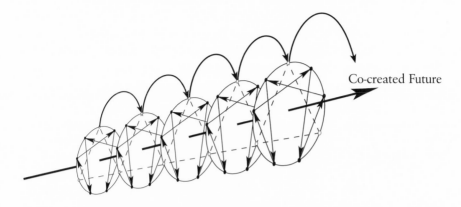

Figure 29 Cycles of the Process Enneagram

Summary

This chapter has shown the fractal nature of the Process Enneagram and the value of using it to deepen our understanding and transform the operation of organizations. Its history helps us understand where this extraordinary tool came from, and where we are in the ongoing evolution of its use. Stories about using the Process Enneagram were shared, with the intent of bringing the theory into practical focus.

In the following chapter, we will look at two more processes, *Rhythms of Change*, and *The Emergence of Meaning and the Will to Act*. They provide ways to understand other processes we find ourselves in as we move through the cycles of change. They can help us adapt to these changes, by deepening our understanding of what is happening and what we need to do. They keep us in touch with what is going on.

Notes

1   One Sunday afternoon in December 1996, I had a grand time in a loft in New York City with Tony Blake and others talking about the way that I've been working with the Process Enneagram. We laid one out on the floor built with a hose, broom handles and pop bottles, and we strode from one point to the other as we talked about it. Tony was quite pleased and comfortable with the work I'd done.

2   See Chapter 9.

· 8 ·

Two More Archetypal Processes

In their writings, George Gurdjieff, Peter Ouspensky, and John Bennett suggest that humans have three relatively separate ways of functioning. They call these three the intellectual, emotional and moving centers. They also suggest that for us to experience life fully, these centers need to mature and learn to act together in harmony.

At this point in the book, we have deeply explored the Process Enneagram. Working with it is primarily related to our intellectual center. To bring this work into harmony and unity, we now need to look at two other archetypal processes that relate to our emotional and moving centers. The first of these processes, which relates primarily to our emotional center, is called *The Rhythms of Change*. The second of these processes related primarily to our moving center is called *The Emergence of Meaning and the Will to Act*.

The Rhythms of Change™

Maggie Moore, whom I met at the Berkana Dialogues, introduced me to the ideas of the Rhythms of Change as a way to look at the flow of our emotions as we go through change. Maggie developed this original work. The emotional side of change is one I've struggled with, both in the organizations I've been with over the years and in myself. As I related The Story of the Journey, you could see the emotional struggles I went through. In my earlier days, when I was operating in the command and control way Richard Orange described in Table 1 in Chapter 6, I was terribly uncomfortable in the emotional side of things. When I got emotional, or those around me got emotional, I did not cope well. As I made the shift and learned to open up, this area has added great richness to my life. Maggie has shown that these emotional experiences have deep patterns associated with them, which occur each time we go through a change experience.

Learning to live in this process was difficult for me. It was important to develop the relationships and trust in others (point 3 in the Process Enneagram) because that's how I learned to trust the process. I began to experience caring and support from those around me. This sort of support was vital for me as I went through the changes myself.

Having an understanding of the deeper processes that are going on as we move through change helps us to keep things in better balance. Knowing what to expect in the emotional patterns helped me to anticipate my feelings and not to be surprised and frightened by them when they happened.

There is a natural sequence to the changes that we move through. In her Rhythms of Change model, Maggie sees these as five stages (Figure 30). The five stages are described in detail in Table 5 (see p.128).

They begin with *Flowing,* where we become aware of new information. The next is *Staccato,* where we hold onto what we're accustomed to in the face of what we need to change. The next stage is *Chaos,* where what we insist on isn't working. The penultimate stage is *Lyric,* where new insights and relationships develop. The last of the five is *Stillness,* where we achieve a new understanding of what is happening and our place in it. The stages can be visualized as a spiral like those in the Process Enneagram.

Figure 30 shows that we move through these rhythms as if in a spiral. Every change is full of potential. The spiral suggests that with every change we move from potential, through a series of feelings (including confusion, resistance, anxiety and fear) to Stillness, where the meaning and purpose of our lives and work is enhanced.

Maggie said in her conversations with me: "We can see where we are in the spiral by noticing what we say. When people are considering new information from the rhythm of Flowing they say, 'Did you know that?' or 'Guess what I just learned! We need to figure out how this fits with what we've already got,' with a tone of curiosity or excitement.

When people are in Staccato, they say, 'There is nothing new here. We've heard all this before. Nothing different is going to happen. This is just a bump in the road and it will go away.'

When people are in Chaos, they say, 'Everything is breaking apart. Things are out of control. Who is in charge? Why don't they do something? What do you mean we have to try harder?'

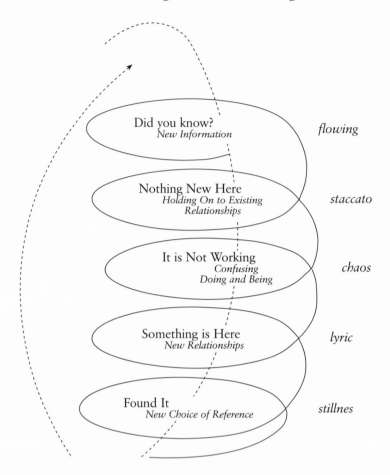

Figure 30 Moore's Rhythms of Change
© **Maggie Moore**

When people are in Lyric, they say, 'Something about this is different. Do you see it? I hadn't noticed it before. What does it mean? How can we learn more about it?'

And in Stillness, they say, 'I see it clearly now. We've found something important. This really makes sense. I wish I had understood it before.'"

Those of us who understand how the spiral of Rhythms can guide us through change can help others by asking questions when we hear them manifesting the patterns of Staccato and Chaos. When we hear people "speaking Staccato," we can ask: What is changing? What does our resistance tell us about what is important? How do we work with the change instead of against it? When we hear people "speaking Chaos," we can ask: What has changed? What new information is being presented to us? Why? What new relationships are required in order to work with the change? In what new ways do we see ourselves moving out of what we're used to and into something different?"

It's very helpful for me to realize that there is a natural progression in the way we experience change. I feel these things each time I go into a period of change. When I get into the stage of chaos, I feel the anxiety and fear, but now that I know that this is just part of the process, I am not seized and disabled by the fear. I know that if I *stay in the process,* I will move through it to Lyric and Stillness.

I also know that I'll be doing this over and over again as I continue to deal with the changes occurring around me. Change is all around us, but I'm handling the emotions better. I still have my good days and bad days, which is why I still need the caring and support of those around me.

Staying in the stage of chaos, feeling the ambiguity, paradox and fear is critical for our growth. Staying in the process is essential for the tension, confusion and disorder (entropy) to build to the point of bifurcation and move us to a new, higher level of organization. As I mentioned before, I developed this insight in private communications with Professor At de Lange in South Africa (de Lange 2000).

In working with teams with Tim Dalmau in Australia and New Zealand, we've seen this same sort of shift occur as the teams struggled in the difficult stage of chaos. At some point in the process, a shift to Lyric occurs. Sometimes it's a sudden shift, and sometimes it happens overnight. It's often profound and wrenching – everyone in the team knows when it happens. The shift I saw in moving from Map 1 to Map 2 in the sugar mill example in Chapter 4 illustrates this well. I have seen the same phenomena unfold while working with groups in Canada and the US as well.

Knowing that we experience change through these natural rhythms is important as we cross the rugged terrain of change. Change is much more than an intellectual exercise. While it's important that we have the intellectual map of the Process Enneagram, we need the emotional map of the Rhythms of Change as well, so that we don't freeze or flee when faced with our changing world. Unless we learn to handle this emotional component of change, we'll fail.

Stage (Rhythm)	Thoughts Associated with the Stage (Rhythm)
FLOWING: We are becoming aware of new information.	When we are moving with the flow of information, our energy is in sync with events. We move easily and feel in control. Our beliefs about how things work or what makes sense are not disrupted or challenged. We seek and handle whatever comes in an easy-going manner.
STACCATO: Holding onto what we're accustomed to in the face of what needs to change.	Questions and clouds appear on the horizon. We experience them as bumps, but we don't know what is wrong. If we are paying attention, we know that Staccato is an indication of disruption or challenge to what we believe should be happening. The disturbance may be one of being startled, surprised, jarred or blocked in some way. If we attend to this sensation, we can direct our attention to what is trying to emerge so we can move with it. If not, we try to recover what we had by forcing it back into place. But it doesn't work.
CHAOS: What we insist on isn't working.	When information and feedback continue to be so disconfirming that we feel things are breaking apart or blowing up, we are in the abyss of Chaos. Our ways of making sense of things no longer hold up. No matter what we do, things are not working as we believe they should. Chaos is less of an abyss if we recognize that its purpose is to break our old habits of thought and action and explore new prospects – if we stop insisting on the way things should work and look for other possibilities.
LYRIC: New insights and relationships are developing.	We slow down so that we can attend to what has changed and learn how to change with it. We are seeing emergence and participating in the re-organizing process with others. We are finding new ways to come together and support one another. Consciousness is expanding to include what we didn't see or what didn't seem important before.
STILLNESS: We have achieved a new understanding of what is happening and our place in it.	We see ourselves as a part of what is happening and actively engaged in creating the new order of things. We have a greater sense of wholeness, relatedness and connection. This awareness quiets and replenishes us, reassures us that we have the capacity to change with the world around us.

Table 5 The Sequence of Rhythms of Change

The Emergence of Meaning and the Will to Act™

Both the emotional and intellectual maps are necessary, but are not by themselves sufficient. A third map that addresses meaning and our will to act is also needed. Even if we do all the thinking and understand our emotions well, if we don't *do* anything, then all the other work is for nothing! It is through our physical bodies that we act and do things. It is in the *Emergence of Meaning* that we find the *Will to Act*. Meaning emerges from the interplay of Identity, Relationship and Information.

The critical role of Identity, Relationship and Information as the conditions and domains of Self-Organization was identified at the February 1993 Berkana Dialogue. They are the conditions for self-organization because through them we develop the clarity about who we are, the access to people, the openness and trust in our organizations and the free flow of information that make it possible. These were discussed in Chapter 6 in the section on Organizations as Living Systems. They are shown here in Figure 31.

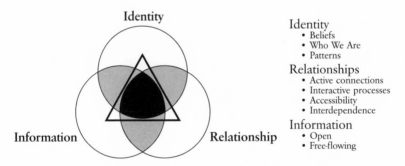

Identity
- Beliefs
- Who We Are
- Patterns

Relationships
- Active connections
- Interactive processes
- Accessibility
- Interdependence

Information
- Open
- Free-flowing

Figure 31 Domains of Self-Organization

Identity, Relationship and Information (I, R, I) can be identified with points 0/9, 3 and 6 of the Process Enneagram and are shown in the diagrams as circles at each point of the inner triangle. The circles are represented as being the same size to show that they have the same level of impact. A simple, qualitative way to measure their levels of impact is discussed in a paper by Kelly Kober and me in the Journal for Quality and Participation (Kober and Knowles 1996: 38). In the process described in the article, we first ask a group to tell us about the things that they believe they need to do. We simply get a list of 40-50 items and then sort the list using Identity, Relationship and Information as the sorting categories. The majority of items will fall into the category where the group has the greatest need and hence the largest area of deficiency. This tends to be around Relationship while the smallest number tends to be around Information, which indicates that they are doing a better job in sharing information than in building and maintaining good relationships. The three regions are dynamic, interacting and functioning all the time.

When we first developed these ideas about the conditions for self-organization at that early Dialogue, I went back to work at Belle, wondering just what to make of them. I first used them to organize a talk I gave about safety to the Texas Chemical Council and found them to work very well as a way to organize the talk. I was invited to speak about how we'd improved our safety at Belle. I was trying to figure out how to cover 5 years of complex work and make sense of it in the 20 minutes I'd been allotted for the talk. When I organized all we'd done to improve our safety performance around the ideas of Identity, Relationship and Information, everything fit beautifully and clearly together. I then realized that they fit perfectly with the work I'd been studying in John Bennett's Systematics on the three-fold nature of relationships.

It was quite important for me to see this connection between the work of those studying chaos and complexity and the work of Bennett in Systematics. When two formerly separate bodies of knowledge come together, I pay attention. I found that Bennett provides a lot of valuable thinking, the language and many models that we can use to talk and think about chaos and complexity.

I began to explore Identity, Relationship and Information (I, R, I) using Bennett's idea of three-fold relationships (see also Bennett 1977, Blake 1996 and Kuchinsky 1985). I consider I, R, I as the interaction of

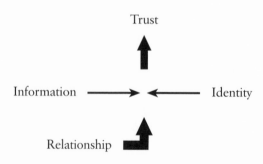

Figure 32 Developing Trust

130

three separate forces. While they interact all the time, for the purpose of the following analysis, I look at them in pairs to see what might be happening.

If we have an abundance of information, and a good sense of our identity and how we fit into the organization, then, as we begin to connect actively with each other and get to know each other, interdependence and trust emerges. This is illustrated in Figure 32.

If we have a good sense of our identity and how we fit into the organization, and have strong interdependent relationships, then as information becomes available, we can move into action. This is illustrated in Figure 33.

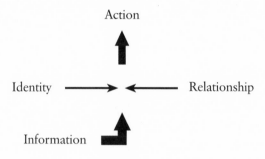

Figure 33 Developing Action

If we have an abundance of information and strong interdependent relationships, as we develop a clearer sense of our identity, of how we fit into the organization and can contribute, meaning emerges. This is illustrated in Figure 34.

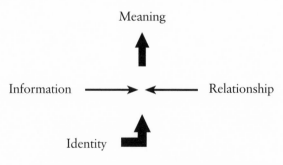

Figure 34 Developing Meaning

When Trust, Action and Meaning come together, people in an organization come alive. As we discover meaning in our work, new energy begins to flow and creativity pours forth. This does not happen automatically. Courage, integrity, commitment and deep caring are needed for it to happen. And then it becomes like a huge spring, pouring forth more and more meaningfulness for everyone. This is illustrated in Figure 35.

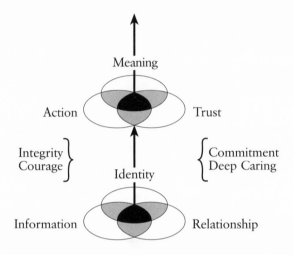

Figure 35 Meaningfulness

Other emergent phenomena are discussed in Chapter 10, which provide many more insights about the deeper patterns and processes that may be operating in an organization.

Conclusion

We can now have a much more complete picture after bringing together into our consciousness, the thinking, feeling and doing parts of ourselves by using these three archetypal processes. We have in the Process Enneagram, an intellectual map that enables us to see and think about a group and/or organization as a whole, and the connections, flow and dynamics within it. We have in the Rhythms of Change Process, a map of the flow of emotions that enables us to know and anticipate how we'll feel as we run the rapids in the river of our life's journey. And we have in the Emergence of Meaning Process, a map that enables us to see how energy and creativity can be released, and how we can move into action. With courage, integrity, caring and commitment we can come more alive.

This all connects back to the work of George Gurdjieff, Peter Ouspensky and John Bennett, who pioneered the idea of the three-fold nature of man with an intellectual center, an emotional center and a moving center. In their view, our work in life is to bring these into harmony as we move through our journey towards Unity. This is illustrated in Figure 36.

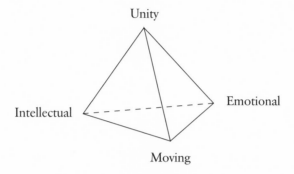

Figure 36 Journey Towards Unity

Encouraging the Journey Towards Unity in people transforms them and their organizations as they discover new purpose and meaning and develop the will to act. It's good for the business, because the results will get better fast, and it's good for the people who become much more alive again. The understanding and use of these processes moves us towards greater wholeness. They can give us guidance as we move into this new way of being. They are maps of a terrain that's largely unfamiliar to us. They help us to see the whole as well as the parts at the same time. They enable us to build the Bowl so we can simultaneously have both order and freedom. They enable us to open up and access the knowledge of the people in our organization. They create the conditions for self-organization to emerge. They enable us to bring coherence into our lives. These processes enable us to live our lives more fully and to participate in creating our future together.

Near the beginning of my journey, Peter Block gave me a boost when he told me that I was on the way to finding my soul. We can rediscover ourselves and at the same time, help make our organizations more effective and humane. In accessing ourselves this way, we also open up our capability to work on the deeper ecology and improve the health of all the systems we're embedded in, including our societies and the global environment.

By moving towards wholeness, we open up the four quadrants that Ken Wilber (1996) uses to look at our individual and collective lives from the inside and from the outside. He studied each of these from the most minute to the cosmic levels. There is a vast difference between our interior and exterior development. From the brief historical summary in Chapter 5, you can see how our focus for hundreds of years has been on the exterior parts of our lives as individuals and as groups. For the individual, for example, a doctor can tell us something about our various parts and how they work, but she or he cannot tell us much about our inner emotions and experiences. At the group level, sociologists describe our material and institutional forms, but they tell us little about our interior meanings, values and identities. This intense focus on the external, materialistic part of our world has resulted in a deep sense of spiritual loss. Figure 37 (Tim Dalmau 1998: private communication) provides some simple questions to illustrate the point. Now, as we move into the living systems paradigm, we can begin to recover this part of ourselves. The bringing together of the interior and exterior views was another step in my journey of healing.

	Interior View	Exterior View
Individual	Who am I? How might I be?	What am I? Tell me what to do.
Group	Who are we? How might we be together?	What are we? Tell us what to do.

Figure 37 Questions About Our Inner World

We have looked very carefully into the patterns and processes of organizations as living systems. By using the approaches to organizational change discussed here, much can be accomplished. But people ask, "Won't all this just disappear and be gone? How do we sustain the changes and learn to build on them?" In the next section, we'll address the issue of sustainability and the long-term health of our organizations.

SECTION 3

SUSTAINING THE WORK WE'VE DONE TOGETHER

· 9 ·

Sustainability: Measuring
the Health of Our Organizations

Moving Towards Wholeness and Health

In the previous Sections of this book we've seen how, in times of crisis, the people in our organizations come alive. We've also seen how we can use the patterns and processes of the Process Enneagram, the Rhythms of Change and The Emergence of Meaning and the Will to Act to help us engage each other and transform our thinking, feeling and acting. We now have good maps of these patterns and processes described earlier in the book.

We in the Center for Self-Organizing Leadership do very significant work with the people in organizations to help them engage the world around them and address, together, the need for constant improvement and change. As people move into these new waters, there is also a need for new tools to guide them and measure their progress. We must pay attention to different things in order to sustain the changes and help to create the more sustainable, healthy organizations we desire. While living all these stories about change at Belle, I continually searched for ways to measure and track the progress of the whole organization. Questions like: "How do we know we're making the needed changes?" and "Are we moving in the directions we intend?" as well as "Are we moving fast enough?" haunted me.

During the thirteen Berkana Dialogues and seventeen Self-Organizing Systems Conferences, I listened to Meg Wheatley, Myron Kellner-Rogers, and Fritjof Capra speak about the work of Humberto Maturana and the late Francisco Varela, and the theory of *autopoiesis* (see Maturana and

139

Varela 1992). After considerable exposure to their ideas and a lot of rumi-
nation about autopoiesis, I developed some ideas and tools that can help
us address these important questions. These tools have helped me to
develop a much deeper understanding of organizations, and in particular,
they have helped me understand how and why those organizations where
the people think and behave more coherently (a healthier organization)
are more sustainable than those where the people think and behave less
coherently (a less healthy organization).

Autopoiesis

Autopoiesis is the pattern of organization of living systems: it is the
defining characteristic of life (see Maturana and Varena 1992). An
autopoietic system has a sense of itself, its identity and its environment.
Such a system senses what is happening around it and decides to which
changes to respond and to adapt in order to maintain its identity. Thinking about systems constantly changing to maintain their identity is a paradox that took some time for me to work through.

An autopoietic system produces the structures that embody the pattern and processes of itself. Structure emerges from the processes. The
system takes in energy from the other systems around it and exchanges
free energy and entropy with those systems to evolve and maintain its
identity. On a moment by moment basis, the system makes adaptations,
and often must adapt again as the environment changes some more. The
ability to adapt is more important than the specific adaptations themselves.

In an autopoietic system there are four main aspects: 1) a structure to
the system, 2) an identity for the system, 3) an awareness of the changes
in the environment around the system and 4) the ability to decide what
changes it must make in itself to maintain it's identity.

Six Key Aspects of Organizations as Living Systems

Since organizations behave like living systems, we can consider them
to have many aspects of autopoiesis. Beyond the four aspects of autopoiesis
that were just mentioned, the people in an organization also have the
ability to self-reflect and to learn from their experience. Furthermore,
they have the ability to be open to new possibilities and to act on them as
they co-create their future. The fifth and sixth aspects are beyond Maturana

140

and Varela's original ideas of autopoiesis. By looking at these six simple aspects in an organization, we can begin to understand what's happening and develop some tools to help us as we move forward. We can also develop, from looking at these aspects, a sense of whether the system is moving towards becoming more life-like, sustainable and healthy, or if it's moving towards becoming more machine-like, less sustainable and less healthy.

The first aspect relates to the *kinds of structures* that people in an organization create as they move forward. In some situations, they will self-organize around the work and in others, more permanent yet fluid structures are put into place. These fluid structures include things like ad-hoc teams, task forces, etc. The fluid structures make the next adaptation much easier because the people in the organization do not have to tear down so much to make the needed change. Design decisions about the specific structures emerge from the nature of their work and from the Issues they engage.

The second relates to the *degree of flexibility that people have in their roles* in an organization and to the need for flexibility to enhance the success of the organization. Both affect the organization's ability to adapt quickly and enable people to step into leaderful roles as the changing conditions demand.

The third relates to the way people in an organization *sense* their environment and feel the *pressure for change*. Disturbances in the environment can be very unsettling or misunderstood. Some organizations choose to ignore these changes because they don't fit into their current thinking. Many times they behave as if they just want the changes to go away. Other organizations choose to pay attention to these changes and try to understand what's happening. They see the new information from the environment as an important part of their life.

The fourth relates to *how people in an organization decide* what, if anything, they want to change, and what impact they want to make on their environment. I was very sensitive to this particular aspect since I worked in the chemical industry for most of my life. I became very aware that just dumping chemicals into a hole in the ground, for example, was an awful practice, so we did a lot to find other ways of working in order to avoid doing this. We had to find ways to make our livings without ruining the environment for our children.

The fifth relates to *how people in an organization learn and improve* their ability to continually adapt. This means that the people must be quite conscious of what they are doing and be open to learning from their mistakes. Self-reflection takes us a step beyond Maturana and Varela's original idea of autopoiesis.

The sixth aspect relates to the people in an organization *being open to and acting on future possibilities and potentialities.* Even though we can't predict the future, we can imagine scenarios and develop a variety of possible actions that might help us as the future opens up to us. We can explore new opportunities for ourselves and for the organization. This aspect also takes us beyond Maturana and Varela's original idea of autopoiesis.

I have found that a concise way to look at these six aspects is to set them up in ratios where the numerator of each ratio represents a tendency indicating that the organization is becoming more alive, sustainable and healthy while the denominator represents the opposite sense of that particular tendency. It indicates that the system is becoming more mechanical, less sustainable and less healthy. All of the ratios apply to all levels of scale in organizations. The six sustainability ratios are the pattern for organizations as living systems.

The Six Sustainability Ratios™: An Overview

Ratio 1: The Formation of Structure

$$\frac{\text{Emergent and fluid design structures}}{\text{Rigid and hierarchical design structures}}$$

This relates to the types of structures that the people in the organization decide to form. As these structures emerge or are created, energy is expended by the system.

Ratio 2: The System's Identity and Sense of Itself

$$\frac{\text{Role flexibility}}{\text{Role rigidity}}$$

From one point of view, this relates to the identity and roles of individual people in the organization and how they see themselves as they continually confront the need to modify their behavior as they encounter their environment. From another point of view, it relates to larger parts of the organization at many different levels, and their self-perception as they confront their continually changing environment.

Ratio 3: Sensing the Environment and the Pressure to Change

Valuing differences, polarity and paradox
_____
Denial and suppression of differences, polarity and paradox

What do we sense is happening when an individual, a group, a larger segment of an organization, or a whole organization bumps into other systems? Everyone and everything is embedded in a variety of systems. To what do we pay attention? What do we decide to do to maintain our identity? It's the energy of these tensions that helps to drive the people in the organization and enables them to move.

Ratio 4: Deciding How to Change and the Impact We'll Have

Positive impact on the systems in which we're embedded
_____
Negative impact on the systems in which we're embedded

This relates to what we decide to do as we engage larger systems, and the world around us. Are our decisions helping or hurting the long-term health of our families, our businesses, our higher-ups, those who are responsible to us, our civic organizations and churches, our communities and our global environment? All the issues of ecology and how we interact and relate come into play here.

Ratio 5: Learning and Our Ability to Adapt

Self-reflecting and self-remembering
_____
Sleep walking, ignoring, compromising or burying problems

In our activities, we sometimes find ourselves doing well while at other times we find ourselves in some sort of a mess. With either success or problems, do we take the time to reflect on what we learned and how to improve, or do we just keep plowing along hoping that things will somehow get better? Because messiness and problems are related to entropy, learning from our problems and doing what we need to do to get better dissipates entropy to the environment. As the entropy, chaos, disorder and stress in an organization builds, do we stay with it and learn from it? Do we stay in the chaos until the tension becomes high enough to cause us to move to a higher level of order (a bifurcation point)? Do we learn to improve our ability to adapt, or do we ignore what's happening around us and try to avoid the chaos until the world around us comes crashing in, forcing change upon us? This entropic process can occur at any level in the system. It can occur in our own individual struggles, in the group's struggles, or even in the struggles of the whole system.

Ratio 6: Being Open to and Acting on Future Possibilities and Potentialities

Openness to and acting on future possibilities and potentialities

Closed and indifferent to future possibilities and potentialities

By openly sharing information in an environment where we can speak freely, explore and learn together, we can consider possibilities and potentialities in the moments, days, months and even years ahead. While we can't predict the future, we can co-create scenarios about it and develop strategies to address the possibilities. Based on our ethical foundations and knowledge of the Bowl, we can develop the fundamental skills we'll need, develop the structures that will most likely sustain us, keep our consciousness high so we can effectively sense our environment to detect early warning changes and stay lean and nimble.

We can also imagine what new possibilities may be open to us and begin to plan how we'll move into this new environment. In our conversations together in our organizations, we need to be constantly open to what might be, and then have the courage to act. In these conversations we co-create our future.

These six sustainability ratios are integral to all aspects of an organization. They are all fractal in nature. By paying attention to them, we see the shifts and get a sense of the direction of movement that we need to be mindful of as we move through change. As we engage change, we need to ask ourselves, "What is the impact we're having on these ratios?" Are we enhancing the numerators and strengthening our sustainability and health or are we enhancing the denominators and weakening our sustainability and health?

Since all the ratios are interdependent and linked, work and movement on any one of them will cause all the others to change to some extent.

A Deeper Exploration of the Sustainability Ratios

The six ratios are a simple, yet powerful way to look at the *impact of the changes* on our sustainability and health as we work through the Process Enneagram. Everything we do is connected to everything around us. It is prudent, therefore, to pay attention to the impact of our actions. We will now consider the content of these ratios in more detail.

Ratio 1: The Formation of Structure

Emergent and fluid design structures

Rigid and hierarchical design structures

Structure is necessary in organizations. "How much structure do we need?" and "What kind of structure do we need?" are important questions for management and others in the organization to ask. It is very important that our organizational structures are as flexible and adaptable as they can be, but they still must be strong enough to maintain the order and focus the Bowl requires.

Structures that emerge from and are embodied by the patterns and processes of the people in the organization we term "emergent and fluid design structures." People's Principles and Standards become alive and can be co-created when they become clearer about their Identity and Intention. Where there is trust and a free flow of Information, they will self-organize around the tasks at hand and do them. Some self-organized teams will be temporary, as the work needs flow and change; others will be longer lasting.

People self-organize in all organizations without exception. It tends to go underground and become covert in mechanistic, command and control organizations. Often, in these organizations, a lot of management effort focuses on trying to prevent and block it. In organizations consciously behaving as living systems, however, self-organization is openly encouraged and becomes a way of life for them. When the Bowl is strong, people can do amazing things by living and working this way. *Ideally, the only behavior that is not permitted is that which is expressly not permitted.*

Self-organization occurs at every level in organizations. We all need to be involved and participating in the organization to experience and understand this (see also Jaworski 1996). If we stand outside the organization reporting to us, as we do in the command and control mode, giving others orders to do things and then sitting in judgment on them, we won't experience the synchronicity and the opening of the flow of energy and creativity.

In addition to temporary emergent structures, there are other times when the people in an organization decide they need some structures that are more permanent than self-organized teams. It is quite appropriate for this to happen. When we do build this kind of organizational structure, like those built around a core function, around a set of special skills, or around a core value like safety or customer service, we need to keep as open and responsive as possible to the changing needs of the system. In trying to do this, one management team I worked with decided to open all of its staff meetings to anyone who wants to come. They provide an empty chair for anyone who wanted to speak, so that they could sit while making their contribution. Using this approach, they can be quite open and receptive to new information and keep changing to maintain their identity. The openness and fluidity of such a structure provides a basis for a high level of adaptability to the changing environment, and as a result, the organization is more sustainable and healthy.

Rigid and hierarchical design structures are what we more typically see in organizations operating out of the machine mode. These will usually take the traditional pyramidal form with several layers of command and control and silos of specialization, with rigid, impermeable barriers that keep people apart. In these, roles are narrowly defined and rules and procedures multiply. *The only behavior that is permitted is that which is expressly permitted.* Things are often done through power, coercion and fear. This highly structured and narrowly defined system will tend to be unresponsive to its environment. Control, reliability, stability and predictability are the desired goals. While these goals are what we want for machines, they don't work very well for people.

Again typically, most of the problems that command and control organizations face are seen to be a result of their organizational structure

146

and work flows. It's believed that if groups and people can just be moved into the right place and the work rearranged, then everything will work better. To solve the problem, the people at the top reorganize. Re-engineering is used in this way to try to solve problems, but the results are most often disappointing and the people are badly used.

These types of rigid structures make it very hard for an organization to be as responsive to the changing environment – as flexible and nimble – as it needs to be to continually adapt, and so, as a result, they are less sustainable and healthy. If we look again at the left side of Figure 8 The Leadership Dance shown in Chapter 2, we can see an illustration of the incoherence that comes from the over use of the operational management approach.

The appropriate use of operational management is an extremely important part of the *Leadership Dance*. In the healthiest organizations, the dance is centered in the *self-organizing leadership* process shown in the center column of Figure 8. When the dance is centered in the self-organizing leadership process, both the operational management and strategic leadership processes shown on the left and right sides of Figure 8 respectively must operate as well. It's not a situation of doing one or the other, but rather of dynamically balancing the processes by using them all and shifting emphasis as conditions and needs change.

Ratio 2: The System's Identity and Sense of Itself

$$\frac{\text{Role flexibility}}{\text{Role rigidity}}$$

The first ratio, The Formation of Structure, is concerned with the nature of *structure*. In this second ratio, we will focus on the behavior of the *individuals* in the organization, and why the need for more flexibility is critical to enhancing our organization's health and sustainability.

The living world in which we find ourselves is always changing and full of surprises. The organizations in which most of us live and work find this ever-increasing rate of change more and more of a challenge. Historically, we have built our organizations to be strong, stable, predictable, reliable and controllable. Our focus has mostly been on the organizational structures and how well they meet our needs. Most of the time, the changes that are made to try to survive and to control our destiny are focused on changing the structures to be more competitive and effective. We move people from one organizational box to another, like so many parts of a machine. While some of these re-organizations are needed, they often do not deliver the results the leadership desired, so another re-organization is made to try to get it right.

People can get lost in organizations, particularly ones going through multiple re-organizations. To protect themselves, they tend to get more and more fixed in their roles. They fixate in the place where they are most comfortable and have the best understanding of their place in the total scheme of things. When there is a lack of clarity about the organization's Identity, Intention and Principles and Standards, people are confused about how they fit in and what's really needed and expected of them. Often our individual identity is entangled in our assigned role and the title the organization has given to that role. When this is combined with the lack of Information about what's really going on, people are left in the dark (the Mushroom Principle). As re-organizations keep occurring, new roles and titles are imposed and people's sense of identity is changed by some overpowering external force. To have someone else messing with our identity does not feel so very good, and so we usually resist the changes being imposed. This resistance to change is often misunderstood by management, frustration grows and the organization begins to turn inward on itself. In this vicious cycle, our sustainability and health become weaker and weaker.

If, however, we've created an environment where Information flows freely, where our Identity, Intention and Principles and Standards are clear and where we have trust in each other, we can co-create our future together as we encounter the changing competitive environment. In this context, our individual identity is much more than our current role and job title; rather it becomes much more connected to the identity and success of the organization as a whole. Our ability to respond to the changing needs can grow in this context. In my experience, when people co-create their future, almost all the resistance to change melts away. A whole new level of being emerges.

We become more sustainable and healthy when we can move easily from one type of behavior to another: from leader to follower, follower to leader, clerical worker to administrative worker, mechanical worker to operations worker. We are more sustainable whenever we can move among various roles to meet the needs of the business and the customers, as long as we do not put the safety of our co-workers, the business or ourselves at risk. We will see the broad picture more clearly and our organization will be more competitive and faster in its response to a changing environment.

There is also a need to be able to move from one way of doing things to another, even within specific roles, in order to be better able to meet the needs of our stakeholders. We need to help everyone to do what is needed for the success of the organization. At home, I needed to share in the cooking and ironing when Claire, my partner and wife, was deeply engaged in her work as Site Services Superintendent at the DuPont Buffalo Plant, which makes Corian® and Tedlar®. At Belle, I picked up trash as I walked the Plant to help to improve the housekeeping and to set an example of role flexibility. There were times at Belle when operators and mechanics would move outside their job functions to help each other and the businesses. Of course, they needed to have the skills to help and to be able to do the work safely.

The ability to move easily without being stuck in our roles is critical. The most important key to being able to do this is to have a clearly established, understandable, workable, widely shared and co-created set of Principles and Standards of behavior in the organization. These Principles and Standards should be established with openness and trust and embedded in the organization through constant conversation and refinement. This is the work on points 0, 1, 4 and 2 in the Process Enneagram discussed in Chapter 7. People will have the confidence and trust to try new things and expand their roles, if we try to live up to the Principles and Standards of behavior as well as we can. A caring and committed leadership is so important here. While we are learning, we'll make mistakes. We need to own up to them and move on, letting everyone know we're trying our best to get better. As Stephen R. Covey points out (1989), it's not the first mistake that you make, it's the second one where you try to pretend that you didn't make the first one that gets people upset.

While I was still in the command and control mode at Belle, the idea of using mistakes as learning opportunities felt very risky to me. More often, I saw them as punishment opportunities. As we learned to live this new way, however, we found that learning as we went resulted in many important adjustments and fine tunings after the little mistakes. We did not ever have the major, disastrous mistakes I had been worried about when I was considering operating this new way.

The people in organizations need to have the capacity to modify their behavior as needs change. In a crisis such as those described in Chapter 1, the organization needs the skill and flexibility to operate in a very different way. Things do change in a crisis; the priorities shift from orderliness and control to effectiveness and nimbleness. Conditions change quickly and often unexpectedly. Those organizations and people that are the most sustainable are those that can live in a chaotic environment, continually adjusting and modifying what they're doing to help each other be effective. A chaotic environment is not to be confused with crisis management. Rank becomes less important because people do what's needed to get the job done and they keep on moving among the various roles to get it done as well as possible. Inflexible and slow organizations, where the people are stuck in their roles, are much less sustainable in the long-term.

Ratio 3: Sensing the Environment and the Pressure to Change

Valuing differences, polarity and paradox
_____
Denial and suppression of differences, polarity and paradox

People in an organization need to be closely linked to those in the larger organizations around them and to be sensitive to the changes in their environment. This is their Context to which they need to be connected, mindful and sensitive. They must be able to decide which changes to respond to in order to maintain the organization's Identity and to achieve its Intentions. They must learn to be very conscious and aware of the Context.

These changes in the environment provide some of the needed tension that helps drive the changes that we need in our organizations. These necessary changes show up in the Process Enneagram at point 8, Structure and Context, and inform and create new Issues at point 2.

In Chapter 6, I wrote about the nature of the boundary of the organization. I repeat this here because this idea is so important to understanding Ratio 3. When we at Belle were operating in the command and control mode, we felt swamped with all the work we had to do to meet all the demands being placed upon us by the external environment. Changes were pouring in from the Environmental Protection Agency, the Occupational Health and Safety Administration, as well as state and local regulators. The businesses always wanted more, faster. The customers wanted more, for less cost, with better service and quality. We had to become ISO 9002 Certified (International Standards Organization). We were pressed to adopt all the best practices that were in fashion. The Company made benefit changes rapidly. All these changes in the world outside of Belle came to us through the top of the organization at Structure and Context point in the Process Enneagram and created a host of new Issues.

The managers and supervisors wanted me to prioritize all these things. But in my experience, today's priorities will not be the same as tomorrow's; the world just doesn't sit still. As I mentioned earlier, in frustration, one day I asked, "How do you prioritize an avalanche?" In order to survive this onslaught, we pushed back a lot. Only a few of us at the top of the organization were in contact with these outside forces. We were trying to make sense of them, translate them for the people in the plant, and get everyone to do all the new stuff. We could not keep up, so we were frequently punished because our performance was not seen to be sufficient.

We didn't want any new information from the outside because it was just more trouble. I viewed the boundary of the organization as if it was like an eggshell, and we put a lot of energy into trying to keep people from the outside from penetrating it and upsetting things again. It's out of these painful experiences that I've concluded that an organization operating in the machine mode is simply unable to respond and be nimble enough to compete effectively in today's rapidly changing world. Interacting with the outside world primarily through a few people at the top of a hierarchy is neither healthy nor sustainable.

When we moved into the living system mode, however, when there was a good sense of the Bowl, when information, energy and creativity were flowing freely, everyone who needed to could interact with our stakeholders. We had operators on business teams, for example. We had adopt-a-customer teams with operators talking directly with the operators in our customers' plants. We had community ambassador teams, and teams who worked with the regulators on things like asbestos and the quality of the bolts we used.

Eventually, the boundary of the organization became like a semi-porous membrane through which information could flow much more effectively. Everyone became part of the process of making sense of what was happening and deciding what we should do. Our coupling to our environment (our Context) was stronger and more effective.

When the environmental factors are not crushing us, we can become much more open to what's happening, and draw energy and value from the environment. The glass now becomes half full. With a clear sense of who we are and what we want to become, with a strong set of Principles

151

and Standards and trust, that is, with a strong Bowl, we can be nimble and quick. We can explore the questions raised about the Tensions shown at Point 2 in the Process Enneagram (see Chapter 7).

We learn to live and function in all the chaos, ambiguity and paradox by entering the conversations, processing all the information and trying to make sense of it all. Just because we can't predict the future precisely doesn't mean we can't prepare effectively for the possibilities. Staying connected to our environment with the help of the Bowl enables us to make the decisions that we need quickly and to act without fear of getting lost in the world around us.

When we are open to what the changes in our environment teach us, new possibilities and potentialities are created that provide the energy for us to move. It's by close contact with our environment, searching for clues and deciding what to do quickly, that we become more sustainable and healthy.

When we are not connected closely to our environment and paying attention to what's going on, we get into trouble. We can ignore it, deny it, even try to explain it away, but none of these things stops the world from changing. The pressures keep building, and eventually we are confronted in such a way that we can ignore it no longer. As the man in the oil filter ad says, "Pay me now or pay me later." There have been many examples of organizations that have been hammered when they tried to ignore a changing environment; some have disappeared. When we choose to behave this way, our organizations become less healthy and sustainable.

Ratio 4: Deciding How to Change and the Impact We'll Have

Positive impact on the systems in which we're embedded

Negative impact on the systems in which we're imbedded

When we are sensitive to our environment and value the differences, polarity and paradox, we become much more aware of the impact we are having on it. As more and more people become involved at the interface, a much richer picture develops. We begin to understand how a narrow focus, such as only focusing on costs and earnings, can limit our ability to see. With more people at the interface, the more abundant the information and the interpretations of what's happening become. We become more inclusive and sensitive. We become more aware of our Context and our connectedness with each other, our communities and our environment. We become much more aware of the richness and importance of our relationships.

As this opens up for us, we need to ask many questions like: "What are we really doing?" and "How do our Intentions, our activities, and our products really impact the world around us?" We begin to realize that when we throw something away, we're just moving stuff around; there is no more "away." Our world is small and the space we have left is being spoiled. Dumping waste into a river, for example, doesn't make it go away. We begin to explore the Issues more deeply. Carl Frankel points out "Life is not only technical and objective, it is also soulful and subjective" (1998: 22). As our consciousness increases, we begin to heal the broken connections among nature, morals and mind (see also Wilber 1996: 276). We become aware of our materialistic orientation, its destructiveness and its unsustainability. We begin to move into the depth dimension of deep ecology.

When we put all our energy into pushing back at the world that's trying to close in on us, however, and do not value the differences, the polarity and paradox (Ratio 3), we remain insensitive and unaware of the systems in which we're embedded. We use very narrowly defined measurement systems to see our progress. As more and more of the financial power of the world rests in the major financial institutions, the focus is almost exclusively on earnings. Jeff Gates discusses this at length in his book, *The Ownership Solution* (1998). Our connections to each other, our communities and to the world as a whole are broken. In the process, we also become disconnected from our own souls. This is not sustainable or healthy for us.

Here is an example to illustrate this ratio. In the Risk Management example in Chapter 1, when we in the chemical plants in the Kanawha Valley were confronted with the request to share our worst-case scenarios, we had many possibilities open to us in how we could choose to respond. Because I had worked in Niagara Falls within the shadow of Love Canal, I knew that trying to stonewall the request would hurt both the plants and the community. Therefore, I chose a path that I hoped would address the issue while bringing the community together in a more sustainable way. Because we used the patterns and processes of the Process Enneagram described in this book, we were successful in helping to build a stronger community.

Ratio 5: Learning and Our Ability to Adapt

Self-reflecting and self-remembering

Sleep walking, ignoring, compromising or burying problems

Self-reflection and self-remembering are critical for people who want to learn and grow and for their organizations. Taking some time each week, say an hour, to reflect on what we are doing is critical. In business, we tend to use many sport analogies that have some utility, but often miss an important point. Sporting teams spend 90-95% of their time practicing and only 5-10% of their time in competition. In business, we want to compete 100% of the time. We all need some practice time. Self-reflecting time is much like practice time. The process can be quite simple. The US Army, for example, uses an "After Action Review" process after each major event, to try to understand what really happened and how they can do better next time.

At Belle, we would spend about an hour each week, in a Staff meeting, asking ourselves "How did we play as a team last week?" Each person was required to talk about the previous week's events, commenting on our play but not on the content. This often included either praise or criticism of various team members; I had to take my share in this process too. Each of us would then pick a number from 1 to 10 (10 being the best score) to summarize how we'd done. We would average these scores and keep them on the wall. This looked just like a statistical process control chart with upper and lower control limits. We could see the common cause and special cause variation in our performance and keep track of our learnings this way. The numbers were just a way to keep track of our progress. The important part of these sessions was the conversation about how to improve.

One of the teams we've worked with in Australia observed that by self-remembering and reflecting for just 6 months, they improved to the point where they can do now in 20 minutes in their staff meeting what used to take 3 to 4 months. There is no more lack of follow through, or lack of commitment. The game playing and politics have stopped. Now when they decide to do something, they are clear and they just go and do it.

Some organizations I've suggested this to complain that they are too busy to do it. This process is a bit like Stephen Covey's Seventh Habit, "Sharpening the Saw" (1989). I agree that this takes precious time in the beginning, but within a month at Belle, we were already ahead of the game and we just kept freeing up more and more time as our effectiveness improved. The Australian team's experience was similar to what we found at Belle. When we're too busy to reflect, when we ignore and bury stuff, we condemn ourselves to making the same mistakes over and over. I have heard it said that one form of insanity is doing the same thing repeatedly, expecting to get different results.

I have been in organizations where better results were desperately needed, and the management process consisted of raising their voices and exhorting us more and more. These managers did not realize that people in the organizations needed to change their patterns and processes in order to get better results. Even though the organization's patterns and processes were invisible to them, they were just as real as the chemical processes we were running. We knew that to improve the yields we had to change the chemical processes. I sometimes got a funny picture in my mind and wondered if these same folks would go stand in front of their cars and shout at them to get better gas mileage. Taking the time for self-reflection and learning is vital for us to improve our health and sustainability.

Ratio 6: Being Open to and Acting on
New Possibilities and Potentialities

Openness to and acting on future possibilities and potentialities

Closed to and indifferent to future possibilities and potentialities

Living in the patterns and processes of the Process Enneagram and being mindful of the sustainability ratios has resulted in the discovery of a sixth ratio. In the final stages of the preparation of this manuscript, Andrew Moyer and I met at a small gathering with Tony Blake near York, PA on April 12-14, 2002. There were 11 of us there to explore Systematics more deeply. In our conversations, Andrew discovered I was working on this manuscript and offered his help. I discovered that Andrew lived in London, Ontario, just 2 hours from my home in Niagara Falls, so it was quite easy for us to get together. In further discussions, I discovered that Andrew had a lot of experience and skills in book editing and publishing from his time as Manager of Claymont Communications, a small publishing business that had published a lot of Bennett's work. Andrew and I acted on these new potentialities and possibilities. We entered into a contract to prepare the book for publication. This relates to the numerator of Ratio

3, valuing new information from my environment.

During the course of this work together, we formed a team (related to Ratio 1 using an emergent structure). There are times when my role shifted from author and employer to student, and Andrew's role shifted from editor and contractor to teacher. This relates to role flexibility in Ratio 2.

Because of our work together, the quality of the book is significantly improved and so potentially, it will have a stronger and more positive impact on leaders and on the way our organizations work. This relates to Ratio 4 (change and impact).

In March 1999, in the early stages of the work on this book, Tom Petzinger who wrote for the Wall Street Journal as well as writing the book, *The New Pioneers* (1999), read a draft. He had two comments. He first said, "This is really important, new work for organizations and leaders." Then he said, "You write pretty well for a plant manager." We both laughed. With Andrew's help, the manuscript has come a long way.

In our work together, Andrew has asked many penetrating questions about what and why I said things in a particular way. He also pointed out gaps that I needed to fill. For me this has led to more reflection and the development of a clearer understanding of this work. This relates to Ratio 5 (learning deeply).

At one point, Andrew suggested that a sixth ratio was needed that related to new possibilities and potentialities. This book has many examples that recount times where I was deeply into new possibilities and potentialities, so making this explicit was a great idea. The stories in Chapter 1, for example, about saving the amines business and the Risk Management Planning, developed and evolved as they did because we were open to and acted on the new possibilities and potentialities. In being open to and acting on them, a stronger, healthier plant was the result in the amines story and a stronger, healthier community developed out of the Risk Management Planning story.

In working in Ratio 6, we have the opportunity to be open to and act on new possibilities and potentialities as we move into the broader issues of the sustainability of our communities and environment. For example, in Eugene, OR, Maggie Moore is already exploring and acting on the new possibilities and potentialities she has found in bringing a wide cross-section of people from the environmental community, business, the academic arenas and the regulators together to explore and to see our environmental and sustainability challenges from an entirely new perspective. New partnerships have already emerged from her pioneering work.

Questions to Get Us Started

These Sustainability Ratios provide patterns we all can use as we engage in the processes that bring our organizations to life. Each time we work through the patterns and processes of the Process Enneagram to make new changes or start new initiatives, we should ask ourselves: "Are we enhancing the numerators and becoming more sustainable or are we enhancing the denominators and becoming less sustainable?"

Questions like those found below are tremendously useful because they provide direct access to the reality of the situation. If we answer "Yes," then we are enhancing the numerators and becoming more sustainable, but if we answer "No," then we are enhancing the denominators and becoming less sustainable. In parentheses, I have put the number(s) for the ratio(s) that I think are related most strongly to the question. You may find that the questions relate to others as well. These questions are great places to begin conversations. As we answer each question, the follow-up questions should be: "How do we know this?" and "What's the evidence?" These follow-up questions are necessary to help the conversations open up for further learning and the discovery of new potentialities.

- Are we in direct conversation with our stakeholders? (2, 3, 4)
- Is information flowing freely? (1, 2, 3, 4, 5, 6)
- Are we becoming interdependent? (1, 2, 3)
- Are we really clear about who we are and what we're doing? (1, 2, 3)
- Are we running experiments? (3, 6)
- Are mistakes used as learning opportunities? (5)
- Do we understand the Bowl well? (5)
- Are people self-organizing around the work? (1, 2)
- Are we encouraging flexible structures and self-organization? (1)
- Are the boundaries permeable? (2, 3, 4)
- Are we partnering with our community? (4, 6)
- Are we encouraging networks? (2, 4)
- Are we being inclusive? (3)
- Do our roles add to the situation? (2, 3)
- Are we being servant leaders? (2, 3, 4)
- Are we encouraging leaderful behavior? (2)
- Are the core values clear? (5)
- Are we being open to the system? (3, 4)
- Do we know what the system is? (4)

- Are we breaking down barriers? (1, 2, 4, 5, 6)
- Are we using less linear thinking? (5)
- Is there less secretive behavior? (3)
- Is decision making more dispersed in the organization? (1, 2, 3, 4, 5, 6)
- Is hierarchy getting flatter? (1, 2)
- Are more people willing to say what's really happening? (3, 4, 5)
- Are new possibilities and potentialities opening up? (6)

These are just examples of the sorts of questions that you can use to be mindful and conscious of the ratios and sustainability.

The Six Sustainability Ratios and the Process Enneagram

It is important that we use the six Sustainability Ratios to help pay attention in all the decision-making. So, when Map 2 (our future state) and successive Maps of the Process Enneagram are being *developed*, each decision about change at any of the 9 points needs to be tested against the guidance these ratios provide. It's important to keep asking ourselves if we are moving towards a more sustainable future or towards a less sustainable one with each decision that is made. For example, encouraging teams to self-organize around the Issues and decide on and do the Work is leading towards a more flexible structure and more sustainability. On the other hand, if a more rigid organizational structure is set up to address some specific Issue, it's important for people to understand this and to be very conscious that they are moving towards less sustainability so that they can do other things that will counterbalance this trend.

Constant, subtle adjustments are needed to move successfully into the future together. When Voyager Space Craft 2 went on its journey in August 1977 to Pluto and Uranus, the engineers knew that they were moving into unknown and uncharted areas. They knew that they needed to be able to make adjustments on the trip as unforeseen conditions emerged. I have been told that the craft was off course over 90% of the time, but was put back onto the path with many fine, subtle adjustments. The mission was highly successful and wonderful pictures of these planets came back to the earth. Its mission continues today as it moves further into the outer reaches of space. This same principle applies as people co-create their future and move into it together.

158

Making constant subtle adjustments as we test our decisions against these ratios is a critical sustainability process. The people on a team need to talk honestly together about how they are living up to the new Principles and Standards that they developed so they can fulfill their Intention. Being honest is not a license to be mean, but rather an important and courageous attempt to talk about the things that are important to them and to learn and grow together. *This is the primary key to sustaining progress as people move forward into their co-created future.*

Without taking the time to self-remember and self-reflect, people will fall back into the patterns and habits of Map 1. This is illustrated in Figure 18 (see p.65), The Workshop Process Schematic. Map 2 must be posted and kept visible to everyone so they can remind each other of the agreements they've made and talk about them. As new insights about their journey emerge, the team members need to write them onto Map 2; this keeps it alive and developing.

When Map 2 gets too cluttered with new things, and/or as new potentialities emerge and develop, people need to develop Map 3 and so on and so forth. For example, the Leadership Team of the City of Niagara Falls is working on the fourth iteration of their Map. Using the six ratios at each decision point in the development and use of the Process Enneagrams helps us to move together into a more coherent and sustainable future.

In keeping the Process Enneagram alive and developing, in using the sustainability ratios as dynamic tools, as in the Voyager Space Craft example, people on a team have constant and active guidance. This evolving sequence of Process Enneagrams is their *dynamic strategic plan*, which is constantly adapting and changing as they move into the future. In using the six ratios to be mindful and conscious of the kinds of decisions they are making, they can co-create a more coherent and sustainable future.

On a deeper theoretical level, the six ratios relate to the points and lines of the Process Enneagram in specific ways. This will be explored and developed in the future with Andrew Moyer.

Mathematical Implications of the Six Sustainability Ratios

As I experimented with these six ratios, I discovered that there are mathematical implications that are useful in qualitatively measuring the health and sustainability of an organization. I am sure that the six ratios interact and influence each other, and that an organization's sustainability relates to all of them and their interaction. We can set up a relationship, therefore, which shows that sustainability is related to the product of the ratios.

Sustainability is related to:
Ratio 1 x Ratio 2 x Ratio 3 x Ratio 4 x Ratio 5 x Ratio 6

Work on the numerators of the ratios tends to move people in an organization towards more flexibility, towards becoming more aware of their environment, towards making intentional changes to preserve their identity, and towards more adaptability, learning and development. Coherent organizations, where the energy and creativity are bubbling up, spend most of their time and efforts doing those things described by the numerators. These are organizations that operate far from equilibrium and behave as if they are living systems. Largely, they are centered in the Self-Organizing Leadership processes shown in Figure 8. They are focused so that 60-80% of their processes and activities are in the numerators and only 40-20% in the denominators.

The denominators of these ratios tend to move people in an organization towards less flexibility, towards becoming less aware of their environment, towards less adaptability and more rigidity, and away from growth and learning. Incoherent organizations, which are near equilibrium, spend most of their time and energy doing those things described by the denominators. They are focused so that only 20-40% of their processes and activities are in the numerators and 80-60% in the denominators.

I am sure that for any given organization, the ratios will be relatively consistent with each other. Since the ratios are all related, finding very large differences from one ratio to another is unlikely. In organizations like those in the example of the coherent organization described above, for instance, all the numerators of the ratios will probably be in the 60-80% range.

We should look at the ratios as tendencies and use qualitative judgments about their approximate values. For the purposes of this analysis, however, it's useful to look at them as if we know them more precisely. This way we can see the mathematical implications much more clearly. In actual use, the qualitative judgments will behave in ways similar to these hypothetical examples.

Let's suppose that there is an extreme command and control organization that is spending only 10% of it's time in the work related to that described in the numerators and 90% of it's time in the work related to that described in the denominators. Below you will find the product of the ratios.

10%/90% x 10%/90% x 10%/90% x 10%/90% x 10%/90% x 10%/90%
= 0.11 x 0.11 x 0.11 x 0.11 x 0.11 x 0.11 = 0.00000177

In these hypothetical examples, I assume that each ratio is the same, and therefore, I have raised the ratio to the 6th power to develop the product of all six of them. By looking across the range of ratios, we can develop the following table:

Ratio	The Ratio to the 6th Power
10%/90%=0.11	0.00000177
20%/80%=0.25	0.000244
30%/70%=0.429	0.00623
40%/60%=0.667	0.088
50%/50%=1.0	1
60%/40%=1.5	11.39
70%/30%=2.33	160
80%/20%=4.0	4096
90%/10%=9.0	531441

One implication that we can draw from this is that we need to work on all the ratios and not just focus on one or two. Since the ratios multiply out, a higher number in only one or two of them is pulled down by the others that have not improved. I have seen many fine conferences and courses offered where the focus would change only one or two of the ratios, but it seems to me that this is not sufficient. Courses focused on improving creativity in an organization, for example, may impact ratios 5 and 6 positively, but the others that are not being addressed will prevent positive change from occurring. This may be one of the main reasons that so many change efforts have not worked as well as people had hoped.

We can derive other implications from the information in the proceeding table if the data are plotted graphically. Since the range of numbers for the Ratios raised to the 6th power is so large, a useful way to present the data is to use their logarithms. Below are two graphs, one that looks at changes occurring over consistent time intervals and another where the time intervals vary in length.

In the first graph, the changes are represented as if they occurred over time intervals of equal lengths. As you can see, the curve is relatively straight and climbs steeply. A new organization or one that is very dynamic, like a sales force in a new high-tech company, could experience changes rapidly. If they go up the curve too fast, they could move so quickly that they may be unable to maintain their identity and will evolve into some, new, emergent organization. This may be good or bad depending on what they want. On the other hand, if they go down the curve too quickly, they can get into deep trouble, perhaps imploding and destroying the organization.

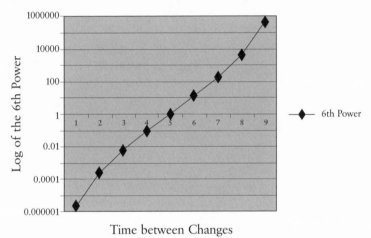

Figure 38 Log of the 6th Power vs. Equal Time Periods

In the second graph (see Figure 39), the changes occur rapidly at the beginning and the end, but take much longer in the middle part of the curve. An established organization with lots of assets will behave more like this, as will an organization engaged in large-scale manufacturing where the processes change slowly. Their inertia will be such, that the rate of change is likely be slow in the middle of the curve. As they move along the curve, such an organization must pay considerable attention to whether they are moving up or down the slope.

Changes in living animal populations behave this way. Changes in cultures also behave this way. They can go for long periods with relatively little change being noticed since they do not change in a linear fashion.

They move slowly along the middle of the curve, but at the extremes, the changes occur very rapidly.

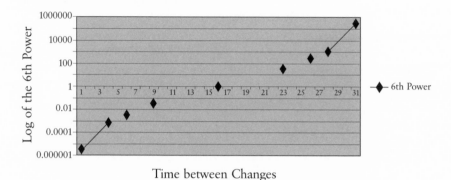

Time between Changes

Figure 39 Log of the 6ᵗʰ Power vs. Variable Time Periods

If an organization is becoming more rigid, less competitive and less sustainable, they are likely to be moving down the middle part of the curve where little change is obvious. The organization can make adaptations to compensate for becoming less sustainable, but if they are not paying attention, they can reach the part of the curve where the slope suddenly becomes much more steep and dangerous. This often catches people by surprise. The sudden collapse of organizations and cultures, however, is well documented. This curve shows how and why this might happen and why we often feel so surprised. At the point of collapse, the rate of decline and the inertia in the organization may make it impossible for it to survive.

If the organization moves too far up the slope, their identity will begin to evolve rapidly (new forms will emerge). I have seen some organizations get into this part of the range, become frightened and pull back; new possibilities can easily be lost when this happens. Early on in the organizational development efforts in parts of DuPont, I saw this happen to us.

The extremes at both ends of the curve are places of hazard for the organization, so a way to pay attention to what is happening in the central part of the curve is critical. We can use the Sustainability Ratios as an effective way to look for clues and get a sense of what's happening in this middle range. The clues can show whether the organization is moving up the curve or down it. They can also show something about rates of change. For me as a manager, knowing where I was on the curve and having a sense of the real rate of change and balance was important.

The next chapter provides specific information about how we can pay attention to emergent behavior, and how I used ideas like these to lead and guide our work at the Belle Plant.

· 10 ·

Building Sustainability:
The Leadership Dance

Introduction

Effective leaders need to have a solid understanding of their business. They need to know business practices like marketing, sales, accounting, manufacturing, human resources, legal and regulatory requirements. Furthermore, they need an understanding of the basic technology that they use in their business, things like chemistry, agriculture, aviation, etc. The business practices and technologies are the visible aspects of work that we see every day. If we consider a tree as a metaphor for an organization, these things relate to the leaves, branches and trunk. This vital work is not the focus of this book.

Effective leaders must also be able to understand and use *Self-Organizing Leadership* and the *Leadership Dance*. These processes tend to be the less visible and are often unseen aspects of the way people in organizations work. *This profoundly important work is the focus of this book.* When people in organizations learn to use *Self-Organizing Leadership,* they often see their effectiveness improve by 30-40%. In the tree metaphor, these things relate to the roots. They are usually unseen and are often ignored and abused.

The main ideas presented in this book are summarized in Figure 1 Congruence Criteria for a Living Organization. The three key features of an organization viewed as a living system are illustrated. These key features are its Structure, Pattern and Process (see Capra 1996: 161).

Structure includes the tangible things like supply chains, buildings and products as well as the less tangible things like hierarchy, networks and teams. The Pattern we can work with consciously is composed of the group of six sustainability ratios. The most effective Process I know uses the three archetypal processes: the Process Enneagram, the Rhythms of Change and the Emergence of Meaning and the Will to Act.

Where do people begin? How can people step into this way of leading? In the Center for Self-Organizing Leadership we coach and help leaders to become more effective and to move into the Leadership Dance. We focus particularly on the four most important pieces of this work. These are:

- developing more flexibility in their roles;
- paying attention in a different way to what's happening around them and thus being able to learn from and respond to what is emerging;
- developing measurement criteria and tools so that they can be sensitive to the potential impact of the changes on and in the organization and their environment, and
- encouraging them to move relentlessly towards building more sustainable organizations and a more sustainable world.

Role Flexibility Within Leadership

Arguably, the most important and challenging role in any organization is that of leading. What's the right style or styles? Who makes the decisions? Is participation or command and control the most appropriate in a particular situation? It is important that people in an organization understand that the necessity for leaders to move among different roles and styles is important for the organization's survival, and that moving among roles and styles is not a sign of weakness in leadership or a lack of clarity or purpose. A flexible leadership style is a very complex mode of operating for an organization and its people. But, if Map 2 is visible and used and people's behavior is grounded in strongly held Principles and Standards that have been co-created by them, everyone will learn to function quite well. At first, when you try to lead with this kind of flexibility, it will feel a little disorganized and chaotic, but it is an important way for us to achieve maximum leadership effectiveness.

As organizations first begin to move through the transition from the machine mode to the living systems one, the message for leaders is often seen as: *"Stop being top-down, autocratic drivers and become relationship builders, team builders and do everything by consensus."* There seems to be a feeling that if the leaders don't do everything in the participative way, they have somehow abandoned the "new religion." We all have a strong tendency to view the world in a polarized way; we think it's either command and control or total participation. However, *it is not either/or, but rather, both/and!* You'll remember this was illustrated in The Leadership Dance in Figure 8.

This challenge of role flexibility within leadership is extremely complex. As we become more flexible and mobile in our roles, the people around us begin naturally to expand their roles, taking on more responsibility for the well being of the whole organization. This can lead to some really interesting surprises, but we don't need to be fearful of having the organization fall apart. When people have a good shared sense of the Bowl, the identity and culture of the organization, then increased flexibility and expanding roles becomes quite effective. There were many nights when I lay awake worrying about this, but as I came to really understand the power of the idea of the Bowl, I realized that people will stay in the Bowl and that we were okay.

Here are two examples to illustrate the idea of role flexibility. One morning at Belle, Becky Dixon called me to tell me how upset she was over a morning talk show she had listened to on the way to start her 6 A.M. shift. The two guys who were the hosts of the show were telling everyone that our plant was causing a lot of pollution. They had noticed our steam plumes and thought they were toxic clouds. Becky, an operator, who was also on our environmental teams knew this was not the case, so she was quite upset by what they were saying and the negative impact they might have on the Plant. She then went on to tell me that she'd called the talk show people, and invited them to the plant. They were scheduled to come the following Monday for the afternoon. She had arranged for me to meet with them for an hour at 1:00 P.M. and give an overview of our plant's environmental work and performance. She also had several other visits set up for them so they could meet people and learn more about what we were doing. She had the whole thing laid out and was in charge. It was one of the best visits we ever had. These talk show hosts spent the next few weeks telling their listeners about all the good things we were doing and the neat people they'd met. As Becky moved into her leadership role, I moved into the role of a follower. This fluid and dynamic leadership dance takes a lot of attention and a high level of consciousness of what's happening around you.

Another example that illustrates clearly a different aspect of the Leadership Dance happened when I was first assigned as Plant Manager at the DuPont Belle, WV Plant. Our safety performance was 10 times worse than the DuPont Co. average injury rate. While I am a very strong advocate of participatory management and involvement, I drove safety from the top, using all I'd learned about using fear and coercion to get the results we needed quickly. I felt that I had to force the organization to move quickly so that we'd stop hurting people and that, in this case, the ends justified the means. The leadership group was so divided and contentious that I decided to just drive right through them. While the process was tough, it worked! Over the next 18 months our injury rates dropped by about 85% to the Company average injury rate.

I let people know what I was doing and why, but they were still confused until we'd gained enough experience and our performance had improved to the point where we could listen to and trust each other. As soon as our standards were reestablished and our performance had improved significantly, I backed away from the heavy-handed, top-down approach. In backing off and moving into a more participatory mode, our performance got even better, to the point where we had between 0 and 3 injuries a year over the next 10 years (about half the Company rate). We could never have achieved the safety and other successes we did without both the total involvement and commitment of everyone and the initial top-down approach. Their caring, their energy and creativity enabled the superior performance that developed after a number of years of working together this way and we achieved really world-class performance. I would still occasionally have to terminate someone for a gross safety violation. I never moved from my absolute insistence on high safety standards. We functioned with multiple leadership styles. This can be done if you are operating out of deeply shared principles. The fundamental principle we operated from, one that was well understood from many conversations together, was this:

"It is not okay to work at a place where it is okay to
hurt people. We do not have a right to make our living
here unless we care enough to do it safely."

This is not an ego driven principle; it came out of our deep need to care about and help each other. We had to be authentic to operate this way; all the cards were face up on the table!

As I stated above, living by our Principles and Standards is basic to this way of leading. Safety Principles and Standards had to apply equally to everyone. This was true for all our other Principles and Standards of behavior as well. As Plant Manager, I was under the same rules as everyone else. In my first year at Belle, for example, we did away with special parking for management people, including me. The only preferred parking was for visitors, the handicapped and those who'd worked with no on-job injuries and no off-job lost time injuries for 25 years. About 15 people qualified at the start, but it took me 4 more years to earn my safety spot because I'd had a recordable injury early in my career in the laboratory. I had to keep sharing the information, listening, trying to keep the deep conversations flowing, admitting my mistakes, trying to improve and change myself. I had to put my ego aside and keep reminding myself to do what's right for the organization, always.

As individuals and as organizations, we need to be very conscious of the idea of role flexibility and help everyone in the organization understand what it is all about if we want to strengthen our organization's sustainability and health. In every decision we make, we need to keep asking ourselves: "Are we strengthening the numerators of the ratios or are we strengthening the denominators?" While you don't learn this overnight, you can begin the journey. Never give up; learn as you go! This is a vital element on the road towards sustainability.

Emergence

In the Leadership Dance, we live in an environment where a lot of things are happening all the time. People interact with each other, with the immediate environment of equipment and things, with the external world of customers, competitors and neighbors. They interact with the patterns and processes of behavior like those illuminated by the Process Enneagram and experience the Rhythms of Change. In all these interactions, novelty is created, new things happen. We can't predict just what these will be because so much is going on. Who can establish just what caused what? We can call this "emergence."

In the Leadership Dance, a high level of consciousness is needed. It's critical to pay attention to what's going on and emerging. Leaders play a key role in setting the conditions embodied in the Principles and Standards *actually* in use. Helping to set the conditions is essential leadership work. In the following descriptions of emergence from self-organizing, operational management and strategic leadership processes, the dynamics of the processes are held still so we can illustrate what's happening. The outcomes will vary depending on the conditions. In actual experience, the processes are all operating and the emphasis on which one we are using shifts as the circumstances change. This is *The Leadership Dance.*

In Chapter 8 the Emergence of Meaning was described. Meaning emerges as we work with Identity, Relationship and Information. This is summarized in Figure 35.

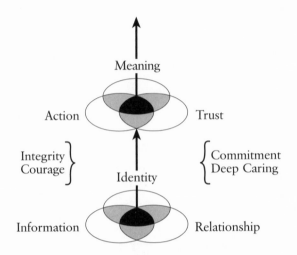

Figure 35 Meaningfulness

Self-Organizing Processes lead to high levels of coherence because we know who we are (Identity), we have reasonably healthy relationships and a good number of strong connections with others both inside and outside the organization (Relationship), and information flows freely so everyone has access to the information they need to do their work (Information).

This self-organizing process is illustrated in the center column of Figure 8 first shown in Chapter 2. When this Self-Organizing Leadership Process is connected to the work of the organization, coherence develops and we have healthy self-organization.

We need to be watchful, however, of the negative side of Self-Organizing processes. It is very important to understand that in self-organizing, the process at points 0, 3 and 6 where Identity, Relationship and Information interact is strongly connected to the process of work where points 1, 4, 2, 8, 5 and 7 where Intention, Principles and Standards, Issues, Structure and Context, Work and Learning interact. If the self-organizing process disconnects from the critical work process of the organization, people tend to sink in to a destructive kind of self-involvement. They will go ever

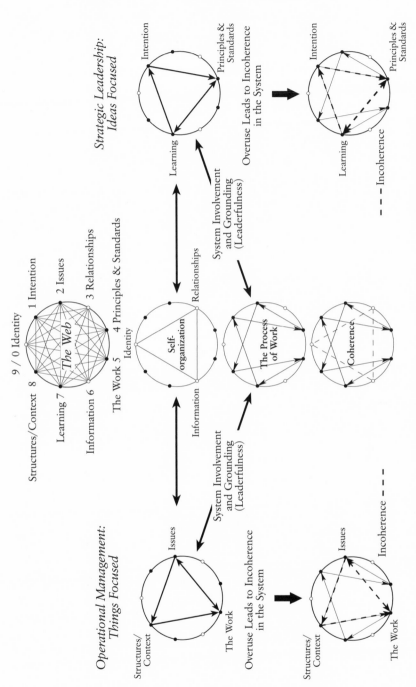

Figure 8 Overview of Living Systems Patterns and Processes: The Leadership Dance

more deeply into exploring Identity and focus too much on building deeper Relationships and become over involved with the details of Information for its own sake.

On reflecting further about Figure 8, it is apparent that the Operational Management Processes (on the left side of Figure 8) and the Strategic Leadership Processes (on the right side of Figure 8) also have emergent properties associated with them. Operational management is concerned with the specific actions we are taking or going to take to do a particular piece of work. Strategic leadership is concerned with exploring the realm of possibilities for actions in the future.

As was mentioned above, the processes are artificially separated so we can see them more clearly. As the reader well knows, these all happen to some degree all the time. There is a constant shifting in emphasis in response to the dynamic environment. In each organization, therefore, the mix of the ever-changing, emergent properties will be unique. High levels of awareness and mindfulness are needed to engage successfully in the Leadership Dance.

Emergence from Operational Management Processes

When we consider the Operational Management Process, we evoke Points 2, 5 and 8 on the Process Enneagram. Thus, we focus on the interaction of Issues, Work and Structure and Context.

The Healthy Side of the Picture

When we work in our organizations centered in the healthy Self-Organizing Processes connected to real work and when we involve people and build the Identity and Relationships and the Information flows abundantly, then *Trust, Action and Meaning* will emerge (Chapter 8). But as I showed in the safety example, when we are centered in the Self-Organizing Processes most of the time, there will be occasions when we do need to be directive about a particular Issue and use Operational Management Processes as part of the Leadership Dance. When people function in highly coherent ways and co-create their future, as is done in healthy self-organization, properties like those following will emerge.

If we have Work that is clearly focused on fulfilling our Intention and our Issues are examined, then, as our Structure self-organizes, *a Sense of Urgency* will emerge. If we have a self-organizing Structure and the Work

172

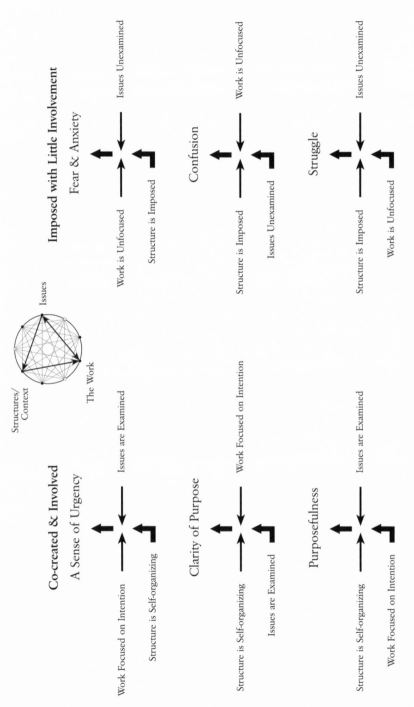

Figure 40 Emergence From Operational Management Processes

is clearly focused on fulfilling our Intention, then, as we examine the Issues, a *Clarity of Purpose* will emerge. If we have a self-organizing Structure and the Issues are examined, then, as the newly developing Work is focused on fulfilling our Intention, *Purposefulness* will emerge.

The Unhealthy Side of the Picture

If we use the Operational Management Processes with an overemphasis on control (becoming command and control) without engaging the people, impose the Structure and the Work, and do not examine the Issues, the level of incoherence will be very high. Most people will not know what's going on, so properties like those following will emerge.

If the imposed Work is unfocused and our Issues have not been examined, then, as a Structure is imposed to do the Work, *Fear and Anxiety* will emerge. If the Structure is imposed and the imposed Work is unfocused, then, as the unexamined Issues come into play, *Confusion* will emerge. If the Structure is imposed and the Issues are unexamined, then, as unfocused Work is imposed, *Reaction and Struggle* will emerge.

This is illustrated in Figure 40 on page 173.

Emergence from Strategic Leadership Processes

When we consider the Strategic Leadership Processes, we highlight the relationship among Points 1, 4 and 7 on the Process Enneagram. The interaction of Intention, Principles and Standards and Learning becomes most important.

The Healthy Side of the Picture

When we work in our organization centered in the healthy Self-Organizing Processes, when we involve people appropriately and build the Identity and Relationships and when the Information flows abundantly, then an enhancement of *Meaning* will emerge. While we operate from the center column of Figure 8 most of the time, there will be occasions when we will need to use the Strategic Leadership Processes as part of the Leadership Dance. In this case, because people function in highly coherent ways and co-create their future, properties like those following will emerge. If we are open and Learning and have developed clear Intentions, then as we develop our Principles and Standards together, *Hope* will emerge.

174

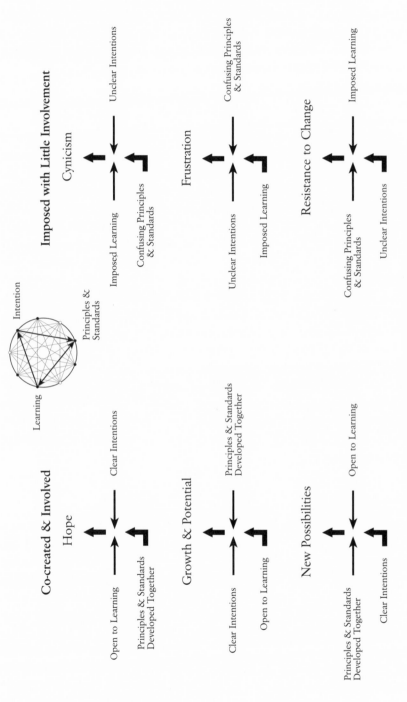

Figure 41 Emergence From Strategic Leadership Processes

If we have developed clear Intentions and have also developed our Principles and Standards together, then, since we are open and Learning, an increase in *Growth and Potential* will emerge. If we have developed our Principles and Standards together and are open and Learning, then, as we become clearer on our Intentions, *New Possibilities* will emerge.

The Unhealthy Side of the Picture

If we are overusing the Strategic Leadership Processes, however, with high levels of control and without engaging the people, the imposed Intention is unclear, the Principles and Standards are confused and the Learning is imposed, the level of incoherence will be high, and properties like those following will emerge.

If Learning is imposed and the Intention is unclear, then, as we engage our work with confusing Principles and Standards, *Cynicism* will emerge. If the Intention is unclear and the Principles and Standards are confused, then as Learning is imposed, *Frustration* will emerge. If the Principles and Standards are confused and Learning is imposed, then as we are faced with unclear Intention, *Resistance to Change* will emerge.

This is illustrated in Figure 41 on page 175.

The analysis of what can happen in our organizations when we notice these emergent properties can give us important clues to what to pay attention to in our own mode of leadership. If we are mindful and see these kinds of things happening, we can continuously make the adjustments in how to engage effectively in the Leadership Dance.

Measuring the Whole System

In addition to role flexibility and paying attention, leaders must have a good sense of how the organization as whole is doing and how fast they are moving. While I was the Plant Manager at the Belle Plant and we were well into our journey, we sensed that things were going very well. Many Plant units were running better. There were fewer disciplinary problems. Safety and environmental incidents were declining. There were fewer quality problems. Our overall sense was that we were doing a lot better, but the only data we had was on the parts. How was the whole of the enterprise running?

I had just read Bart Kosko's book *Fuzzy Thinking* (1993) and H. Richard Priesmeyer's book *Organizations and Chaos* (1992) and I began to wonder if we could use fuzzy (but not sloppy) thinking to measure our system. Kosko talks about qualitatively measuring things to see if they are about right, things like asking if the carpet is clean enough after we've run the vacuum cleaner over it. Priesmeyer talks about chaos and looks at how things impact each other in an organization. In his examples, he looks at earnings, investment and growth of organizations. I began to wonder what we'd see if we tried to get some qualitative sense of the impact on the organization that had resulted from all the changes we had made over the past 5 years. We needed something simple that would lend itself to a fuzzy thinking approach.

We decided to try to make judgments of the impact of all the plant-wide changes we'd made over the previous 5 years. We looked at these in three aspects (see Figure 42 below). The first one we looked at was how we felt the changes had impacted our teams and the way we worked together (i.e. organizational effectiveness). The second aspect measured the impact on our skills and learning (i.e. functioning effectiveness). The third was the impact on our business performance (i.e. business effectiveness). Each of the eight people on the leadership team was asked to give their judgment on the changes in each of these three aspects. We used a scale ranging from +3 for the most positive impact to -3 for a strong negative impact. We used 0 for no impact. We then averaged the scores for the impact of each change on each aspect, and thus each change had three different scores. We then simply added the scores up algebraically for each impact area and plotted them on a graph.

To see if this qualitative approach had any real merit, there were some tests we decided to use to try to see if things really hung together. From an intuitive perspective, one would expect that the way we worked together (organizational effectiveness) and our functional skills would show stronger improvements than the business performance (business effectiveness) at the beginning of our change efforts. The graph shows that this is exactly what happened. At some point, however, you'd expect the curves to cross, with the business impact curve becoming the strongest. The graph shows that this happened as well.

There should also be some key places where we could relate significant changes in this graph to the business results. While the changes that show on the small version of the graph aren't very clear, the larger versions of the graph show an inflection point occurred in February 1991, which is in the same quarter that our earnings curve reversed and turned upwards.

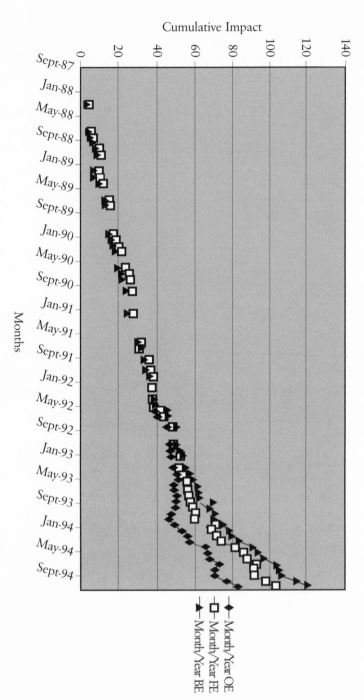

Figure 42 Cumulative Impact of the Changes at Belle

The curves also show that we were getting into a significant problem in early 1993, when there were a number of negative things hitting the plant from the outside. We had lost several potential projects to sister plants and there were some difficult employee relations issues, such as when the Company tried to get its health insurance costs under control (this needed to be done). We saw the negative things manifest in the dip in the organizational effectiveness curve, which represents the impacts on the way we worked together. We were concerned that with the curves diverging, we might not be able to sustain our momentum. Later in the year, we were able to pull that this curve back onto an upward trend. To do this, we communicated extensively, spent time with our people helping them understand where we were, and then fortuitously, we got several new projects as well.

This attempt to develop a way to measure the whole did give us some very useful insights. We could now get a sense of the progress of the whole system and the balance of the major components within the system. When we did this analysis for the first time in the fall of 1992, after we had sensed that we were doing a lot better, we discovered that the inflection in the curve and its relationship to the positive change in the earnings curve had actually occurred 18 months earlier in 1991.

We were criticized by some for using this unusual, qualitative approach based on our subjective judgments. I was not particularly disturbed by this because every business decision I have ever been involved in has had qualitative and subjective aspects. We never have all the information we need or want, but we have to decide anyway.

Because we were using subjective measures and fuzzy math, we kept testing our thinking against the external environment to see if the thinking, the behavior and results corresponded. Since then, I've tested this thinking with a lot of people and, so far, it makes sense to everyone. Furthermore, as we made these changes at Belle, our performance continued to improve and the plant's performance just kept getting stronger. In the organizations where I'm working now, like the City of Niagara Falls, NY, the numerators are getting stronger, and the organization is becoming more adaptable and resilient with better performance on the one hand and stronger teamwork on the other.

Another way in which I tried to measure the whole was to relate all the changes we had made to the Sustainability Ratios. I did this after I'd left Belle and had developed the ratios. A mechanic from Belle, Eddie Long, and I met at an Association for Quality and Participation meeting, and over lunch we did the analysis. We had worked closely together while I was at Belle, and he had gone through all the changes with me. For each of the changes we'd made, we asked ourselves whether the change had a positive (score + 1), neutral (score 0) or negative (score -1) impact on the Sustainability Ratios.

For example, in going to teams across the plant, we felt that this improved our structural fluidity, role flexibility, and valuing differences (score +3). It caused us to spend a lot of time looking inward trying to get the teams up and running so the impact on the way we interacted with the systems around us was negative (score -1). We didn't feel it had any impact on the self-reflection ratio (score 0). So, for the change in moving to teams, the net score was a +2. We simply added the scores up. Going to teams: Fluid structures (+1) + Flexible roles (+1) + Valuing differences (+1) + Impact on the systems around us (-1) + Self-reflection (0) = +2.

I found it quite remarkable that Eddie and I had pretty consistent scores. I don't think that I particularly influenced his answers because I was no longer his plant manager. Eddie and I had a very open relationship, so that we could and did disagree on things without it getting in the way of our relationship.

We averaged our scores for each change, added them up and plotted them on the graph shown in Figure 43.

This curve has a similar shape to the cumulative impact curves in

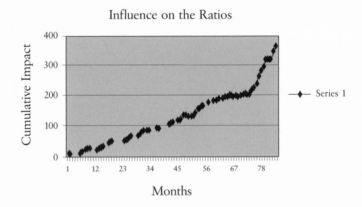

Figure 43 Impact of the Changes at Belle on the Ratios

Figure 42. It's another way to see movement and the rate of change of the whole. It is less complicated to prepare, but it also has less detail. The tool

180

is sensitive enough to use when the numerators are in the 30-70% range, where the curve is fairly flat, as a way to keep track of the direction of movement towards or away from more sustainability.

Another way to map the organization and to begin to track its progress is to measure responses to 66 questions I have developed. There are 11 questions relating to each of the 6 sustainability ratios. Teams can use this tool among themselves to get a sense of how they're doing. For each of the 66 questions, you are asked to indicate:

I agree	5 points
I slightly agree	4 points
I am neutral or don't know	3 Points
I slightly disagree	2 Points
I disagree	1 Point

The scores are then totaled to give you a picture of your team. As you do this over a number of months, you can get a pretty good sense of your progress. This questionnaire is currently being used by one of the teams we've worked with in Australia. In addition to the mapping, they use it to develop questions for their ongoing conversations, which they also feel, are helping them to make progress.

Sustainability

The whole focus of this book is to help develop ways for organizations to become more effective and sustainable. The word "sustainability" means a lot of things to a lot of people. Paul Hawken (1993: 139) defines sustainability in terms of the carrying capacity of the ecosystem. "Sustainability is an economic state where the demands placed upon the environment by people and commerce can be met without reducing the capacity of the environment to provide for future generations."

Carl Frankel expands this definition beyond the "Three E's": Economics, Environment and Equity. "Sustainable development implies a new and healthier balance in how we conduct our human affairs, one that celebrates depth along with surfaces, community along with individuality, spirituality along with materialism, art along with linear technique" (1998: 22). Sustainability, he says, "has a vertical as well as a horizontal dimension." These ideas are quite consistent with the work of Fritjof Capra and others at the Elmwood Institute.

The ideas about sustainability and living systems are deeply interconnected; they are probably two aspects of the same thing. The six

Sustainability Ratios and the way they can be seen to interact and behave are very much in keeping with the way Frankel and Capra look at sustainability. These ratios help to reveal the pattern of the whole so that as we use the Processes of the Living System we can be ever mindful of the path towards improved sustainability, and build more health and sustainability into our organizations, our families, our communities, our civic and church groups, our businesses and ourselves.

We Now Have Some Clear Choices We Can Make

I hope you've enjoyed our journey together. In looking beneath the surface, we've found some powerful and useful maps as well as some archetypal patterns and processes. We've also learned some qualitative means to measure our progress towards a more healthy and sustainable future. These maps can be our guides as we move into the world of organizations as living systems. When we do this, we will come more into dynamical balance and wholeness with each other, our global environment and ourselves.

I think we need to be in a dynamic dance, paying attention to the six Sustainability Ratios and to what is emerging as we move among the self-organizing, strategic and operational processes described in Chapter 2. I think we need to be in constant conversation. We live in many planes of existence simultaneously, mixing theory with the reality of our own experiences and of those around us. It seems to me we are required to open up our consciousness. In conversations and processes like those described in this book, we move into more harmony with each other and our environment. It's a purposeful harmony, aimed at making our world a better, more sustainable place for us all.

We've blended chaos, complexity, autopoiesis, fractal geometry, dissipative structures, synchronicity, fuzzy logic and math with less well-known developments in the Systematics of John Bennett and Tony Blake. So many insights emerged as we brought together two, very different areas of thinking and seeing. The coming together of these bodies of thought and work have resulted in the emergence of a new way to look at the whole of an organization and see what's going on. It's enabled us to see deeper, archetypal patterns and processes. It's enabled us to come together in a different way to address the challenges and issues before us all. We've only been on this journey a few years. Many of you reading this book will move further on, opening new vistas and opportunities to help us all build a healthier, more sustainable world.

The insights we've shared in this book offer a new choice, a clear choice, about how we want to be together. A new way of seeing is offered. We can stay in the *command and control mode,* seeing men and women and our organizations as machines to run until we've squeezed everything out of them and they wear out. We can see our earth as a thing to exploit, taking all we can from it, or we can choose to see women and men and our organizations as well as our world as *living systems,* seeing that we're connected together in a shared destiny and needing to come together in new ways in conversation and work. We can choose to be in the *Leadership Dance* centered in Self-Organizing Leadership processes and use the operational management and strategic leadership processes as the situation demands (see Figure 8 again). We can understand and use the principles and practices of Self-Organizing Leadership.

One day, as we worked and learned this way together at Belle, Mike Murphy, a Shift Supervisor, said to me, "I don't have to be different at home, or at church or at work any more." He said it all! As we became more coherent in our thinking and our work, most aspects of the business got a lot better and we all felt a lot better about how we were personally growing and learning together.

Perhaps we can use these processes and strategies to help to save ourselves and all that comes after us. We, ourselves, are the only barriers to getting started. It does not require money or new laws; it just depends on our courage and willingness to step into it and the commitment to stay with it. These are patterns and processes of *Self-Organizing Leadership* that can change the world.

Appolinaire said:
"Come to the edge."
It's too high.
"Come to the edge."
We might fall.
"Come to the edge."
And they came.
And he pushed them.
And they flew.
(Source unknown)

Bibliography

Abram, David. *The Spell of the Sensuous.* New York: Vintage Books, 1996.

Alexander, Christopher. *The Timeless Way of Building.* New York: Oxford University Press, 1979.

Andrews, Lynn V. *Medicine Woman.* New York: Harper and Row, Publishers, 1981.

———. *Flight of the Seventh Moon.* New York: Harper and Row, 1984.

———. *Jaguar Woman.* San Francisco: Harper and Row, 1985.

———. *Star Woman.* New York: Warner Books, 1986.

———. *Crystal Woman.* New York: Werner Books, 1987.

———. *Windhorse Woman.* New York: Warner Books, 1989.

Argyris, Chris. *Flawed Advice and the Management Trap.* New York: Oxford University Press, 2000.

Autry, James A. *Love and Profit.* New York: Avon Books, 1991.

Axelrod, Robert. *The Evolution of Cooperation.* New York: Basic Books, 1984.

Bandler, Richard and Grinder, John. *Frogs into Princes.* Moab, Utah: Real People Press, 1979.

Bardwick, Judith M. *Danger in the Comfort Zone.* New York: American Management Association, 1991.

Barker, Joel Arthur. *Paradigms.* New York: William Morrow and Company, 1992.

Barks, Coleman. *The Essential Rumi.* New York: Harper Collins, 1995.

Baskin, Ken. *Corporate DNA.* Boston: Butterworth-Heinemann, 1998.

Bennett, John Godolphin. *Deeper Man.* Edited by Anthony G. E. Blake. Charles Town, West Virginia: Claymont Communications, 1977.

———. *Transformation.* Charles Town, West Virginia: Claymont Communications, 1978.

———. *Enneagram Studies.* York Beach, Maine: Samuel Weisner, Inc., 1983.

———. *Witness: The Autobiography of John Bennett.* Charles Town, West Virginia: Claymont Communications, 1983.

185

——. *The Dramatic Universe. 4 Volumes.* Charles Town, West Virginia: Claymont Communications, 1987.

——. *Is There Life on Earth?* Santa Fe, New Mexico: Bennett Books, 1989.

——. *Creative Thinking. 4th Edition.* Charles Town, West Virginia: Claymont Communications, 1989.

——. *Sacred Influences: Spiritual Action in Human Life.* Santa Fe, New Mexico: Bennett Books, 1989.

——. *Hazard, The Risk of Realization.* Santa Fe, New Mexico: Bennett Books, 1991.

——. *Needs of a New Age Community.* Santa Fe, New Mexico: Bennett Books, 1990.

——. *Gurdjieff, Making a New World.* Santa Fe, New Mexico: Bennett Books, 1992.

——. *Elementary Systematics.* Edited by David Seamon. Santa Fe, New Mexico: Bennett Books, 1993.

Bennis, Warren. *On Becoming a Leader.* Reading, Massachusetts: Addison-Wesley Publishing Company, 1989.

Bergquist, William. *The Postmodern Organization.* San Francisco: Jossey-Bass Publishers, 1993.

Berne, Eric. *Games People Play.* New York: Grove Press, 1967.

Berry, Wendell. *The Hidden Wound.* San Francisco: North Point Press, 1989.

——. *What Are People For?* New York: North Point Press, 1990.

Blake, Anthony G. E. *The Intelligent Enneagram.* Boston and London: Shambhala, 1996.

Block, Peter. *The Empowered Manager.* San Francisco: Jossey-Bass Publishers, 1987.

——. *Stewardship.* San Francisco: Berrett-Koehler Publishers, 1993.

Bracy, Hyler; Rosenblum, Jack; Sanford, Aubrey and Trueblood, Roy. *Managing From the Heart.* New York: Delacorte Press, 1990.

Bortoft, Henri. *The Wholeness of Nature.* Hudson, NY: Lindisfarne Books, 1996.

Bridges, William. *Transitions.* Reading, Massachusetts: Addison-Wesley Publishing Company, 1980.

——. *The Character of Organizations.* Palo Alto, CA: Consulting Psychologists Press, Inc., 1992.

Briggs, John and Peat, David. *Turbulent Mirror.* New York: Harper and Row Publishers, 1989.

Bibliography

Brown, Michael H. *The Toxic Cloud*. New York: Harper and Row, Publishers, 1987.

Caine, Renate Nummela and Caine, Geoffrey. *Education on the Edge of Possibility*. Alexandria, Virginia: Association For Supervision and Curriculum Development, 1997.

Callenbach, Ernest; Capra, Fritjof; Goldman, Lenore; Lutz, Rudiger and Marburg, Sandra. *EcoManagement*. San Francisco: Berrett-Koehler Publishers, 1993.

Campbell, Joseph. *The Power of Myth*. New York: Anchor Books Doubleday, 1988.

——. *The Hero With a Thousand Faces*. Princeton: Princeton University Press, 1973.

Capra, Fritjof. *The Tao of Physics*. Boston: Shambhala, 1991.

——. *The Web of Life*. New York: Anchor Books Doubleday, 1996.

Capra, Fritjof and David Steindl-Rast. *Belonging to the Universe*. New York: HarperCollins, 1991.

Carson, Rachel. *Silent Spring*. Boston: Houghton Mifflin Company, 1962.

Castaneda, Carlos. *The Teaching of Don Juan*. New York: Ballantine Books, 1968.

——. *Journey to Ixtlan*. New York: Pocket Books, 1972.

——. *A Separate Reality*. New York: Pocket Books, 1973.

——. *The Fire From Within*. New York: Pocket Books, 1984.

Casti, John L. *Complexification*. New York: HarperPerennial, 1994.

Cherniack, Martin. *The Hawk's Nest Incident*. New Haven: Yale University Press, 1986.

Cohen, Jack and Stewart, Ian. *The Collapse of Chaos*. New York: Viking, 1994.

Combs, Allan and Holland, Mark. *Synchronicity*. New York: Marlowe and Company, 1996.

Cong Huyen Ton; Nu Nha Trang and Pensinger, William L. *The Moon of Hoa Binh. Vol 1 and 2*. Bangkok: Craftsman Press, Ltd., 1994.

Cooper, Robert and Sawaf, Ayman. *Executive EQ*. London: Orion Business, 1997.

Covey, Stephen R. *The Seven Habits of Highly Effective People*. New York: Simon and Schuster, 1989.

——. *Principle-Centered Leadership*. Provo, Utah: The Institute for Principle-Centered Leadership, 1990.

Crosby, Philip B. *Quality is Free*. New York: The New American Library, 1979.

Daniels, Aubrey C. *Performance Management*. Tucker, Georgia: Performance Management Publications, 1989.

Davis, Stanley M. *Future Perfect*. Reading, Massachusetts: Addison-Wesley Publishing Company, 1987.

de Lange, At. *Staying in The Rhythms of Change*. Gold Fields Computer Centre for Education, University of Pretoria, Pretoria, South Africa. Personal communication, 2000.

DePree, Max. *Leadership is an Art*. New York: Doubleday, 1989.

Dertouzos, Michael L; Lester, Richard K. and Solow, Robert M. *Made in America* Cambridge, Massachusetts: The MIT Press, 1990.

Drucker, Peter F. *Management*. New York: Harper and Row, 1973.

——. *Technology, Management and Society*. New York: Harper and Row, 1970.

Durant, Will and Durant, Ariel. *The Story of Civilization, Volumes I-XI*. New York: Simon and Schuster, 1935-1975.

Efron, Edith. *The Apocalyptics*. New York: Simon and Schuster, 1984.

Frankel, Carl. *In Earth's Company*. Gabriola Island, BC: New Society Publishers, 1998.

Frankl, Viktor E. *Man's Search for Meaning*. New York: Pocket Books, 1984.

Fromm, Erich. *The Art of Loving*. New York: Bantam Books, 1963.

——. *Man For Himself*. New York: Fawcett World Library, 1966.

Fulghum, Robert. *All I Really Need To Know I Learned in Kindergarten*. New York: Villard Books, 1993.

Garcia, Linda. *The Fractal Explorer*. Santa Cruz, CA: Dynamic Press, 1991.

Garratt, Bob. *The Learning Organization*. Hants, England: Gower Publishing Company Ltd., 1987.

Gates, Jeff. *The Ownership Solution*. Reading, Mass.: Addison-Wesley, 1998.

Gell-Mann, Murray. *The Quark and the Jaguar*. New York: W. H. Freeman and Company, 1994.

Gibb, Jack. *Trust*. North Hollywood, California: Newcastle Publishing Company Inc., 1978.

Gibran, Kahlil. *The Prophet*. New York: Alfred A. Knopf, 1985.

Gladwell, Malcolm. *The Tipping Point,* London, UK: Little, Brown and Company, 2000.

Gleick, James. *Chaos*. New York: Penguin Books, 1987.

Goldstein, Jeffrey. *The Unshackled Organization*. Portland, Oregon: Productivity Press, 1994.

Greenleaf, Robert K. *Servant Leadership*. New York: Paulist Press, 1977.

Griffin, Douglas. *The Emergence of Leadership*. London and New York: Routledge, 2002.

Gurdjieff, George Ivanovich. *Meetings with Remarkable Men*. New York: E. P. Dutton, 1974.

Hammond, Sue Annis. *The Thin Book of Appreciative Inquiry*. Plano, Texas: Kodiak Consulting. 1996.

Hanna, David P. *Designing Organizations for High Performance*. Reading, Massachusetts: Addison-Wesley Publishing Company, 1988.

Handy, Charles. *The Age of Paradox*. Boston: Harvard Business School Press, 1994.

Harden, Garrett. *Filters Against Folly*. New York: Viking, 1985.

Hawken, Paul. *The Ecology of Commerce*. New York: HarperBusiness, 1993.

Hillman, James. *Kinds of Power*. New York: Currency Doubleday, 1995.

——. *The Soul's Code*. New York: Warner Books, 1997.

Hock, Dee. "Thoughts on Change." *Wired Magazine,* Aug-Sep, 1999. p. 90.

——. *Birth of the Chaordic Age*. San Francisco: Berrett-Kohler Publishers, Inc., 1999.

Holdrege, Craig. *Genetics and the Manipulation of Life*. Hudson, New York: Lindisfarne Press, 1996.

Holland, John H. *Hidden Order*. New York: Helix Books, Addison-Wesley Publishing Company, 1995.

——. *Adaptation in Natural and Artificial Systems*. Cambridge, Massachusetts: The MIT Press, 1995.

Hurley, Kathleen and Dobson, Theodore. *What's My Type?* San Francisco: HarperCollins Publishers, 1991.

——. *My Best Self*. San Francisco: HarperCollins Publishers, 1993.

Hurnard, Hannah. *Mountains of Spices*. Wheaton, Ill.: Tyndale House Publishers, Inc., 1977.

——. *Hinds' Feet On High Places*. Wheaton, Illinois: Tyndale House Publishers, Inc., 1984.

Hurston, Zora Neale. *Moses, Man of the Mountain*. New York: HarperPerennial, 1991.

Janov, Jill. *The Inventive Organization*. San Francisco: Jossey-Bass Publishers, 1994.

Jacobs, Robert W. *Real Time Strategic Change*. San Francisco: Berrett-Koehler Publishers, 1994.

Jaworski, Joseph. *Synchronicity*. San Francisco: Berrett-Koehler Publishers, 1996.

Johnson, H. Thomas. *Relevance Regained*. New York: The Free Press, A Division of Macmillan, Inc., 1992.

Juran, J. M. *Managerial Breakthrough*. New York: McGraw-Hill Book Company, 1964.

Kabat-Zinn, Jon. *Wherever You Go, There You Are*. New York: Hyperion, 1994.

Kaplan, J. D. *The Dialogues of Plato, Jowett Translation*. New York: Pocket Books, 1951.

Kauffman, Stuart A. *The Origins of Order*. New York: Oxford University Press, 1993.

———. *At Home in the Universe*. New York: Oxford University Press, 1995.

Keen, Sam. *Hymns to An Unknown God*. New York: Bantam Books, 1994.

Keirsey, David and Bates, Marilyn. *Please Understand Me*. Del Mar, CA: Prometheus Nemesis Book Company, 1984.

Kellert, Stephen H. *In the Wake of Chaos*. Chicago: The University of Chicago Press, 1993.

Kelly, Kevin. *Out of Control*. Reading, Massachusetts: Addison-Wesley Publishing Company, 1994.

Kelly, Susanne and Allison, Mary Ann. *The Complexity Advantage,* New York, BusinessWeek Books, 1999.

Kleiner, Art. *The Age of Heretics*. New York: Currency Doubleday, 1996.

Kober, Kelly and Knowles, Richard N. "Measurement in Self-Organizing Systems." *The Journal for Quality and Participation* Vol. 19, No. 1, Jan/Feb, 1996.

Kohn, Alfie. *Punishment by Rewards,* Boston: Houghton Mifflin Company, 1993.

Korten, David C. *When Corporations Rule the World*. San Francisco: Berrett-Koehler Publishers, 1995.

Kosko, Bart. *Fuzzy Thinking*. New York: Hyperion, 1993.

Kouzes, James M. and Posner, Barry Z. *Leadership Challenge*. San Francisco: Jossey-Bass Publishers, 1988.

Kuchinsky, Saul. *Systematics: Search for Miraculous Management*. Charles Town, West Virginia: Claymont Communications, 1985.

Land, George and Jarman, Beth. *Breakpoint and Beyond*. New York: HarperBusiness, 1992.

Levy, Steven. *Artificial Life*. New York: Vintage Books, 1992.

Lewin, Roger. *Complexity*. New York: Macmillan Publishing Company, 1992.

Lewin, Roger and Regine, Birute, *The Soul at Work*, New York: Simon and Schuster, 2000

Lewis, C. S. *Mere Christianity*. New York: Macmillan Publishing Company, 1960.

———. *The Four Loves*. New York: Harcourt Brace Jovanovich, Publishers, 1960.

———. *The Problem of Pain*. New York: The Macmillan Company, 1962.

Lissack, Michael and Roos, Johan. *The Next Common Sense*. London: Nicholas Brealey Publishing, 1999.

Lorenz, Edward. *The Essence of Chaos*. Seattle: University of Washington Press, 1995.

Lynch, Dudley and Kordis, Paul L. *Strategy of the Dolphin*. New York: William Morrow and Company Inc., 1988.

Mackay, Charles. *Extraordinary Popular Delusions and the Madness of Crowds*. New York: Crown Publishers Inc., 1980.

Makower, Joel. *The e Factor*. New York: Times Books, 1993.

Maturana, Humberto R. and Varela, Francisco J. *The Tree of Knowledge*. Boston: Shambhala, 1992.

Maynard, Herman Bryant, Jr. and Mehrtens, Susan E. *The Fourth Wave*. San Francisco: Berrett-Koehler Publishers, 1993.

McMaster, Michael D. *The Praxis Equation*. Douglas, Isle of Man: Knowledge Based Development Co, Ltd., 1997.

Merrill, A. Roger. *Connections, Quadrant II Time Management*. Salt Lake City: Publishers Press, 1989.

Moore, Thomas. *Care of the Soul*. New York: HarperPerennial, 1992.

Morgan, Gareth, *Images of Organization*, Thousand Oaks, CA: SAGE Publications, Inc., 1997.

Nair, Keshavan. *A Higher Standard of Leadership, Lessons from the Life of Gandhi*. San Francisco: Berrett-Koehler Publishers, 1994.

Nicolis, Gregoire and Prigogine, Ilya. *Exploring Complexity*. New York: W. H. Freeman and Company, 1989.

Nicoll, Maurice. *The New Man*. Boulder and London: Shambhala, 1984.

Olson, Edwin E. and Eoyang, Glenda H. *Facilitating Organizational Change*. San Francisco: Jossey-Bass/Pfeiffer, 2001.

Orr, David W. *Earth in Mind*. Washington, DC: Island Press, 1994.

Ottoboni, M. Alice. *The Dose Makes the Poison*. Berkeley: Vincente Books, 1984.

Ouspensky, Peter Damien. *The Psychology of Man's Possible Evolution.* New York: Vintage Books, 1974.

Palmer, Parker J. *The Active Life.* San Francisco: HarperCollins, 1991.

——. *To Know as We Are Known.* San Francisco: HarperCollins, 1993.

Peat, F. David. *Synchronicity.* New York: Bantam Books, 1987.

Peck, M. Scott. *The Road Less Traveled.* New York: Simon and Schuster, 1978.

——. *People of the Lie.* New York: Simon and Schuster, 1983.

——. *Further Along the Road Less Traveled.* New York: Simon and Schuster, 1993.

Percy, Walker. *Lost in the Cosmos.* New York: Simon and Schuster, 1984.

Peters, Thomas J. and Waterman, Robert H., Jr. *In Search of Excellence.* New York: Harper and Row, Publishers, 1982.

Peterson, Ivars. *Newton's Clock, Chaos in the Solar System.* New York: W.H. Freeman and Company, 1993.

Petzinger, Thomas, Jr. *The New Pioneers.* New York: Simon and Schuster, 1999.

Priesmeyer, H. Richard. *Organizations and Chaos.* Westport, Connecticut: Quorum Books, 1992.

Prigogine, Ilya. *The End of Certainty.* New York: The Free Press, 1996.

Ray, Michael and Rinzler, Alan, eds. *The New Paradigm in Business.* New York: G. P. Putnam's Sons, 1993.

Reina, Dennis S. and Reina, Michelle L. *Trust and Betrayal in the Workplace.* San Francisco: Berrett-Koehler Publishers, 1999.

Renault, Mary. *The Nature of Alexander.* New York: Pantheon Books, 1976.

Renesch, John, ed. *Leadership in a New Era.* San Francisco: NewLeaders Press, 1994.

Renesch, John, ed. *New Traditions in Business.* San Francisco: Berrett-Koehler Publishers, 1992.

Riesman, David; Glazer, Nathan and Denny, Reuel. *The Lonely Crowd: A Study of the Changing American Character.* New Haven: Yale University Press, 1950.

Riso, Don Richard and Hudson, Russ. *The Wisdom of the Enneagram.* New York: Bantam Books, 1999.

Roberts, Monty. *The Man Who Listens to Horses.* London: Arrow Books Ltd., 1997.

Rubin, Theodore Isaac. *Compassion and Self-Hate.* New York: Ballantine Books, 1976.

Russell, Bertrand. *A History of Western Philosophy*. New York: Simon and Schuster, 1963.

——. *Human Society in Ethics and Politics*. London: Routledge, 1994.

Sanford, John A. *The Invisible Partners*. New York: Paulist Press, 1980.

Sardello, Robert. *Love and the Soul*. New York: HarperCollins Publishers, 1995.

Saul, John Ralston. *The Unconscious Civilization*. Ringwood, Victoria, Australia: Penguin Books, 1997.

Savory, Allan. *Holistic Management: A New Framework for Decision Making*. Washington, DC: Island Press, 1999.

Schaffer, Robert H. *The Breakthrough Strategy*. New York: Ballinger Publishing Company, 1988.

Scherkenbach, William W. *The Deming Route*. Washington, DC: CEEPress Books, 1988.

Schuster, John P.; Carpenter, Jill and Kane, Patricia M. *The Power of Open-Book Management*. New York: John Wiley and Sons, Inc., 1996.

Senge, Peter M. *The Fifth Discipline*. New York: Doubleday/Currency, 1990.

Shah, Idries. *The Commanding Self*. London: The Octagon Press, 1994.

Silver, Brian L. *The Ascent of Science*. New York: Oxford University Press, 1998.

Smuts, Jan Christiaan. *Holism and Evolution*. Edited by Sanford Holst. Sherman Oaks, CA: Sierra Sunrise Publishing, 1999.

Sogyal Rinpoche. *The Tibetan Book of Living and Dying*. San Francisco: HarperCollins Publishers, 1992.

Stacey, Ralph D. *Managing the Unknowable*. San Francisco: Jossey-Bass Publishers, 1992.

——. *Complexity and Creativity in Organizations*. San Francisco: Berrett-Koehler Publishers, 1996.

——. *Strategic Management and Organizational Dynamics*. London: Financial Times, Prentice Hall, 2000.

——. *Complex Responsive Processes In Organizations*. London: Routledge, 2001.

Stacey, Ralph D.; Griffin, Douglas and Shaw, Patricia. *Complexity and Management, Fad or Radical Challenge to Systems Thinking,* London and New York, Routledge, 2000

Tannen, Deborah. *You Just Don't Understand*. New York: Ballantine Books, 1990.

Bibliography

Tillich, Paul. *The Courage To Be.* New Haven: Yale University Press, 1952.

Troffler, Alvin. *Power Shift.* New York: Bantam Books, 1990.

Untermeyer, Louis. *Robert Frost's Poems.* New York: Washington Square Press, 1971.

Vollmar, Klausbernd. *The Secret of Enneagrams.* Shaftesbury, Dorset: Element Books, 1997.

Waldrop, M. Mitchell. *Complexity.* New York: Simon and Schuster, 1992.

Wesson, Robert. *Beyond Natural Selection.* Cambridge, Massachusetts: The MIT Press, 1993.

Weisbord, Marvin R. and Janoff, Sandra. *Future Search.* San Francisco: Berrett-Koehler Publishers, 1995.

Weisman, Alan. *Gaviotas: A Village to Reinvent the World.* White River Junction, VT: Chelsea Green Publishing Company, 1998.

Whyte, David. *The Heart Aroused.* New York: Currency Doubleday, 1994.

Wilber, Ken. *A Brief History of Everything.* Boston and London: Shambhala, 1996.

Wheatley, Margaret J. *Leadership and the New Science.* San Francisco: Berrett-Koehler Publishers, 1992.

Wheatley, Margaret J. and Kellner-Rogers, Myron. *A Simpler Way.* San Francisco: Berrett-Koehler Publishers, 1966.

Wilson, Mitchell, *American Science and Invention.* New York: Simon and Schuster, 1954.

Youngblood, Mark D. *Life at the Edge of Chaos.* Dallas: Perceval Publishing, 1997.

Zimmerman, Brenda; Lindberg, Curt and Plsek, Paul. *Edgeware.* Irving, Texas: VHA Inc., 1998.

Zuckerman, Marilyn R. and Hatala, Lewis J. *Incredibly American.* Milwaukee, Wisconsin: ASQC Quality Press, 1992.

Zukav, Gary. *The Dancing Wu Li Masters.* New York: Bantam Books, 1979.

——. *The Seat of the Soul.* New York: Simon and Schuster, 1990.

Richard N. Knowles
Biographical Information

Richard N. Knowles graduated the McDonogh School in Maryland in 1953 and then from Oberlin College in 1957. He received a Ph. D. in Organic Chemistry from the University of Rochester in 1961. He then joined the DuPont Company at the Experimental Station in Wilmington, Delaware where he worked for 12 years in the fields of agricultural chemicals, industrial chemicals, animal repellents, process development and flame retardants. He received 40 US Patents and a number of foreign patents in this work.

He served as a Research Supervisor for about 2 years, and then spent 3 years in supervising a market development group commercializing new products. After 1976, he was engaged in manufacturing assignments at Repauno in Gibbstown, NJ, Chambers Works in Carneys Point, NJ (Assistant Plant Manager), Niagara Falls, NY (Plant Manager: August 83 to March 87) and Belle, WV (Plant Manager: April 87 to January 95). In 1995, he began his last assignment, focused on building local sustainability, in Wilmington, DE as Director of Community Awareness, Emergency Response and Industry Outreach. Part of his efforts was focused in DuPont plants and part was in other plant communities on behalf of the Chemical Manufacturers Association. On September 30, 1996, he retired from DuPont after 37 years of service.

He serves on the National Institute for Chemical Studies Board, the EPA Office of Chemical Emergency Planning and Preparedness, the Board of the Berkana Institute, and Co-Founded and is a Director for the Center for Self-Organizing Leadership™. He was the 1992 Recipient of the DuPont Agricultural Products Crystal Award for the Championing of Human Potential. In 1995, he received the EPA Region III Chemical Emergency Planning and Preparedness Partnership Award.

He helped establish industry/community dialogue groups such as the Industrial Liaison Committee in Niagara Falls in March of 1985, and the Belle Community Advisory Panel in early 1990. He was on the CMA Community Awareness and Emergency Response Task Group from September 1987 to December 1996, serving as Chairman in 1995-1996. From 1990 to 1995, he was a member of the West Virginia State Emergency Response Commission. In order to develop more dialogue between the chemical plants and the community, he helped to found the State Chemical Working Group of the West Virginia Environmental Institute in 1991. He played a leading role in Safety Street, Managing Our Risks Together in which, on June 3-4, 1994, 8 chemical plants in the Kanawha Valley shared 29 worst case scenarios with a community of 300,000 people, and...trust went up! His work in Belle is featured in Tom Petzinger's *The New Pioneers,* published by Simon and Schuster in1999 and Roger Lewin and Birute Regine's *The Soul at Work,* also published by Simon and Schuster in 2000.

He is married to Claire E. F. Knowles, his business partner and Co-Founder of the Center for Self-Organizing Leadership. He has 3 daughters, a stepdaughter, 3 granddaughters and a grandson.

In September 1996, he formed his own consulting company. He was associated with Kellner-Rogers and Wheatley for 6 years, and is currently a member of the Dalmau Network, which focuses on organizations as living systems, and the forms of organizations for the 21st Century. He is deeply involved in the United Kingdom through Frank Smits and Tim Morley in Symphoenix, Ltd.

In addition to the US Patents mentioned earlier, he has published a number of papers on community outreach and self-organizing systems. For several years, he was deeply involved in the Leading Organizational Change course in Australia with Tim Dalmau. Bringing all this together, he and his partner Claire E. F. Knowles founded the Center for Self-Organizing Leadership™ in November 2001. The Center is a learning community of people drawn together around this emerging way of leading. The Center for Self-Organizing Leadership is focused on helping people in organizations develop coherence, significantly improving their performance.

Key Thoughts on Effective Leadership

More and more people are coming to realize that the most effective leaders are those who are able to open and guide conversations in their organizations. This releases the creativity and energy of the people with whom they work. These are leaders who treat their organizations as living systems rather than machines, believing in the inherent creativity and vitality of people. We call this *Self-Organizing Leadership™*.

The tree is a helpful metaphor when thinking about leadership in organizations. The leaves and small branches holding them, reaching out into the open air, can be seen as strategic leadership. They are reaching to the future. The trunk and main support branches, which hold everything up and provide nutrient flows through all parts of the tree can be seen as operational leadership. The root system, which provides food and grounding and enables us to thrive is usually outside our notice – invisible and taken for granted. The roots draw in many nutrients, and ultimately determine the health of the system. Attending to the roots characterizes Self-Organizing Leadership. This form of leadership develops coherence in the organization.

Self-Organizing Leadership™

Leaders learning to use the Self-Organizing Leadership approach know the importance of engaging their people deeply. They know that sharing information, developing relationships and interconnections, and inviting the people to be partners in co-creating their future develops coherence in the organization. They know there is value in having the people involved, although they usually have no quantitative data to support this nor, often, the language to describe it. These leaders also know that, while they need to be centered in the self-organizing approach, from time to time they will need to manage operationally to deal with immediate issues. They know there is a need to move among the various leadership approaches as conditions and circumstances change. We describe effective leadership as a *dance,* which requires a high level of consciousness on the part of both the leader and people throughout the organization.

When we teach organizational change, we bring intact teams together to look at their organization as a living system. We share and develop the patterns and processes of organizations seen as living systems, emphasizing their application in the working environment. Inevitably, significant improvements in relationships develop in the teams. We have used this approach in a variety of settings including a large number of successful safety leadership improvement programs. A number of examples of extraordinary change in large organizations have emerged from this work including:

·   superior financial performance;

·   significantly improved safety performance, and

·   strengthened relationships with employees, managers and other stakeholders.

The Self-Organizing Leadership approach is also being used with Mayor Irene Elia, Ph. D. and her leadership team in Niagara Falls, NY.

The Center for Self-Organizing Leadership™
Guides for Turbulent Times

At the Center for Self-Organizing Leadership (C-SOL), we view organizations and communities as if they are living systems that have the inherent capability to co-create their futures consciously. When organizational leaders have this overt intention, their organizations experience a release of energy, creativity, capability and meaning that is not available by any other means.

Our task at C-SOL is to guide and support people to find, recognize and develop the inherent leadership capabilities of people within their organizations and communities. The most effective leadership practices are a vital necessity if our organizations are to thrive and become more sustainable.

The Center for Self-Organizing Leadership offers opportunities to learn powerful ways to understand the deep processes in your organization, and shows you how to develop the most effective leadership practices. We help you to learn the *Leadership Dance*.

In our approach, we help you to look at your organization from nine different interconnected perspectives by engaging people in a dialogue of discovery. Although this information resides in the organization, you have never seen it all presented and connected before. Through these conversations, the organization becomes much more coherent and effective and able to adapt as change occurs.

Claire E. F. Knowles offers opportunities for people who may feel "stuck," feel a lack direction in their lives or who are in the midst of life transitions and high stress through her Lights On Workshop (www.lightsonworkshop.com). The living systems approach invokes wholeness and coherence for the people engaged in the Workshop.

Self-Organizing Leadership has been used successfully in many different leadership and organizational development efforts, including:

- designing new organizations;

- aligning various functions to corporate goals;

- aligning various departments in municipal government;

- developing management and work teams;

- coaching executives on leadership issues and practices;

- improving safety practices and reducing injuries and incidents;

- exploring issues that undermine organizational performance;

- identifying and overcoming obstacles to increase the effectiveness of work teams;

- sensing what is going on within organizations – making issues visible so that they can be appropriately addressed;

- personal path-finding and development through the Lights On Workshop, and

- helping organizations and communities to improve their sustainability.

If you want additional information about the Center and how it may be of help to you, please contact us by e-mail at Ctrsol@aol.com or through our web site:

www.centerforselforganizingleadership.com